Human Rights in
Chinese Foreign Relations

PENNSYLVANIA STUDIES IN HUMAN RIGHTS

Bert B. Lockwood, Jr., Series Editor

A complete list of books in the series
is available from the publisher.

Human Rights in Chinese Foreign Relations

Defining and Defending National Interests

Ming Wan

PENN

University of Pennsylvania Press

Philadelphia

10 9 8 7 6 5 4 3 2 1

Published by
University of Pennsylvania Press
Philadelphia, Pennsylvania 19104–4011

Library of Congress Cataloging-in-Publication Data
Wan, Ming, 1953–
    Human rights in Chinese foreign relations / Ming Wan.
        p. cm. — (Pennsylvania studies in human rights)
    Includes bibliographical references and index.
    ISBN 0-8122-3597-5 (cloth : alk. paper)
    1. Human rights—China.   2. China—Foreign relations—1976–   I. Title.
II. Series.
JC599.C49 W36   2001
323′.0951—dc21   00-048933

To Anne

Contents

Chapter One
Introduction

No issue in the relations between China and the West in the past decades has inspired so much passion as human rights. Much more is at stake here than moral concerns and hurt national feelings. To many Westerners, the Chinese government appears ultimately untrustworthy on all issues because it is undemocratic. To Beijing, Western human rights pressure seems designed to compromise its legitimacy, and this threat hangs over what might otherwise be considered "normal" disputes on issues like trade and arms sales. And neither side harbors its resentment silently; rather, both bring their rights views to the table in seemingly unrelated official business. All these factors make human rights an important subject for the study of Chinese foreign relations.

This book examines China's human rights relations with the United States, Western Europe, Japan, and the United Nations human rights institutions. Two sets of questions form the core of the research behind it. The first group focuses on the states and international institutions that initiate human rights pressure on China. What is the nature and impact of external pressure on China from key actors? Why have years of intense human rights pressure on the Chinese government yielded few tangible results? The second group puts China at the center. Has Beijing's engagement with the international human rights establishment affected how it defines its national interests, particularly how it approaches relations with the initiators of rights pressure? What tactics has Beijing employed in response to such pressure? Does China's response vary according to the initiating state or institution? Why has rights pressure contributed to rising nationalist sentiment within both government and society?

Answers to these questions shed light on China's foreign relations. As an ongoing contemporary diplomatic issue for Beijing, human rights offers new means for studying Chinese foreign policy. As the most important remaining nondemocratic country, and one subject to constant external pressure, China provides a good test for the relevance of human rights in the conduct of world diplomacy today. Comparing the normative dimension of U.S., European, and Japanese foreign policy toward China and the Chinese response will contribute to a better understanding of the interplay of ideas and power in the dynamic interaction among major powers.

This book addresses these questions by examining the views on human rights and democracy that serve as a foundation for Chinese diplomacy. Interviews conducted in China, the United States, and Japan and sources in Chinese, English, and Japanese provide a basis for an analysis of China's human rights relations with the United States, Western Europe, Japan, and UN institutions. The book thus tells a complex story based on a broad survey of China's human rights relations with the West. It offers two key findings. The first is that, while the idea of human rights is important in Western policy toward China, it has seldom prevailed over traditional power calculations when push comes to shove. Western governments have not committed as many policy resources to pressuring Beijing on human rights as on other issues. And they have not united except for a short period following the 1989 Tiananmen crackdown. The different degrees of commitment to rights-oriented foreign policy and the importance of rights relative to other considerations explain why Japan, Western Europe, and the United States, in that order, gradually retreated from confronting China on human rights issues.

The second finding is that, after a decade of persistent external pressure, Beijing still plays human rights diplomacy as traditional power politics, and its rights exchanges with the West have mainly led to adaptive learning about how to fend off Western pressure rather than to cognitive learning about the importance of human rights per se. China has mobilized its propaganda machine to refute Western criticism. Beijing has also made compromises when intense foreign pressure has threatened its core interests. Respecting power, China is more accommodating to the United States than to Western Europe and Japan. At the same time, China has offered commercial incentives and promised human rights dialogues to prevent a unified Western front from developing. At the United Nations, Beijing has largely succeeded in rallying developing nations to defeat Western attempts at censure. The main reason for Beijing's intransigence, of course, is that the Chinese Communist Party leadership has no incentive to yield to foreign rights pressure, pressure that undermines its political legitimacy and control. But another reason is that, while human rights has become an important theme in international relations, power remains a central factor shaping the conduct of human rights diplomacy. It is a structural conundrum that, as ideas of human rights become more important in Western policy formulation toward China, it becomes more necessary to resort to conventional power to implement human rights policy. As a result, human rights pressure appears to target nations like China just as old-fashioned power politics has targeted such nations, albeit with new motivations. In Beijing this induces a perceived need to defend national interests and simultaneously makes it harder for the Chinese government to accept the enlightened ideas embedded in external pressure. Foreign countries' power plays against China, ironically, also generate resentment and contribute to rising nationalist sentiment among the same ordinary Chinese citizens in whose name pressure is exerted in the first place.

The first two sections of this chapter summarize my arguments about China's human rights relations with the West and illustrate the contributions of my work to the study of China's foreign policy. The last section highlights the implications of the China case for international relations theories.

Human Rights in China's Foreign Relations

Human rights in China became a subject for Western media coverage and academic research in the late 1970s. Ross H. Munro published a series of articles on China's rights abuses in the *Toronto Globe & Mail* in October 1977, and Amnesty International issued a detailed study, "Political Imprisonment in the People's Republic of China," in November of the same year.[1] Significantly, a democratic movement also emerged in China in the late 1970s.[2] The movement is yet to win popular Chinese support, but it has been persistent.

Persecution of Chinese citizens fighting for democracy and rights has helped rally Western human rights advocates to pressure their governments and international organizations to take action against Beijing. With better access to Chinese society, Western reporters and scholars have written extensively on human rights in China.[3] This work lays the foundation for the study of China's human rights diplomacy, elucidating the substantive focus of external pressure.

At the same time, scholars have given insufficient attention to the state-to-state interplay at the heart of rights diplomacy. Andrew J. Nathan and James D. Seymour have offered article-length overviews of human rights in Chinese foreign policy, but the depth of their analysis is limited by space constraints.[4] Ann Kent has produced a book-length treatment of China's human rights diplomacy, but her principal focus is UN human rights activities.[5]

The main reason for this "neglect" is that human rights in China has become a serious diplomatic issue only in the past decade. When the United States and Western Europe started incorporating human rights into their foreign policy in the 1970s, China was "exempted" from Western criticism.[6] The U.S. State Department started including China in its annual human rights report in 1979, and several isolated diplomatic incidents—over a Chinese political asylum seeker, the Chinese family planning program, and China's policy toward Tibet—occurred in the 1980s between Beijing and Washington. Still, human rights was basically a nonissue in China's diplomatic relations with the West through the decade. The reasons for China's exemption included an information gap about China's situation, guilt about imperialism, respect for Chinese civilization, and an absence of a strong lobby concerned with human rights in China.[7] It is now also widely recognized by both American and Chinese analysts that the United States and other Western nations ignored human rights in China due to the Cold War imperative of containing the Soviet Union.[8]

The Chinese government's brutal crackdown on demonstrators in Tiananmen in June 1989, televised live around the globe, dramatically pushed human rights in China onto the diplomatic agenda of Western nations and UN human rights organizations. The subsequent collapse of communist governments in Eastern Europe and the end of the Cold War removed the common strategic bond that had existed between China and the West in their opposition to the Soviet Union, and this allowed Western governments to pressure the Chinese government, now considered a political laggard. Human rights became an issue sharply contested between China and the West in the 1990s.

Works published in the West on China's human rights diplomacy are largely devoted to Beijing's exchange with the United States.[9] Little has been written on other international sources of rights pressure.[10] A similar bias exists in Chinese writings on Chinese foreign policy. Chinese writers have written books on the Sino-U.S. human rights exchange,[11] but they have given little attention to rights issues involving other Western nations.[12] This disparity between works on Sino-U.S. relations and on China's relations with other countries certainly reflects the reality that the United States has been the leader of Western criticism. However, the disparity also results from an imbalance in intellectual resources and research interests between the United States and other countries. Most China specialists are based in the United States and tend to look at China mainly through the prism of the United States. As for scholars based in China, most see studies of the United States as more prestigious and more financially rewarding than studies of other countries, thanks to the Chinese public's fascination with the "beautiful country" and opportunities to visit the United States with American funding.[13]

It is important to study China's human rights exchanges with other players, especially Western Europe and Japan. The obvious reason is that we need to have a comprehensive picture of China's human rights diplomacy. Beijing has engaged continuously in human rights exchanges with Western Europe, Japan, and others, and these interactions are worthy of study. From an analytical point of view, by examining similarities or differences in China's human rights relations with a variety of countries, we can differentiate characteristics of human rights diplomacy in China from the idiosyncrasies of Chinese relations with any one state. In fact, China's relations with Western Europe and Japan are better cases than its relations with the United States to test how important human rights has become in current international relations. After all, it is not surprising that Americans promote human rights abroad. As the world's sole superpower since the end of the Cold War, the United States can satisfy both ideological and strategic objectives by promoting rights and democracy in the world. By contrast, China's human rights exchanges with Western Europe and Japan test the relevance of rights in the conduct of international relations between nonhegemonic powers.

To better understand Chinese human rights diplomacy, this book includes an in-depth discussion of Chinese views on human rights and democracy. It pays particular attention to the evolving opinions and calculations of the Chinese "silent majority" and to the dynamic state-society relationship that helps explain the possibilities and limits of Western rights pressure.

In the early 1990s a wide range of external actors pressured Beijing on behalf of universal values. The United States, more convinced of the values of human rights and democracy with the end of the Cold War, led the way in exerting pressure on China. Washington acted in a high-profile manner and linked human rights explicitly and implicitly to other issues such as trade and international security. Western European governments joined the United States in pressuring China in a public and critical fashion, though they engaged in less confrontation after 1993. Japan, unlike the West, chose a nonconfrontational approach and struck a balance between the West and China. Given the importance of its relationship with the West, Japan could not afford to do nothing. But given the importance of its relationship with China, it could also not afford to do too much. In the United Nations Commission on Human Rights, the West unsuccessfully sponsored resolutions on human rights in China. Latin American and Eastern European members leaned toward supporting the West while Asian and African members were mostly supportive of China.

Beijing adopted a defensive human rights diplomacy. To avoid international isolation, the Chinese actively cultivated relations with neighboring nations. To fend off Western pressure, the government stood firm on principles of sovereignty and noninterference in domestic affairs but remained flexible in making opportune concessions, such as release of prominent dissidents, signing international human rights treaties, and publishing human rights white papers. It also employed economic statecraft to influence Western policy and strengthened a propaganda campaign to counter Western ideas of human rights and democracy. To drive a wedge between the United States and its main allies, China identified Japan as a weak link that could be helpful in ending its international isolation, and Beijing also adopted a more conciliatory approach to Western

Europe than to the United States. Also, China was more willing to accommodate international human rights institutions than bilateral human rights diplomacy because China respected the legitimacy of these institutions—and recognized that their enforcement mechanisms were weak.

China paid dearly for its clash with the West over human rights. Needless to say, Chinese citizens suffered when they continued to be denied basic civil and political rights, but the government paid a high price too. It expended considerable diplomatic resources, which could have been used for other purposes, on rights issues. More significant, China's need for support over human rights weakened its bargaining leverage regarding other issues. And Beijing's loss in reputation compromised its core value in territorial integrity: a democratizing Taiwan gained diplomatic ground and the Tibetan cause, led by the Dalai Lama, received greater international sympathy.

Washington also paid a high price for its cause. By treating human rights as a central issue in its relations with a major power, the United States jeopardized other important interests such as trade and security and found it difficult to maintain a working relationship with a rising power over a range of key international issues. Human rights disputes arguably led to a deteriorating bilateral relationship, which slipped to the brink of military confrontation in March 1996 when President Clinton sent two carrier battle groups near Taiwan in response to China's massive military exercises aimed at influencing Taiwan's first direct presidential election and preventing the island's perceived move toward independence.

Western Europe did not pay such a high price for its human rights pressure on China. This is because Europeans preferred approaches that imposed less cost on China than did those pursued by Washington. While almost as vocal about China's rights problems as Americans, they did not link trade with human rights. Conversely, the Chinese did not feel as threatened by Western Europe as by the United States. Thus, in a reciprocal relationship, Beijing did not focus on Western Europe as much as on the United States for rhetorical counterattack.

Japan avoided offending its giant neighbor, from concern more about the negative impact of a collapsed China on itself than about Chinese domestic practices. Tokyo worked hard at the sometimes awkward task of preventing deterioration in relations between Beijing and Washington; it actually benefited diplomatically and commercially from China's efforts to improve bilateral relations with Japan.

While ensuring release and better treatment of prominent dissidents and forcing the Chinese government to engage in human rights discourse with the West, Western rights pressure largely failed to improve human rights in China. It is true that China continued to relax economic and social controls on citizens, but mainly as a continuation of domestic reform, not as a result of explicit foreign pressure. Beijing continued to repress political dissent and, in its exchanges with the West, defended its human rights policy. China did not fundamentally redefine its national interests in a way that appealed to the West.

Since the mid-1990s, human rights in China has settled in as a mere diplomatic issue with the United States. While human rights remains an issue between Chinese and Western governments as a result of domestic pressure in the West, Beijing has succeeded in marginalizing human rights disputes in its official relations with the West. While insisting on a vigorous stance on human rights in China, the U.S. government now sees human rights as only one of a whole series of issues with China. Western Europe, Japan, and other advanced nations have now largely replaced pressure tactics with symbolic, toothless rights dialogues. In the UN Human Rights Commission, Beijing has won solid support from most developing members and has divided the Western camp, complicating the already difficult task of passing a resolution concerning human rights in China.

Beijing has won a "diplomatic victory" because overcoming determined resistance of a major power to foreign interference in its internal affairs is inherently difficult. As a rapidly rising economic, political, and military power, China has considerable resources at its disposal. At the same time, human rights is yet to prevail consistently over traditional realist calculations for Western governments, despite its periodic rise to the top of the issue pile.

Equally important, Western criticism does not resonate with Chinese society at this stage. Since the 1989 mass demonstrations, the government has offered Chinese citizens an implicit bargain: they will be left alone to engage in nonpolitical affairs, especially if they want to get rich, but they will pay a high price if they dare to mount a direct challenge to the Communist Party. The government increasingly uses economic performance as the basis of its legitimacy. Having observed expanded economic opportunities and personal choices and the government's demonstrated resolve in crushing dissent, most Chinese citizens have chosen to focus on economic gain rather than political protest at this point.

More significant, based on China's rapid economic growth and Russia's collapse as a world power, most Chinese, who are averse to political turmoil, have concluded that the party leadership is a necessary evil to ensure political stability and economic success. They also doubt that Western notions of democracy and human rights can help them advance economically. The country's rising power has also contributed to growing national pride and anti-Western sentiment when the West has continued to criticize Beijing over a wide range of issues.

However, the current societal support for the government will not last indefinitely. First, contingent as it is on economic performance, the support would be upset by a serious downturn, a prospect the party understands and dreads. Second, a large segment of Chinese society has not benefited from economic reform, making it a hotbed for antigovernment sentiment and activities. Even organized "nonpolitical activities" such as the Falun Gong spiritual movement have struck fear in the party leadership, whose harsh reaction ensures continuation of human rights as a contentious issue between China and the West. Third, a more affluent and better-educated Chinese society is bound, sooner or later, to embrace civil and political rights as essential to its quality of life. In short, the Chinese government's success in marginalizing human rights pressure may well be only a temporary victory.

The Study of Chinese Foreign Policy

China's human rights diplomacy is both unique and indicative of its general foreign policy. On the one hand, human rights is much more sensitive than "traditional" issues. As the Chinese government sees it, Western human rights pressure challenges the very existence of its political regime. This political sensitivity sets human rights apart and explains why, for example, a few months after the accidental NATO bombing of the Chinese embassy in Belgrade, Beijing resumed negotiations on the WTO and struck a deal, and then resumed military-to-military exchanges and arms control talks but has shown no signs of resuming human rights dialogue. On the other hand, human rights is indicative of current Chinese foreign policy. As the country continues to integrate into the global economy and global institutions, "nontraditional" issues such as human rights have become diplomatically unavoidable for Beijing.

This book examines how the Chinese government defines and defends its national interests in its human rights relations with the West. National interest is a term used frequently by policy makers and analysts but it is elusive and vague. It is difficult to determine a country's national interests independent of its behavior; we often explain government actions on the basis of interests we infer from the actions we are attempting to explain in the first place. To minimize this tautological problem, I devote Chapter Two to a detailed analysis of the Chinese definition of human rights, and the following four chapters to how Beijing defends its interests in its relations with the United States, Western Europe, Japan, and the UN human rights institutions. Also, we need to consider the basic question of whose national interests we are talking about. This book examines mainly the evolving views of the state and a dynamic state-society nexus. From a critical perspective, one may argue that the Chinese government's definition of national interests is fundamentally flawed, that the society should not be thinking the way it does at this point and that dissidents' views should be taken more seriously. However, my objective in this book is not to add to a long list of existing critiques of human rights problems in China but to produce a comprehensive study of human rights as an official policy issue between China and the West. In this context, it is necessary to analyze Beijing's human rights views and behavior as they are rather than as they should be.

This book contributes to the study of Chinese foreign policy in three ways.[14] First, to understand Chinese foreign policy we need to examine the national objectives the government pursues at a particular historical moment and how committed the leadership is to those objectives. A country's national purpose determines its most fundamental national interests. China's national purpose since 1978, as defined by Deng Xiaoping and his successor Jiang Zemin, is to achieve economic modernization through economic reform and to maintain party dominance in the process. This book shows that the Deng line sets the parameters for Chinese human rights diplomacy and explains why Beijing has doggedly engaged in a defensive approach, not yielding to foreign pressure but also not withdrawing from international entanglements. Rather, the government has stayed the course of furthering economic reform while repressing challengers to party rule. This strategy leads to continued Western criticism but also has so far ensured the strong economic performance and relative political stability that have strengthened Beijing's ability to withstand Western pressure.

Second, Chinese foreign policy has become more pragmatic and effective than before. Beijing is no longer as ideological as it was through the 1970s. Rather, the Chinese government has become focused on maximizing its national interests even though it still thinks it adheres to high principles.[15] This pragmatic foreign policy is consistent with Deng's approach to solving China's problems. As China has shifted priorities from revolution to modernization, the government has realized the need for flexibility in advancing the country's interests in a complex and uncertain world. This book shows that a pragmatic diplomacy allows Chinese human rights diplomats to design and carry out strategies in a result-oriented fashion to advance Chinese goals, operating within the parameters of the central leadership's basic national program. They have learned quickly how the international system works. And they have worked hard to defend the nation.

Third, the book confirms the conventional wisdom that Chinese foreign policy is still based on a traditional notion of sovereignty, driven by narrowly defined national interests.[16] While making concessions to fend off foreign human rights pressure and maintain cooperative economic ties with the West, Beijing has engaged mainly in adaptive learning, with no serious change of mind about its domestic practices. Based on its narrow notion of state sovereignty, the Chinese government continues to block society's participation in foreign policy-making despite pluralization of government agencies involved in foreign policy.

Human Rights in International Relations

This book is not designed to test international relations theories. Nevertheless, as the book examines China's relations with major Western powers and UN human rights institutions in a nontraditional issue area, it has theoretical implications for our understanding of current international relations.

Human rights has become a central research topic for international relations scholars.[17] The issue illustrates some of the "great debates" in the field. Neorealists, for example, argue that international power structure determines state behavior. Human rights norms are not persuasive in and of themselves; instead they are imposed as the values of the dominant state.[18] By contrast, neoliberal institutionalists maintain that international norms such as universal protection of human rights help shape state preferences by setting authoritative standards that condition how states calculate the costs and benefits of a particular course of action.[19] Unlike realists and institutionalists, who largely take interests as a given, constructivists argue that principled ideas like those on human rights produce a fundamental shift in the way states define their interests. As norms emerge and take hold, states undergo a learning process that includes gradual internalization of norms and eventually alters states' perceived interests.[20]

This book shows that the interplay of ideas and power is the central issue of international relations, necessarily drawing on all three schools. The constructivist approach effectively explains why initiating states have come to accept human rights as an important issue on which to engage China. The idea of human rights now affects the behavior of not only liberals who are already convinced that promotion of rights is important in its own right, but also conservatives who see promoting rights overseas as facilitating pursuit of traditional interests such as security and trade. The constructivist approach also offers a partial explanation for why countries vary in their behavior. Those countries most convinced of the importance of promoting human rights in world politics, such as the United States and some small Western European nations, are most willing to pay a price to engage in rights diplomacy; those less convinced of the wisdom of incorporating human rights into foreign policy, such as Japan, are less willing to confront offending governments. Constructivists can also predict, correctly, that Beijing would act differently if, independent of its power status, it adopted a more liberal view of human rights and democracy.

However, the constructivist approach does not explain why states holding the same principles behave differently. The institutionalist approach explains how an evolving international human rights regime influences member states' calculations of interests. This book shows that the international human rights regime has affected China's human rights relations with the West. For the West, the presence of the rights regime legitimizes its pressure on China and offers a less costly alternative to bilateral clashes. For China, its participation in the rights regime means that it needs to adapt its behavior. At the same time, the regime's impact on China is limited due to its weak enforcement mechanism.

While recognizing the contributions of the constructivist and institutionalist approaches, this author concludes, based on the empirical evidence in this book, that the realist approach offers a better explanation of China's human rights relations with the West. To start with, for strategic reasons, Western governments did not pressure China on human rights until the late 1980s. Soon after they initiated vigorous human rights diplomacy with China, their resolve weakened significantly because their human rights policy compromised other diplomatic issues. Realists can also fully understand why the United States has been more willing to pressure smaller countries such as Cuba while engaging with a major power like China. As for China, Beijing would not pay much attention to Western criticism and pressure if the West did not have superior power to back its moral claims. The Chinese government also sees its diplomatic activities in the UN Human Rights Commission as centered on defending its national interests against the West. And its rising power is a decisive reason that it has largely succeeded in fending off the Western human rights offensive.

Moreover, realism explains how external pressure is interpreted in China. To carry out human rights diplomacy, initiators still need to use conventional means of power—not only moral suasion but also threats, sanctions, and occasionally, as we saw in Kosovo, force. For people in the target nations, it is difficult to tell the difference between the nobly motivated idea that drives external pressure and the traditional power instruments by which that pressure is brought to bear. What China experiences directly is the latter, no matter the motivation. In particular, it makes practical sense for the external power to link human rights with other issues like trade or technology sales or aid disbursement. But from the point of view of the target state it seems as though the true interest is trade and strategic concerns—that human rights serves as a mere cover for power concerns.

A Note on Conventions

Chinese and Japanese names in this book generally have their surnames listed first, as is the custom in China and Japan. When Chinese and Japanese scholars choose to reverse their names when writing in English, names are presented in Western style. The pinyin system is used for Romanization of Chinese words, except names of individuals living outside mainland China.

Chapter Two

Chinese Views of Human Rights

Western diplomatic pressure has produced little progress on human rights in China. Indeed, human rights advocacy rarely yields immediate results whenever target governments, especially major powers such as China, put up strong resistance. But a lack of understanding of political and social developments in China has also aggravated the situation and led to misjudgments about timing and degrees of pressure. What has been missing in the public debate in the West is the Chinese voice. Western attention has focused mainly on Beijing's declared policies and Chinese dissidents' opinions. Hence, U.S. policy prescriptions and media commentaries are too often based on the simplistic view of a repressive Communist government ruthlessly frustrating a society composed of aspiring democrats, as represented by courageous human rights fighters like Wei Jingsheng. But does anyone know what China's "silent majority" think? The evidence suggests that they are in fact quite vocal in their own circles, expressing strong opinions about China and U.S. policy toward it.

Decision-makers and observers should know and care about the views of ordinary Chinese since what is being debated in the West is not conventional diplomacy but rather a campaign to pressure the Chinese government according to the Western notion of how a "civilized" member of the international community should behave. That implies an attempt to reweave the very fabric of Chinese political and social life; hence the receptivity of Chinese society is central to the wisdom and feasibility of such an interventionist approach.

One basic assumption in much Western writing about China is that its repressive government is standing in the way of progress and is thus "on the wrong side of history." That assumption is what legitimizes Western pressure on China. Since the end of the Cold War, the West has displayed increasing confidence in the inevitable triumph of human rights and democracy and can point to some evidence to substantiate such a view. The 1989 Tiananmen incident illustrated, on prime-time TV, the extent of discontent within China, and Chinese dissidents strike Western audiences as sympathetic speakers for democracy. But what if such impressionistic evidence does not reflect the normal situation? What if Chinese society as a whole does not share the same fundamental values as American society at this point of history? Should the West still exert pressure on China over human rights and democracy?

This chapter discusses the views on human rights and democracy held by the Chinese state and Chinese society and, to a lesser extent, what these views tell us about the legitimacy of the Chinese regime. The chapter's goal is to present Chinese views as objectively as possible. This is a difficult task because Chinese views on human rights and democracy are increasingly diverse, not only among officialdom, civil society, and the dissident community, but also within each of these broad categories. Chinese views are also evolving as domestic and external circumstances change. Nevertheless, mounting empirical evidence and personal observations suggest that we should be neither too optimistic nor too pessimistic about the prospect for human rights and democracy in China.

Optimism must be tempered with the realization that Chinese society is neither ready nor willing at this stage to push for democracy and human rights. For despite serious social and economic problems, Chinese society appears to be largely content with the country's economic performance. A broad developmentalist consensus has emerged, in government and society alike, that emphasizes stability as a precondition for economic development. The concern for stability and growth on the part of ordinary Chinese conditions their cautious and even suspicious views on human rights and democracy. Even most Chinese intellectuals have adopted an instrumentalist view, asking what these Western ideas and institutions can do to improve the lives of the people. As a result, the current regime enjoys significant popular support while the dissident movement attracts little sympathy. What this means for China's relations with the West is that human rights in China is a Western concern rather than one that strikes a chord with the

Chinese nation. In fact, human rights is now largely a foreign, not domestic, policy issue for the majority of Chinese.

But excessive pessimism is also unwarranted. Chinese society has evolved markedly since the present era of reform began in 1978. Ordinary Chinese have become more individualistic and conscious of their rights, especially property rights. More important, popular support for the political regime in China today does not mean that Chinese people have fallen in love with the party-state all over again. Rather, the society supports the regime because of a cynical but rational calculation of its best interest. The party-state is widely considered a necessary evil for the achievement of economic goals that society supports. Hence, a dialogue between the West and China on human rights is not quixotic, but only so long as the West continually takes the pulse of Chinese society while it communicates with Beijing.

Official China on Human Rights and Democracy

As Hungdah Chiu has noted, not a single article devoted exclusively to human rights was published in China before Mao Zedong's death in 1976.[1] The Chinese government's engagement in human rights dialogue with the outside world started with the reform in 1978. Ironically, Western scrutiny of China's human rights situation intensified just as China started making progress in this area.

The Information Office of the State Council has issued twenty one White Papers (listed below) since November 1991, thirteen of which deal with human rights. Eight of the thirteen respond to specific Western criticism of China's criminal justice system, its policy toward Tibetans and other minorities, its family planning program, its religious policy, and the status of Chinese women and children. The other five White Papers discuss human rights in general, and all of these five cover similar issues, thereby shedding light on changes in government views during the 1990s.

Human Rights in China	November 1991
Criminal Reform in China	August 1992
Tibet—Its Ownership and Human Rights Situation	September 1992
The Taiwan Question and Reunification of China	August 1993

The Situation of Chinese Women	June 1994
Intellectual Property Protection in China	June 1994
Family Planning in China	August 1995
China: Arms Control and Disarmament	November 1995
The Progress of Human Rights in China	December 1995
The Situation of Children in China	April 1996
Environmental Protection in China	June 1996
The Grain Issue in China	October 1996
On Sino-U.S. Trade Balance	March 1997
Progress in China's Human Rights Cause in 1996	March 1997
Freedom of Religious Belief in China	October 1997
New Progress in Human Rights in the Tibet Autonomous Region	February 1998
Development of China's Marine Program	Undated
China's National Defense	July 1998
Progress in China's Human Rights Cause in 1998	April 1999
National Minorities Policy and Its Practice in China	September 1999
Fifty Years of Progress in China's Human Rights	February 2000

The general human rights White Papers treat people's rights to subsistence and development as taking precedence over civil and political rights in China's current situation. Economic rights are therefore given priority in all these documents. The 1991 Human Rights White Paper maintains that "the right to subsistence is the most important of all human rights, without which the other rights are out of the question." It also begins with a six-paragraph discussion of imperialist aggressions against China. The 1995 White Paper toned down the anti-imperialist theme and summarized past Chinese humiliation in a single sentence. The paper highlights instead China's rapid economic growth, its rising incomes, the declining mortality rate, and government efforts to assist the poor. The 1997 and 1999 White Papers follow the format of the 1995 document and focus on China's economic performance in 1996 and 1998 respectively. The 2000 White Paper maintains that China has achieved major progress in human rights in all areas. All five documents treat political and civil rights in China as an afterthought to economic rights. The 1991 document asserts that Chinese "did not have any democratic rights to speak of in semifeudal, semi-colonial China" and that they "gained real democratic rights after the founding of New China." It emphasizes the Chinese constitution, the people's congresses at all levels, and multiparty cooperation led by the Communist Party. The next four White Papers omit the historical discussion. The 1995 paper discusses the Administrative Procedural Law of 1990 and the State Compensation Law of 1994, which have given citizens more rights against arbitrary state actions. The 1997 and 1999 papers highlight laws passed in the previous year that gave further protections to citizens. The 2000 paper reflects these themes. All five papers detail how local elections have become more democratic.

The arguments of the five documents have found echoes in statements and publications of other party and government organs. In addition, the government has established some research centers on human rights such as the China Society for Human Rights Studies. Although the association is supposed to be a nongovernmental organization, it is in essence, judging by its origin, mission, funding, membership, and privileged position, an extension of the party propaganda apparatus. The Society was created in response to Western criticism. In 1990 a group of leading foreign scientists wrote a letter to Zhou Guangzhao, head of the Chinese Academy of Sciences, criticizing China's human rights record and threatening to sever scientific exchanges with the country. Zhou showed the letter to Jiang Zemin, who instructed an organized response as China could no longer avoid the issue. China's official human rights studies kicked off in 1990, paving the way for the group's creation in 1993. The mission of the group is to engage foreign human rights NGOs, develop Chinese theories of human rights, and defend the Chinese government in the international arena. The Society has ten permanent staff members and more than a hundred members, mostly retired government officials and scholars. Leading members are mostly from the Xinhua News Agency. The funding for its activities and operational expenses for its four-room office at Tibet Tower in Beijing comes from the Human Rights Research Foundation, which is headed by Lu Dong, an influential former cabinet minister. Lu has used his influence to solicit more than ten million yuan in donations from large state enterprises since 1994, when the foundation was created. Leaders of the Society do not accept the suggestion that they might be controlled by the government. After all, they are party propaganda veterans and mentors of those now serving in the government and in party agencies. Zhu Muzhi, the president of CSHRS, headed the Central External Propaganda Small Group of the Central Party Committee before 1988, which means that he was essentially in charge of the party's external propaganda.[2] Moreover, truly nongovernmental groups intended to study and monitor human rights in China have not been allowed to exist. In Shanghai, a group called the Human Rights Association applied to the authorities as an organization in March 1993 but never heard a reply. Three members of another group, the Study Group on Human Rights in China, were sentenced to three years in labor camps in October 1994.[3]

Chinese government agencies and semi-official groups have produced hundreds of papers and dozens of books on human rights. They express a diversity of views.[4] For instance, the human rights articles (twenty-six essays between mid-1989 and mid-1994) in *Beijing Review*, an official English language news magazine aimed at a foreign audience, repeatedly deny that there are human rights problems in China, defend Chinese policies in Tibet especially, and condemn Western human rights pressure as interference in China's domestic affairs. Several authors claim that the Beijing regime does indeed protect human rights and, in any case, argue that different countries have different situations. An increasingly important theme is the preference for economic and social rights over civil and political rights. Other articles criticize human rights violations in the United States and thus point out contradictions in U.S. human rights policy.

The volume of Chinese writing on human rights decreased for a time after President Clinton delinked human rights and China's most-favored-nation trading status in May 1994. However, since the issue remains important in Sino-American relations, there is renewed interest in the topic in the official Chinese media, which now take a more aggressive approach. For example, in retaliation for a January 1996 Human Rights Watch report that alleged that children in some Chinese orphanages have died of neglect and starvation, the Chinese government sponsored a commentary in *People's Daily* that criticized the conditions of children in the United States.[5] In another case, the China Society for Human Rights Studies authored a paper in March 1996 entitled "A Comparison of Human Rights in China with Those in the United States." This paper was a response to the U.S. State Department annual report and concluded that China is doing better than the United States. In March 1999, the Society published "Human Rights Record in the United States," an explicit response to the State Department 1998 report released on February 26, 1999.

The Chinese media rallied against the United States and NATO after NATO's accidental bombing of the Chinese embassy in Belgrade in May 1999. Besides sensational coverage of the bombing, the Chinese media focused on a few themes. One theme is that the Western notion of "humanitarian intervention" is unacceptable. One article in *People's Daily* argues that humanitarian intervention is based on the incorrect assumption that human rights are more important than sovereignty. The article argues that, in fact, the United States is using the notion of "humanitarian intervention" to justify the use of military means to practice hegemony.[6] Another article in *People's Daily* asserts that the United States is using internal issues such as human rights as an excuse for interfering in the internal affairs of the countries that refuse to follow its leadership.[7] Another important theme is that the West used the bombing of the Chinese embassy to create chaos in China to keep it from becoming stronger. An editorial in *People's Daily* urged people to rally around Jiang Zemin and the party leadership to build a stronger nation, and it emphasized that stability is the key to China's success.[8]

Interpreting Chinese Human Rights Commentaries

When we examine subtle changes in tone and focus in Chinese texts to try to determine whether the Chinese state has made progress in human rights, we should exercise caution. One may conclude that the published views of the government show considerable progress. After all, the government no longer denies the importance of human rights and has come to embrace more rights than before, in rhetoric if not in action. One may hypothesize that Western rights pressure has forced the Chinese government to confront human rights issues, which in time has led to a change in government viewpoint, due to the persuasiveness of the rights arguments. There are surely reasons for optimism. In order to engage in discussion or debate over human rights with the West, the Chinese government has allowed translation and publication in China of virtually all important human rights documents and treaties.[9] Also, the government has given more leeway to more open-minded and independent scholars to discuss rights issues.[10] All this may help spread the idea of human rights and democracy in the country and contribute to healthy long-term developments. However, shifts in Chinese propaganda at this point in history are more indicative of an adaptive learning process through which Chinese government agencies and "unofficial" study centers search for a better propaganda pitch. A relative conception of human rights works better than a flat denial of human rights or an outright rejection of interference in domestic affairs. An emphasis on subsistence rights over political and civil rights resonates with many developing nations and with Chinese citizens.

The views of Chinese propaganda agencies do not automatically translate into state policies. In the Chinese configuration of power, the agencies directly involved in human rights issues are the propaganda and education (*xuanjiao*) system or *xitong*, and the foreign affairs (*waishi*) *xitong*.[11] The propaganda *xitong* serves as the mouthpiece of the party. The Central Propaganda Department of the party is the leading agency, and its Bureau of Overseas Propaganda orchestrates propaganda targeted at foreign countries. The White Papers discussed earlier were the products of the Bureau.[12] In contrast, the foreign affairs *xitong* is responsible for China's foreign policy, including human rights diplomacy, with the Foreign Ministry as the key implementing organization.[13] The propaganda and foreign affairs *xitongs* are parallel institutions and are not well coordinated. Foreign policy bureaucrats generally ignore propaganda functionaries.[14] The UN Human Rights Division of the Foreign Ministry conducts its own research on human rights laws and treaties and has little contact with human rights scholars in universities or research institutes.[15] With the foreign affairs *xitong* charged with defending Chinese national interests, career diplomats consider it humiliating if China is condemned in the UN Human Rights Commission, regardless of their personal convictions. More than their counterparts in democratic nations, Chinese diplomats are interested in self-preservation, which means avoiding diplomatic failures. As a result, China's human rights diplomacy is much more pragmatic and flexible than government rhetoric would suggest. Despite the lack of coordination, the propaganda and foreign affairs *xitongs* are connected at the top. The party leadership sets guidelines for both *xitongs* to coordinate what the government says and does. Although the propaganda *xitong* is at times more zealous than the party leadership, the rhetoric reflects the political environment in China, which conditions the country's foreign policy as well. Commentaries by the Xinhua News Agency or in *People's Daily* and statements by the Foreign Ministry now sound strikingly similar, an indication of converging views on human rights and democracy among government officials.

Deng Xiaoping set the tone for China's human rights theories.[16] The third volume of his speeches (from September 1982 to February 1992) published by the party includes extensive discussions of human rights and Western democracy.[17] The dominant themes in his discussions are that economic development should be China's priority and that stability is absolutely essential for realizing this goal. Only the Communist Party is capable of leading the country to economic success and international prestige. To ensure stability, the party needs to be resolute in dealing with challenges to its authority from inside and outside the party, challenges that undermine stability. Western democracy is unsuitable for China. Specifically, Deng believed that improvement of economic welfare is a foremost human right and also the prerequisite for other rights, that collective rights take precedence over individual rights and that sovereignty is far more important than individual rights.

Deng's candid discussions also give us important clues for understanding his thought process. It is apparent that his views had been shaped by China's past humiliation, his revolutionary experience, and his personal suffering during the chaotic Cultural Revolution. China's past committed him to an overarching goal of making the country strong and glorious again. His revolutionary experience committed him to a firm belief in the party leadership and legitimacy. His humiliation during the Cultural Revolution committed him to an orderly society and to maintaining stability at all costs. It is important to note that current leaders share with Deng a collective and selective memory of China's past and the Cultural Revolution, events which have shaped their conservative attitude toward political change. The only difference is that the current leaders, who lack revolutionary experience, want party primacy due to a vested interest in power rather than revolutionary convictions.

Government views on human rights and democracy are now represented by President Jiang Zemin, who echoes Deng's thoughts. His 1997 state visit to the United States provided a rare opportunity for the outside world to hear his personal views on these issues. Jiang presented himself as an open-minded leader, but he differed sharply with his American hosts on human rights issues. The spontaneous exchange between Jiang and Clinton at a joint press conference on October 29 illustrated this in striking fashion. Responding to a reporter's question about the Tiananmen incident, Jiang claimed that "the Communist Party of China and the Chinese government have long drawn the correct conclusion on this political disturbance, and facts have also proved that if a country with an over 1.2 billion population does not enjoy social and political stability, it cannot possibly have the situation of reform and opening up that we are having today." Clinton responded that the Chinese government "is on the wrong side of history" on this issue. Jiang also held spirited debates over human rights with U.S. congressional leaders.

Jiang has talked about human rights a few more times since his U.S. trip, with little notable change in his views. He discussed human rights with Clinton again during the American president's visit to China in June 1998. In fact, he has become more confident and assertive in discussing rights issues. In a twenty-minute speech given to a gathering of world business leaders organized by Time-Warner's *Fortune* magazine in Shanghai in September 1999, Jiang spent much time expressing China's view on human rights, emphasizing that without rights to survival and development one cannot think of other rights and that China is making a major contribution to the global human rights cause by assuring rights to survival and development for more than 1.2 billion people. "We oppose any efforts by any country to impose its own social system and ideology on another country," he told his audience.

Jiang's remarks reflect the dominant view in the Chinese government. What has emerged as a convergence point for most government and party agencies is "developmental authoritarianism," which calls special attention to China's *guoqing* or state conditions.[18] According to this view, stability is critical for achieving the country's primary objective of economic development. Some would go further and argue that the party leadership is necessary for ensuring political stability. The government agencies not centrally involved with human rights have more pressing issues at hand: to promote economic reform, raise living standards for their districts or working units, and promote the careers of their officials. My discussions with Chinese officials have repeatedly confirmed that developmentalism prevails among Chinese officials. As a typical example, a deputy head of a major state enterprise from a northern city concluded during his first visit to the United States that the "beautiful country"— the literal translation of the Chinese name for the United States— is blessed with natural resources, giving it leeway to allow greater personal freedom than China, which is not as endowed with resources. Chinese should focus on improving their living standards and therefore they need stability.[19]

Dissent assuredly exists within the party and the government. In 1978, Deng Xiaoping's supporters advocated a pragmatic theory of "seeking truth from facts" and won an ideological battle against then party chairman Hua Guofeng and other beneficiaries of the Cultural Revolution, who dogmatically advocated following Mao's instructions verbatim. This first "thought liberation" helped Deng establish his dominance in the party and launch economic reform. The second thought liberation in 1992 (socialist or capitalist) and the third thought liberation in 1997 (public or private) were essentially part of an ongoing debate over the growing strength of the private sector, which had come about as a result of Deng's widening and deepening economic reforms. As Ma Licheng and Ling Zhijun see it, the first thought liberation broke the personality worship of Mao, the second broke the worship of planned economy, and the third broke the worship of public ownership; all three liberations had the common theme of battling leftists who at first tried to prevent and still continue to challenge Deng's economic reforms.[20] The Deng Xiaoping theory was enshrined in the new party constitution adopted at the 15th Party Congress in September 1997. The core of Deng's theory is to conduct economic reform while strengthening the party leadership to ensure political stability. Such a theory will prevent fundamental political reform toward greater democracy in the system and will also prevent citizens' getting more civil and political rights.

More liberal views and policy prescriptions for political reform have challenged the party orthodoxy in the past and will continue to do so in the future.[21] To cite a recent example, Li Shenzhi, former vice president of the Chinese Academy of Social Sciences, wrote shortly after the fifty-year anniversary of the founding of the PRC that it is high time for democratization in China.[22] Some have also worked quietly to improve grass-roots democracy.[23] One may hope that liberal dissent will spread and someday become the mainstream view within the party and the government. But Deng's "voice" clearly dominates in China at this point, compared to other voices characterized by dogmatism, nationalism, feudalism, and democracy.[24] It is thus important to note that an effective and coherent opposition force for political reform in China will take time to emerge. Until then, the outside world should base its analysis on the actual current level of political development in China rather than on wishful thinking.

It is also important to note that liberals within the party and government, unlike dissidents outside the political system, do not necessarily support outside criticism and pressure on the issue of human rights. In fact, support within the government for the American position on human rights has weakened even further in the past few years, particularly since NATO's bombing of the Chinese embassy in Belgrade on May 8, 1999. Even some previously liberal-minded officials have come to believe that Americans are indeed using human rights pressure to weaken China. It is also important to recognize a clear trend of declining liberalism and rising nationalism in China in the 1990s. The government's continuous repression partly explains declining liberalism. But China's rising economic power, widening economic opportunities, and mounting Western pressure over a wide variety of issues have also contributed to this trend. In this context, Chinese commentaries on human rights currently reflect the dominant opinion of official China, a fact that has boosted the confidence and conviction of commentators themselves.[25]

China's "Silent Majority" Speak

It is difficult to know precisely the opinions of ordinary Chinese in the absence of systematic national polls to allow time-series and cross-section analyses of public opinion. Since the views of the majority of the society are not easily heard, both the government and dissidents claim to represent Chinese society. The Chinese government routinely refers to itself as "the Chinese government and Chinese people" and charges any foreign criticism or actions it does not like as "hurting the feelings of the Chinese people." Such claims are rightly challenged by dissidents. For example, Xiao Qiang, executive director of Human Rights in China, which is based in New York, commented that "the world rarely hears Chinese (or Tibetan) voices for democracy and human rights, because they have been totally suppressed by Jiang's government."[26] However, the fact that the voice of Chinese society is not heard does not necessarily mean that society shares the views of dissidents. Observers outside China normally speculate based on anecdotal evidence and reasoning. More important, their assessments are often shaped by explosive media events like the 1989 Tiananmen Incident. But the opinions expressed at moments of passion do not necessarily represent the views and calculations of the society under normal circumstances.

In this section I sketch a portrait of Chinese society based on occasional opinion polls conducted in China in recent years, on interviews, and on participation in seminars, conferences, and internet groups. This rough picture displays four interesting features about Chinese society regarding human rights and democracy.

First, the majority of Chinese today prefer social order and stability to freedom. Based on a survey conducted in Beijing in December 1995, Yang Zhong, Jie Chen, and John M. Scheb II found that 33.8 percent of those polled agreed that they "would rather live in an orderly society than in a freer society which is prone to disruption" and another 61.8 percent strongly agreed with the statement. Only 3.6 percent and 1.6 percent respectively disagreed or strongly disagreed.[27] To be sure, the survey question was based on the premise that more freedom risks instability, which is not necessarily so, although the government clearly emphasizes such a connection to its own advantage. The phrasing of the question may well have skewed the results in the direction of support for order over freedom. However, the notion that freedom may lead to instability is persuasive to many ordinary Chinese, given their collective experience with past political experiments and turmoil. The answers to the poll question suggest widespread worry among ordinary citizens about any political change that promises greater freedom but may also undermine stability. Chinese are generally cautious toward political and economic change. The extraordinary energy exhibited during the 1989 Tiananmen incident illustrated the potential of Chinese society for political change, but the broad support shown for student protesters stemmed more from a desire to end official corruption than from a desire for democracy. Under normal circumstances, most Chinese are not active politically. In addition, when many Chinese consider the fate of the former Soviet Union, they draw a negative conclusion about the wisdom of promoting democracy at all costs.

Second, Chinese citizens are more preoccupied with economic advancement than political freedom at this point. This is even the case among college students, traditionally the most politically aware and active social group. According to a survey of 1,512 members of the Chinese elite conducted by *Far Eastern Economic Review* in Beijing, Guangzhou, and Shanghai in July–August 1999, 60 percent of the respondents agreed that economic prosperity should take precedence over political freedom, with 15 percent disagreeing and 24 percent saying neither was more important than the other. One would expect China's upper middle class to be most interested in political rights. In fact, when asked about their most important values, 65 percent chose hardworking, followed by accountability (54 percent) and respect for learning (47 percent), while only 15 percent chose personal achievement and 14 percent personal freedom.[28] Chinese society's strong preference for economic prosperity is certainly related to its strong preference for social stability.

Third, Chinese political culture still exhibits some undemocratic attributes that might create problems if the country were to undergo democratization now. Based on a national survey conducted in China in 1990, Andrew J. Nathan and Tianjian Shi identified the following potential difficulties for immediate democratization in Chinese political culture although there is no reason to believe that "Chinese political culture is an absolute bar to democracy." Compared with citizens in more advanced nations, Chinese show lower levels of awareness of the government's impact on their daily lives, lower expectations of fair treatment from the government, and lower tolerance of ideas with which they disagree. Although educated Chinese score higher in perceived government impact and political tolerance than their less-educated countrymen, they are still "substantially less likely to hold democratic orientations than people of the same educational levels elsewhere."[29] The Chinese are thus caught in a sort of "Catch-22": they cannot acquire the attributes necessary for democratization in the absence of democratic experience itself.

Fourth, Chinese are becoming more individualistic, the young especially so.[30] According to a Gallup poll conducted in China in 1997, more than half the Chinese polled described their life philosophy as "work hard and get rich," while only 3 percent nationally saw their basic attitude toward life as "never think of yourself, give everything in service to society."[31] Chinese are also increasingly aware of their rights, property rights in particular. A poll conducted in 1994 in Beijing indicated that when presented with "stories" of rights violations, an absolute majority of people were aware of their rights, with urban residents more informed than rural residents.[32] In fact, Chinese people are more concerned about economic rights than social and political rights. This pattern is illustrated by a project entitled Social Development and Protection of Civil Rights in China, which was conducted by a Chinese research team from 1992 to 1995.[33] Its nationwide survey showed that while 50 to 60 percent of respondents would be highly resentful if the fruits of their labor were seized by government cadres, almost one-third of those polled would exhibit no resentment if someone entered their house without permission. Chinese are even less assertive about their political rights: only 15 percent of those polled had considerable or strong resentment about having no opportunity to voice their opinions on policy and law.[34]

If China replicates the experience of Taiwan and South Korea, a greater awareness of property rights will, in the end, lead to a greater awareness of political and civil rights.[35] But based on the evidence to date, this connection has yet to be made in China. In fact, according to the 1992–95 national survey mentioned earlier, between one-third and one-half of the respondents answer that rights to personal safety, to election and dismissal of cadres, and to humane treatment in confinement are granted by the state. And only 1 to 3 percent think people are born with these rights. Since the start of the reform, almost all new rights have been granted to the people by the state and only a few civil rights initiatives have come from below.[36]

A powerful combination of aversion to political instability and awareness of economic interests and rights provides a fertile ground for developmentalist and instrumentalist views of human rights, now shared by the government and most of society. According to these views, China's paramount objective should be economic growth; political stability is essential to assure China's continued success in development; and democracy may not suit China's current needs given the country's unique and difficult *guoqing*. This perspective is reinforced by general satisfaction among Chinese with their rising living standards, the country's rising status on the world stage, and their wish to see a powerful and prosperous China. The 1997 Gallup poll cited earlier showed that Chinese adults rate their quality of life as 29 percent better than it was five years ago and expect quality of life to improve by a further 32 percent over the next five years. The 1999 *Far Eastern Economic Review* survey of the Chinese elite revealed a high degree of satisfaction with China's economic development among the Chinese elite, with more than half of the respondents agreeing that China is already a developed nation and 87 percent agreeing or agreeing strongly that the country "must assume a stronger leadership role in the world."[37]

The prevalence of such views among ordinary Chinese explains why human rights and democracy continue to be perceived as foreign concepts remote from daily life. Indeed, the most striking trend in China today is strong political conservatism combined with nationalist emotions, even among intellectuals. While the government has appealed to nationalism as a substitute for discredited communist ideology, U.S. pressure has arguably also contributed to rising nationalist sentiment among Chinese. In fact, merely four years after the 1989 Tiananmen incident, independent Chinese intellectuals sharply reversed the very positive views of the United States they had had in the 1980s, publishing books and articles and expressing views against the West. One key reason for such a reversal was that these intellectuals started questioning the motives of American human rights diplomacy and came to believe that the West was seeking strategic and economic advantages for itself without real concern for Chinese freedom.[38] While these intellectuals carefully distanced themselves from government positions and avoided appealing to nationalism, nationalist sentiment did grow in the 1990s, with encouragement from the government. The massive demonstrations in front of the American embassy and consulates in May 1999 were triggered by NATO's accidental bombing of the Chinese embassy in Belgrade, but resentment against Western criticism and pressure had been building for several years. Human rights pressure was in fact often identified as a reason for anti-Western sentiment, especially among young Chinese.[39] Although misconceptions to the effect that the United States is attempting to destabilize China may be fanciful, they nonetheless condition policy debates and decisions in China.

Conditional Popular Support for the Regime

Contrary to the perception in the West that the Chinese government is an illegitimate regime that has survived solely by coercion, there is now considerable public support in China for the government. Jie Chen, Yang Zhong, and Jan William Hillard found strong popular support for the regime in a survey conducted in Beijing in December 1995.[40] What is more, popular support appears to have grown. In a nationwide survey conducted by a team of American-trained Chinese scholars in 1986 and 1987, there was only "moderate" support for the political regime, even though support for the country was strong.[41] It is difficult to draw definite conclusions based on the two surveys, which followed different procedures. But the findings confirm rather than contradict the impression one gets that there is stronger public support for the government now than in the mid-1980s.

Opinion surveys have not posed specific questions about Chinese society's views toward human rights and democracy advocates, but anecdotal evidence suggests little support from ordinary Chinese citizens. Dissidents play, at most, a marginal role in shaping China's political, economic, and social developments. Chinese dissidents, prone to infighting and factional politics, have consistently failed to form a united front against the government.[42] Moreover, Chinese advocates for democracy have had difficulty forming associations with peasants and workers. An important reason for this is that the dissidents often take an elitist attitude toward peasants, whom they judge to be unable to understand democracy, and toward militant workers, whom they perceive as a threat to a functioning democratic system.[43] Such attitudes undermine society's sympathy for human rights advocates regardless of government actions.

Such data, of course, must be handled with circumspection. One obvious objection to these surveys is that Chinese respondents may be afraid to give their true opinions. This is a common concern for pollsters conducting surveys in China. But pollsters alleviate people's fear of government retaliation by keeping strict confidentiality. Nor is there a single known case of the government tracking down survey respondents for retaliation. This is due in part to the absence of government regulations on academic survey research before 1997. Now researchers need advanced government approval of the content of their surveys. As of August 1999, the Chinese government has also imposed limits on market surveys. Now market researchers have to present their questionnaires for prior approval from the State Statistical Bureau and their results for review by the bureau before giving them to clients. The government is clearly worried about market researchers asking politically sensitive questions and engaging in espionage.[44] Ironically, government concern gives us more confidence in the surveys that were done before the restrictions.

We also need to question whether the respondents actually understand abstract concepts differently. This is a serious problem that we need to take into consideration even though some surveys have made adjustments by giving respondents scenarios rather than asking them about abstract concepts.

Another possible objection is more important. The calculations and views expressed in the polls reflect in large part the harsh political reality that the communist regime created in the first place. There is not a level playing field between the government and dissidents. The government has forcibly prevented dissidents from presenting their views and alternative programs to ordinary Chinese by sending almost all leading dissidents abroad or to prison, thus separating them from the larger society. Wei Jingsheng, who was expelled from China in November 1997, had resisted going abroad precisely to prevent diminishing his influence in China. Likewise, the government monopolizes the carrots (financial benefits) and sticks (violence and imprisonment) by which public opinion is molded. Thus, the Tiananmen incident was a reminder to Chinese that the government is willing and able to use brutal force, while at the same time it alone possesses the financial resources to benefit society. No wonder most Chinese people keep their distance from political protests and dissidents. One may thus speculate that opinion polls and interviews might produce decidedly different results if Chinese society were more openly exposed to the views of human rights advocates. But neither should that possibility be exaggerated. After all, most Chinese scholars in the United States continue to lend considerable support to Beijing and largely share the premise of developmentalism despite constant exposure to alternative views and protests against Chinese government policies. Chinese dissidents have had, in fact, only a limited impact on the political attitudes and behavior of Chinese scholars overseas. Liberal-minded Chinese intellectuals have been seizing every conceivable opportunity to advocate a more open political system and more respect for human rights. Unlike dissidents who openly challenge the communist authority, these political reformers seek to operate within the system while testing the limits of party tolerance at any given moment. Encouraged by Zhu Rongji's selection as prime minister and Clinton's scheduled June 1998 visit, some daring intellectuals published books and organized discussion forums or internet groups to openly advocate Western-style liberalism, political reform, and respect for human rights in the first half of 1998.[45] Despite some cautious optimism, this turned out to be another short-lived "Beijing Spring." Soon after Clinton left China, the government shut down political discussion groups and issued new regulations for the internet. As during previous Beijing springs, more open intellectual discussions were accompanied by dissidents' seizing the opportunity to mount a direct challenge to party authority. Hundreds of long-term and recent dissidents took advantage of Clinton's visit to seek official registration of a new opposition party, the China Democracy Party (CDP). Although hesitant at first, the government eventually initiated a crackdown. In typical fashion, the government punished organized dissidents severely, sentencing dozens of CDP members to long jail terms, though liberal-minded intellectuals were treated more gently.

We would not know for sure whether the public would have responded massively to the appeal of political reform and human rights if the government had allowed the 1998 Beijing spring to continue and had tolerated the CDP's existence. However, it appeared that ordinary Chinese citizens did not pay close attention to the intellectual debates or dissident activities. Most Chinese continue to avoid the dangerous minefield of politics and focus energy instead on family and career, an option open to them and encouraged by the government. Even among college students, the most potent sentiment in 1998 was nationalist rather than liberal, which explains why thousands of students came out to protest against the United States and NATO in May 1999.

In short, Chinese society's broad developmentalist and instrumentalist views on human rights and democracy provide a partial explanation for the growing popular support for the party-government and the lack of support for dissidents. Society supports the state because it supports the state's goals of developing the national economy and building a strong nation and because it agrees that political stability is necessary to realize these goals. Popular support rises when the nation makes progress in achieving these goals.

Living Dangerously

It must be said, however, that the real story is more complicated than can be suggested by a simple linear relationship between popular support and shared goals. The evidence suggests that Chinese society supports the government not because it closely identifies with the regime, but because it sees it as a necessary evil for achieving what it wants. Thus, Chinese society has "distanced" itself from the party-state, both physically and mentally. Such distancing is the inevitable result of reform, which fundamentally is about adjusting the relationship between the state and the society. As economic reform deepens and widens, ordinary Chinese enjoy greater freedom in areas such as employment, travel, residence, and schooling. The party-state has retreated from one area after another even though it has remained stubborn in cracking down on open and organized attempts to challenge its power. This distancing applies to all major social groups, from farmers to intellectuals, who are now identified more with the society than with the party.[46] The rural majority, meanwhile, has become more independent of the state in economic, social, and even political life.[47]

More significant, the society has become estranged psychologically from the party and the government. Ordinary Chinese are not thrilled with the government's performance in specific areas. Chen, Zhong, and Hillard found that Chinese graded their government poorly on controlling inflation, providing job security, minimizing the income gap, improving housing conditions, maintaining social order, providing adequate medical care, providing welfare to the needy, and combating pollution.[48] There is no blind faith in the party-state. Quite the contrary, there is widespread distrust of the party-state. In the 1986–87 survey cited by Chan and Nesbitt-Larking, while there was moderate support for the political system and goals of the party (62 percent approval rating), over 80 percent of respondents claimed that party members are not good models for them.[49] While 57 percent of those polled were satisfied with the party's current line and policy, only 30 percent thought the party's performance satisfied their expectations (62 percent answered no). Some 57 percent did not want to be Communist Party members, and only 56 percent of those who were party members were proud of that fact.[50] As a dramatic example of the party's loss of moral authority, Falun Gong (law wheel practice), a sect founded by Li Hongzhi that combines traditional breathing practices with Buddhist teachings, acquired millions of followers in a short period of time, including many party cadres and government officials.

How does one explain the apparent paradox of significant popular support for the regime combined with low satisfaction with the party-state? Media control and government propaganda do not provide a sufficient explanation. If the party's brainwashing had worked, public estrangement from the state would not exist. The logical hypothesis would seem to be that the polling data is a product of people's cold calculations rather than any affection for the party-state. Consistent with its views on human rights and democracy, Chinese society has increasingly adopted an instrumentalist view: what is important is not the form or ideology of the state but its success in promoting growth. Lack of alternatives and aversion to chaos and instability encourage such calculations, and while no survey data address this question directly, it is a mentality that emerges repeatedly in interviews and discussions with Chinese from all walks of life.

This development actually bodes well for human rights and democracy in China. All the courageous challenges to the state by individuals or groups will avail nothing unless ordinary Chinese are capable of a sophisticated, rational assessment of their own best interests. The evidence is that they are—and that they understand that democracy cannot be sustained in a country in which the society and the state are locked in a perpetual, uncompromising struggle.

There now exists an implicit contract between the state and the society. To maintain its power, the state needs to respond to societal needs and leave enough space for societal self-expression. In return, the society concentrates on nonpolitical pursuits and avoids open and organized challenges to the state. The party understands that its existence is largely contingent upon its willingness and ability to address issues that are of immediate concern to the people. In recent years the government has responded to public concerns about inflation, crime, corruption, and unemployment, if not always in a timely and exact fashion.

At the same time, the party-state is living dangerously. Public support is contingent upon performance. The challenge facing China is daunting as the nation goes through several transformations simultaneously: from a planned to a guided market economy, from a rural to an urbanized society, from a highly centralized to a more decentralized state, from revolutionaries to technocrats in top leadership, and from a self-sufficient economy to one closely integrated with the global economy. China needs to address poverty, the environment, population, education, ethnic conflicts—and the list goes on. Ironically, while society is gaining more independence from the state, it has also come to expect more from the state. As Tianjian Shi demonstrated, Chinese citizens have always engaged in voluntary participatory acts such as appeals, adversarial activities, cronyism, and boycotts to articulate their interests. Chinese citizens have not been able to articulate collective demands directly to the state due to the *danwei* or working unit system in which they compete with each other for scarce resources.[51] However, as the *danwei* system is eroding, collective problems such as unemployment and official corruption may serve to mobilize the masses against the government. In fact, labor unrest has grown drastically. Labor disputes increased from 8,150 in 1992 to 120,000 in 1999, but labor disputes still make up a small percentage of total disputes, a mere 7 percent in 1998. While violent protests have been reported, there is no evidence that workers from different enterprises have sought to strike simultaneously.[52] But Beijing is clearly worried.

Chinese scholars and officials often suggest that the country needs to maintain an 8 percent growth rate in gross national product to prevent social chaos. But such rates are difficult to sustain. China was shielded from the financial crisis that began in Asia in 1997 due to its enormous foreign trade surplus, massive reserves, and relative insulation from global financial markets. But the crisis still had a major negative impact on the Chinese economy and alerted investors to the problems in China. A slowdown in the economy is now aggravating the problem of failing state enterprises and the weak banking system. The China National Bureau of Statistics announced on December 29, 1999 that China's GDP growth for 1999 had reached 7.1 percent, surpassing the target of 7 percent. But most analysts believe that China's actual growth for the year was significantly lower. China is in a bind. If the government keeps pumping money into state enterprises, it will face more serious banking and budget deficit problems. If the government proceeds with a drastic reform of state enterprises, it will have to face the problem of millions more unemployed and angry workers. The government has slowed down the pace of state enterprise reform to prevent an already serious problem from getting worse, but this will only defer the crisis to a future time.[53]

The party is a danger to itself, judging from the widespread corruption among its officials. Persistent and serious corruption erodes public confidence. To make matters worse, unemployed workers readily relate their economic hardship to government corruption, which is a potent source of public protests against the state. In response, the party has periodically launched anticorruption campaigns, often using some high-profile cases to address public anger. However, the party has proven incapable of dealing with its own problems. As absolute power corrupts absolutely, the only way for the party to rid itself of structural corruption is to conduct fundamental political reforms, allowing a free press to serve as a public watch dog, an independent judiciary system to investigate and prosecute corruption cases, and a more competitive political process to enable citizens to select more qualified officials who possess greater integrity.

As the party has so far refused to conduct meaningful political reform, it has mainly resorted to repressive measures to prevent organized protest. The leadership has been hypersensitive about social stability since late 1998, and it adopted excessive measures to prevent social unrest. In particular, the party has waged a major political campaign against the Falun Gong sect. On April 25, 1999, about ten thousand followers of the sect surprised the party leadership by staging a silent demonstration around Zhongnanhai, a compound that houses the party headquarters. The protest's purpose was to pressure the government to allow the group to practice legally, and it was the largest demonstration in the center of Beijing since 1989.

This organized and disciplined sect represents a serious challenge to the Communist Party because it presents an alternative belief system. After careful preparations, the government announced its ban of the group on July 22. On December 26, a Chinese court sentenced four sect leaders to jail terms ranging up to eighteen years. But repression only breeds long-term problems for the party and the nation. In an impressive display of civil disobedience, Falun Gong followers continue to demonstrate silently throughout the country and thousands of them have engaged in a quiet campaign of defiance in Tiananmen Square.

It is never easy to forecast China's political future. The government has consistently surprised observers with brilliant successes and mind-boggling blunders. But what we can say is that the way in which the party-state adapts itself to challenges facing it will in part shape its destiny, determine whether it is dumped into the dustbin of history or whether it continues to dominate China's political development. It should also be recognized that precisely because of Chinese society's instrumentalist views, the party-state will face serious challenges when the calculations of society change as a result of its enhanced political awareness and belief in viable alternatives.

Implications for China's Relations with the West

This discussion of Chinese perspectives on human rights and democracy has important implications for China's relations with the West. While U.S. policymakers must continue to bow to Americans' moral concerns and their own political interests, they also must recognize how concerned, or relatively unconcerned, a majority of Chinese are about human rights and democracy at a given time. As Chinese society evolves, a dialogue between China and the West is possible and can prove productive. Certainly when Chinese citizens are ready to push for greater democracy and human rights, they will seek inspiration from the experience of existing democratic nations. However, it is important to recognize that although Western concerns and the concerns of Chinese society overlapped somewhat from 1989 to 1990, there is at present a chill. If China's "silent majority" does not respond to Western pressure, then interventionist diplomacy is unwise and counterproductive: unwise because any pressure that does not strike a sympathetic chord with ordinary Chinese will fail, and counterproductive because human rights pressure only contributes to rising nationalism in China. The Chinese have the same right to evolve morally and politically, on their terms and at their own pace, as the West has had. And the one thing the United States cannot do is hasten the process through its own impositions in an attempt "to save China from the Chinese."

Chapter Three

Human Rights and Sino-U.S. Relations

Convenient Negligence in the 1970s

Human rights was not an issue between the United States and China in the 1970s. Human rights in China was rarely mentioned by the government, the media, or human rights nongovernmental organizations (NGOs) in the United States. China was a "human rights exception" even when the United States pursued a global human rights policy after 1974.[1] Human rights in China emerged as an issue for the media, NGOs, and some scholars in the United States in the late 1970s.[2] Nevertheless, human rights remained largely a non-issue between U.S. administrations and the Chinese government until the early 1980s when Ronald Reagan became president.

There were good reasons why human rights was not an issue between China and the United States in this period. The United States and China shared strategic interests in containing the Soviet Union. There was a general understanding that both sides should set aside drastic differences in social values and political systems and that their bilateral relationship should be based on noninterference in internal affairs. This understanding was evident in the Shanghai communiqué signed during Richard Nixon's 1972 visit to China; the United States would not criticize the Chinese government for its internal policies and the Chinese government would refrain from exporting revolution to the United States. "What is important is not a nation's internal political philosophy," Nixon told Mao. "What is important is its policy toward the rest of the world and toward us."[3] In addition, U.S. officials were sensitive to Chinese feelings at this early stage in their relationship.[4]

Sino-U.S. interaction in this period did have a normative dimension. The Americans had high hopes that China would change through its closer ties with the outside world. As for the Chinese government, there was increasing concern over "corrupt" Western influence on Chinese society. It is true that there was a greater awareness in China of human rights in this period than in previous times, but this official awareness was more acknowledgment than endorsement of the Western idea of human rights.

While the Chinese government refused to confront the human rights issue during this period, it was gradually losing its control over Chinese people's thinking. After a spontaneous protest movement in Tiananmen Square in Beijing in April 1976 on the occasion of the death of the premier, Zhou Enlai, a small but persistent dissident movement grew. Chinese dissidents caught world attention during the 1979 "democracy wall" movement, when posters openly expressing political opinions and sometimes challenging the Communist Party were put up on a wall near the center of Beijing. Although the movement was eventually suppressed by the government, the increasing voluntary involvement of Chinese society and intellectuals in the process of politics and economics in China would have an important impact on the human rights interaction between China and the West in later years.

Increasing Tensions in the 1980s

Human rights as a diplomatic issue between China and the United States emerged in this period. The first human rights incident was Reagan's granting of political asylum to the Chinese tennis player Hu Na in 1983 despite strong protest from the Chinese government. In 1984 eighteen U.S. Representatives wrote to the Chinese government expressing concern over China's human rights record. In August 1985, Congress passed an amendment attacking China's forced abortion policies. In October 1987, Congress passed an amendment regarding China's violation of human rights in Tibet. When George Bush, a former U.S. ambassador to Beijing, became president, he chose China as one of the first countries to visit and hoped to restructure the Sino-U.S. relationship on a broad basis.[5] However, what dominated U.S. media coverage during his 1989 visit was "the Fang Lizhi Incident," which highlighted the human rights situation in China.[6] This foreshadowed the storm to come later that year.

There were several reasons for the shift in U.S. policy over human rights in China. First, after the United States and the Soviet Union resumed annual summits in 1985 to improve bilateral relations, the United States did not need China as a strategic balance against the Soviet Union as much as it had previously. The United States was now "freer" to criticize China. Second, as China became more involved in international politics, it was held to higher standards. There was hope that China could be pushed to make further improvements in human rights. After all, the Chinese government under Deng Xiaoping had been rehabilitating the cadres and citizens wronged in previous political campaigns. Third, closer interaction between the two nations connected human rights NGOs in the United States to emerging dissidents in China. Fourth, with a more open China, the Western media acquired better knowledge of the extent of past and present human rights violations in China. Ironically, the West became aware of the human rights issue in China just after China had made its greatest progress in this area in decades.

Despite increasing tensions over human rights, the issue did not dominate the agenda between the two nations in this period. "Naturally, there have been some incidents, in a technical sense, but not in a political sense," Deng told U.S. National Security Advisor Brent Scowcroft and Deputy Secretary of State Lawrence Eagleburger during their visit to Beijing in November 1989.[7] One important reason for low U.S. human rights pressure was that Deng was widely perceived to be a pioneering reformer leading China down a path of economic and political liberalization. In fact, Deng was selected by *Time* magazine as the "Man of the Year" in 1984. Despite the Fang Lizhi incident, Bush and his key foreign policy advisors chose not to confront China on human rights issues based on their strategic view about United States relations with China.[8]

Explicit Linkage in 1989–94

In June 1989, the Tiananmen incident seriously strained the Sino-U.S. relationship. Congress, the media, the public, human rights NGOs, and Chinese students in the United States exerted tremendous pressure on the White House to take strong action against the Chinese government. A Harris Poll conducted June 3–6, 1989 showed that 90 percent of the polled believed that the Chinese students were "right in their demands" and 67 percent believed that "the U.S. should issue a strong protest against the shooting of the students by the Chinese troops, even if that sets back U.S. relations with China."[9]

Bush found himself in a difficult situation. He could not ignore public sentiment and the intense pressure from Congress, but he did not want Sino-U.S. relations to deteriorate beyond repair. Based on his experience in China and his friendship with Chinese leaders, Bush personally took charge of China policy in the crisis period of 1989–90. He attempted to engage China while avoiding criticism at home, adopting calculated and moderate measures. The Bush administration suspended military sales to China, exchanges between the U.S. and Chinese military, and extended the stays of Chinese students. A few days later, Bush suspended high-level government exchanges with China and decided to seek suspension of new loans to China from international financial organizations. But he secretly sent Scowcroft and Eagleberger to Beijing in November 1989 to open a channel of direct communication with Deng and the Chinese government.[10]

The dominant issue in 1990–94 was the linkage between China's human rights record and its most-favored-nation (MFN) status with the United States. There was pressure from Congress and the public to use MFN status as a weapon to force China to improve its human rights record. The annual renewal of China's MFN status became a highly contentious political issue in the United States. In the first annual renewal of MFN status in 1990, which coincided with the first anniversary of the Tiananmen incident, China initially ignored U.S. protests due to its focus on domestic politics.[11] But China responded to Bush's obvious displeasure early in 1990 and made some gestures based on pragmatic calculations rather than a willingness to change domestic policies.[12] In this period, China was reactive to foreign pressure on human rights. Using China's gestures as evidence to support a positive engagement approach, Bush renewed China's MFN status.

Bush came under heavy criticism for "kowtowing" or bowing to the "Beijing butchers." His critics wanted him to take into consideration the new realities of the post-Cold War era. China's strategic significance was perceived to have drastically diminished with the collapse of the Soviet Union. With the former Soviet Union, Eastern

European nations, and South Africa taken off the list of "human rights offenders," China moved up in the priority list for the United States and Western Europe. A wide range of human rights issues caught the attention of the United States and the international community, such as political imprisonment, religious repression, criminal justice procedures, capital punishment, Tibet, family planning, and labor camp exports.[13]

As a presidential candidate, Bill Clinton criticized Bush's China policy and promised a firm stand against China on human rights, but he modified his attitude soon after he was elected in 1992. In September 1993, in a major policy shift, he announced that his administration would adopt an "enhanced engagement" policy toward China instead of a "confrontation" approach.[14] Secretary of State Warren Christopher visited Beijing in March 1994 and, as a journalist later commented, was "treated scandalously."[15] Partly due to domestic politics and partly in defiance of the Americans, the Chinese government detained several high-profile democracy activists, including Wei Jingsheng and Wang Dan, on the eve of Christopher's visit. In fact, a number of activists were arrested while John Shattuck, Assistant Secretary of State for Democracy, Human Rights, and Labor, was in China discussing the human rights issue with the Chinese. Still, as expected, Clinton delinked China's human rights record and its MFN status in May.

Several factors explain the Clinton administration's decision to yield on the MFN issue. First, China adopted a comprehensive strategy to deal with the United States and the West, including propaganda, diplomacy, and economic statecraft. In propaganda, the Chinese government gradually shifted from denial and silence to a head-on approach, launching an intense media campaign on the human rights issue.[16] Articles in Chinese newspapers and magazines both defended China's record in human rights based on its historical and development circumstances and criticized U.S. human rights practices. The effectiveness of such publicity campaigns should not be dismissed quickly. China's official response strengthened its position in two important ways. By engaging in a "dialogue," the Chinese campaign created some doubt about the validity and applicability of Western ideas in the Chinese context. More important, the campaign helped to create a strong "collective Asian voice" that the Western decision-makers could not ignore.

In fact, China engaged in active diplomacy to both avoid isolation in the international community and isolate the United States on the human rights issue. China cultivated closer relationships with other Asian nations, some of which were also targets of criticism on human rights by the United States and other Western nations.[17] There emerged an Asian versus a Western perspective on human rights,[18] as reflected in documents from the UN Human Rights Conferences held in Bangkok and Vienna in 1993. Indeed, one reason for Clinton's decision to delink human rights and MFN status for China was the negative response from most Asian governments.

China's strategy also included the use of its UN Security Council seat and its growing market to exert pressure. Because China is a permanent member of the UN Security Council and an influential political and military power in Asia, the United States needs China's cooperation on both global and regional affairs. The most important component of the Chinese strategy was to further economic reform. China's economy bounced back from the dip in growth in 1989–90 to enjoy the fastest economic growth in the world in the early 1990s. This had two implications for the United States. One was that democracy might indeed come if economic reform continued. The other was that a growing economy gave China greater bargaining leverage with the West.

However, economic interaction was a double-edged sword. As the largest market and the most crucial source of high technology in the world, the United States was important for China. China would lose more than the United States if such an economic tie were cut. As a result, Beijing made what some hard-liners believed to be excessive concessions to the United States, releasing some dissidents in advance of the annual review of MFN status and the International Olympic Committee's vote on the site of the Summer Olympics in 2000.

Clinton faced a difficult choice. China's growing economic clout and strategic significance in the region, mixed with U.S. frustration in the human rights area, polarized the U.S. policy community into pragmatists and idealists.[19] As a result of this division Washington sent mixed signals to the Chinese, undermining Christopher's human rights policy. Human Rights Watch complained that the former treasury secretary, Lloyd Bentsen, had visited Beijing in February 1994 and hinted at Washington's intention to delink human rights and MFN status. Then the visit by Shattuck to China was crippled when Undersecretary of Commerce Jeffrey Garten visited China at the same time to strike commercial deals for American businesses.[20]

Chinese scholars who offered advice to the Chinese leadership confirm this point. Their assessment was that since the United States would give China MFN trade status there was no reason to make concessions, although some gesture should be made to allow Christopher and Clinton to save "face."[21] In addition, the Chinese students in the United States,[22] the Chinese Americans, and the Taiwan and Hong Kong business communities generally did not support withdrawing MFN status from China. In the end, Clinton sided with the economic officials backed by the business community and the trade caucus in Congress.[23] His decision was welcomed across Asia.[24]

Drift to Confrontation in 1994–96

Human rights remained a contentious issue in the relationship between China and the United States between May 1994 and early 1996. Although the United States no longer demanded improvements in human rights as a condition for economic and political dealings with China, it continued to press China on human rights in both bilateral and multilateral contexts. More important, there was an implicit linkage between human rights and other issues in dispute between the two nations. However, U.S. human rights policy toward China largely failed except for securing the release or better treatment of a few high-profile dissidents.

Bilateral Human Rights Exchange

The Clinton administration remained critical of China's human rights record, but it refrained from using pressure tactics to push for human rights in China. As Human Rights Watch/Asia complained, Clinton's decision to delink human rights and MFN status removed the "last vestige of meaningful pressure on China from the international community" since "other governments and key trading partners with China had long since given priority to expanding economic ties."[25] The basic thrust of the new U.S. policy was to demonstrate to the Chinese that unless the Chinese government improved its human rights the Sino-U.S. relationship could not be fully developed. For example, there would be limited normal interactions such as exchanges of visits by high-level officials.

The Clinton administration talked about the "unacceptable" human rights record in China when China's MFN status was extended on June 3, 1995. Clinton had promised to create an "honor code of conduct" for American businesses operating in China as an indirect way of improving the human rights situation in China. In April 1995, the White House offered a draft, which invited much criticism from human rights NGOs for being too broad and lacking enforcement mechanisms.[26] A staff member from Amnesty International complained that the code "has no teeth, no enforcement, no technical support from the Commerce Department, and only vague language."[27] But the draft was welcomed by the business community precisely because the voluntary code would not constrain their business activities in China.[28] The code has not been heard of since then.

The State Department concluded in its 1995 human rights annual report (released in March 1996) that the human rights situation in China had deteriorated. But there was little advocacy for using trade as leverage over China. Even Shattuck admitted that "there is little evidence that denying trade to China would lead to major improvements in human rights." In fact, he argued that "it's possible that the contrary could occur."[29] As expected, Clinton renewed China's MFN status on May 21, 1996. On June 27, the House voted 286 to 141 to block a resolution to revoke China's MFN trade status.

Besides the State Department report on China's human rights and the renewal of China's MFN status, other incidents tested the Sino-U.S. relationship. One case was China's arrest of the China-born American human rights activist, Harry Wu, who went to investigate the forced labor situation in China in 1995. In response to pressure from the United States, the Chinese government expelled Wu on August 24 after sentencing him to fifteen years in jail. It was believed that he was released to pave the way for Hillary Clinton's participation in the Fourth International Conference on Women in Beijing in September 1995. In another case, Wei Jingsheng, widely considered to be China's most famous dissident, was sentenced to fourteen years' imprisonment in a one-day trial on December 13, 1995. Wei had already been in detention since April 1994. The Americans protested. Shattuck stated at a Congressional hearing that "Wei Jingsheng and his case have been at the forefront of all of our public and private statements about the human rights situation in China," as his sentence was "far beyond anything that was expected."[30]

The UN Commission on Human Rights

The United States has played a leading role in sponsoring and lobbying for resolutions criticizing China's human rights record at the UN Human Rights Commission in Geneva. As Shattuck suggested, "the UN Human Rights Commission is probably the single-most important instrument for, at least on a multilateral basis, addressing the human rights violations in China."[31] In contrast to trade sanctions, a UN Human Rights Commission resolution would allow Washington to pressure China without putting U.S. trade and investment opportunities at risk. Instead of being forced to behave, human rights violators might be "shamed" into changing their behavior.

Americans came to see the commission as a more important instrument to pressure China after Clinton's delinking of human rights and MFN status. Unlike in the previous years, the U.S. government engaged in active lobbying for the 1995 session.[32] In 1995, the U.S.-led coalition, for the first time, defeated China's procedural maneuvering and brought a resolution criticizing China up for a vote at the commission. But when voting on the substance of the resolution, Russia changed its vote from opposition to the no-action procedural vote to opposition to the substantive vote, sending the resolution to defeat by a single vote. The small margin did produce much anticipation on the U.S. side that a China resolution might be passed in 1996. "We are renewing and stepping up the effort this year," Shattuck told the International Operations and Human Rights Subcommittee of the House of Representatives shortly before the 1996 session, "working with the European Union and a coalition of democratic countries from Latin America, Asia, and Africa, as well as Central and Eastern Europe."[33]

However, of the 53 countries at the commission, 27 voted on April 23, 1996 to put aside both discussion and a vote on a modified draft resolution. Most of the members supporting Chinese were from Asia and Africa. Twenty countries voted in favor of the resolution, mainly Western nations plus nine countries from developing nations and the former Soviet bloc. Six countries abstained. Shattuck called the result "another day in China's failure to recognize the fundamental power of human rights." China's Xinhua Agency concluded, on the other hand, that the outcome, "contrary to the expectations of the United States and certain other Western countries, is evidence that power politics, confrontation and the imposition of Western values upon others are doomed to fail."[34]

The Chinese side believes that the United States worked hard to pass the resolution. But "we had confidence that the resolution would not pass," said a senior Chinese diplomat. He then suggested that the Chinese delegation had not been nervous in 1995 either because of the dialogues they had had with developing nations. He also insisted that the adoption of a China resolution would not damage China, but instead would put the United States in a difficult position. The Sino-U.S. relationship would suffer seriously if the U.S. intention of undermining China became apparent. In addition, the United States would then have no easy way out of continuously backing UN resolutions against China since such resolutions would now attract more public attention.[35] To put such remarks in perspective, it is certainly in China's interest to discourage the United States from sponsoring anti-China resolutions at the commission. Trying to convince the United States and others that the Chinese do not care about such resolutions and that the United States has no chance of winning is one strategy for doing that. In fact, some Chinese scholars believed that the Chinese Foreign Ministry was indeed nervous and worked hard to prevent the passage of such resolutions.[36] After all, the margin of China's success in no-action moves decreased from 12 in 1992 to 5 in 1993 to 4 in 1994 and to 1 in 1995.

The principal reason for China's narrow victory was that the Chinese government waged a vigorous campaign, winning the support and sympathy of developing nations. "China obviously takes this extremely seriously," Shattuck observed. "It lobbies around the world, it presses other governments very aggressively not to take up these issues in the UN Human Rights Commission."[37] The Chinese UN ambassador, Wu Jianmin, told the delegates before the vote that if a resolution criticizing China were passed, similar things "could happen to any other country tomorrow."[38] Developing nations sent supporting correspondence to the Chinese Foreign Ministry. In fact, even Europeans and Japanese privately expressed reservations and reluctance about supporting Americans.[39]

Implicit Linkage

At first glance, human rights did not look important in this period. After all, human rights was only one of the issues between China and the United States. The two nations had disputes over a wide range of issues such as military buildup, trade balances, intellectual property rights, nuclear proliferation, and Taiwan. In fact, the U.S. administration gave more attention to issues other than human rights after 1994. "The administration is willing to exert major political and economic pressure on China to press Beijing to abide by global trading rules," Mike Jendrzejczyk of Human Rights Watch/Asia complained. "But when it comes to moving China to respect its international human rights obligations, the administration has yet to develop a credible and effective strategy, analogous to its stance on intellectual property rights and the use of the threat of sanctions to obtain results."[40] In early 1996, the United States threatened to impose economic sanctions over China's sale of nuclear-related materials to Pakistan and its violation of an intellectual property rights agreement with the United States. But there was little mention in the administration regarding sanctioning China over human rights.

However, there was an implicit linkage between human rights and other disputes between the two nations. Human rights affected the U.S. relationship with China in important ways. First, due to the human rights situation in China, the Clinton administration refrained from conducting normal high-level official exchanges, seeing such visits as "rewards" to the Chinese government and potential political liabilities at home. Clinton did not visit China. Clinton agreed to meet Jiang Zemin in the White House for a working visit after the fiftieth anniversary of the UN in New York in October 1995, but he refused to invite Jiang for a state visit as requested by the Chinese. "A state visit is reserved for allies, for countries with which we have excellent relations," a State Department official was quoted as saying. "It would have been inconsistent with relations that have been in the deep freeze."[41] In the end, a meeting was arranged in New York.

As for Warren Christopher, he was most interested in the Middle

East during his tenure. Between 1993 and 1996, he paid two visits to China—the failed mission on human rights in March 1994 and a farewell visit after his resignation in November 1996. In contrast, he had visited Israel twenty-six times, Syria twenty-four times, Egypt thirteen times, and Jordan eleven times as of June 8, 1996.[42] This unwillingness on the U.S. side to conduct high-level exchanges represents a drastic change from before 1989, when American dignitaries saw visits to China as a boost to their prestige and political fortunes. This change in elite thinking is a reflection of a changed environment in the United States. U.S. domestic politics is an important factor in shaping policy toward China. As long as there is a sizable constituency in the United States lobbying for a strong stance on human rights in China, human rights will not go away in Sino-U.S. relations. In the period of 1994–96, Congress remained interested in human rights issues in China. Human rights concerns combined with trade disputes and China's arms sales to produce a strong anti-China sentiment in Congress.

Implicit linkages with human rights showed up in other disputes as well. Human rights was linked with the arms buildup. There has been much discussion in recent years in the U.S. academic and policy-making circles on "democratic peace," the notion that democracies do not fight each other. Logically, nondemocratic countries like China pose a potential threat to the United States and its allies. From this perspective, it is in the U.S. interest to promote democratization and human rights in China, a move that ultimately promotes U.S. security interests. Human rights was linked with trade. There were allegations in the United States that China tolerated inhumane labor standards and even used forced labor to export cheap goods to the United States. Human rights was also linked with intellectual property rights in the sense that the rule of law, a fundamental characteristic of societies that respect human rights, was a better guarantee for foreign intellectual properties than was the prevailing situation in China.

Most important, human rights was linked with the Taiwan issue, which became a flash point after the Clinton administration allowed—under heavy pressure from Congress—the Taiwanese president, Lee Teng-hui, to pay a visit to Cornell in June 1995. The U.S. decision and Lee's diplomatic efforts to expand diplomatic space for Taiwan greatly angered Beijing. China temporarily recalled the Chinese ambassador to the United States and subsequently tested missiles near Taiwan. The Chinese political and military leadership has repeatedly stated Beijing's determination to use force if Taiwan declares independence or "foreign forces" interfere in Taiwanese affairs. But democratization in Taiwan means that Taiwan is unlikely to reunify with the mainland any time soon and may seek greater autonomy in the international community since this is what most voters in Taiwan want. Respect for human rights and respect for values and institutions that Americans hold dear led to increasing U.S. support and sympathy for Taiwan in Congress, the media, and the public at large. Taiwan came to be seen as a new democracy worthy of U.S. support while China was perceived as lagging in political reform. In fact, Beijing was seen as reacting mainly against the threat of Taiwanese democracy rather than against the threat of Taiwanese independence.

For the Chinese government, human rights has an impact on the very survival of its political regime. "U.S. human rights policy toward China is in essence about China's one-party system," even an open-minded senior Chinese diplomat asserted. "But China cannot learn everything from the U.S. China has its own tradition and situations."[43] Such views are common among Chinese government officials. There is increasing anger over the idea that the United States would never deal with China fairly unless China modeled itself after the United States. Some simply see U.S. human rights foreign policy as an excuse for interfering in other countries' internal affairs and practicing hegemonism.[44] The importance of this assessment is that disputes over human rights between China and the United States provided a strong reason for the Chinese to see U.S. pressure on China regarding other issues as evidence of a comprehensive U.S. design to weaken, contain, and undermine China. In other words, human rights disputes gave the Chinese a different perspective on what may be called "normal" disputes between states in international relations.

Attempting Strategic Partnership Since Mid-1996

March 1996 was an important turning point in Sino-U.S. relations. China staged waves of military exercises across the Taiwan Strait in response to Lee's visit to the United States, a visit Beijing interpreted as a calculated effort by Lee to move Taiwan toward independence. China timed its military exercises, which included firing missiles near the island of Taiwan, to intimidate Taiwanese voters before Taiwan's first fully democratic presidential election. To counter the Chinese exercises, Clinton sent two carrier groups to the Taiwan area, the largest show of U.S. military force in East Asia since the end of the Vietnam War. The U.S. and Chinese military thus found themselves confronting each other, albeit not directly. The March crisis was a wakeup call for both China and the United States. The U.S. and Chinese governments attempted to create a strategic partnership after mid-1996.[45]

On the U.S. side, the objective of achieving a strategic understanding with China, now widely perceived to be a rising power and one of only few countries capable of posing a serious challenge to the United States in the future, gained support in the policy community. The second-term Clinton administration treated China as a priority issue. "The United States has no interest in containing China," Clinton commented in November 1996. "What the United States wants is to sustain an engagement with China . . . in a way that will increase the chances that there will be more liberty and more prosperity and more genuine cooperation in the future."[46] Christopher visited Beijing in November 1996 to pave the way for an exchange of state visits by Clinton and Jiang Zemin. Clinton and Jiang met for 85 minutes during the APEC forum on November 24 and confirmed Jiang's visit to the United States in 1997 and Clinton's return visit to China in 1998.

China also made concessions to improve relations with the United States, especially on the nuclear nonproliferation issue. The U.S. intelligence community confirmed the Chinese statement that the Chinese are complying with a promise made in May 1996 to stop selling nuclear-related materials to Pakistan. In addition, during discussions with the U.S. Undersecretary of State Lynn Davis in November, the Chinese indicated that China may cancel the proposed sale of a nuclear facility to Iran. At a press conference on November 20, Christopher announced that China had agreed to establish a comprehensive, nationwide system to monitor the export of nuclear materials. This step would allow U.S. companies to export nuclear technology and equipment to China.[47] Chinese cooperation in controlling weapons of mass destruction, along with other issues such as environmental protection, intellectual property protection, and the Korean peninsula, provided incentives for the United States to continue a strategic dialogue with China.

In this context, while continuing to spar over human rights in bilateral and multilateral contexts, the U.S. and Chinese governments made conscious efforts to avoid letting rights issues take precedence over other issues. The U.S. government downplayed the importance of human rights because the United States was now more focused on common strategic concerns rather than divisive issues such as human rights. Madeleine K. Albright, the new secretary of state, made it clear at a press conference on her first full day in office that she would "tell it like it is" to Beijing about human rights, but she stressed that the U.S.-China relationship "cannot be held hostage to any one issue."[48] Two weeks earlier at her confirmation hearing, she defined the U.S. goal as "to expand areas of cooperation, reduce the potential for misunderstandings and encourage China's full emergence as a responsible member of the international community."[49] This argument became the party line for the administration in defending its engagement with China.

Although the Chinese would certainly prefer to take the human rights issue off the table altogether, they had realized by now, given their better understanding of American political culture and domestic politics, that the rights issue would not die.[50] Beijing's second best choice was to minimize the impact of rights disputes while pursuing its main goal in improving relations with the United States, which was to reduce U.S. support for Taiwan and to pressure Washington to use its own influence to persuade Taipei to enter political negotiations with Beijing. "It is amazing that Taiwan can be independent from China for such a long time. That is all because the United States is behind Taiwan," a top-level Chinese diplomat reasoned. "If the United States withdraws support for Taiwan, things will change quickly."[51] In typical Chinese fashion, the Chinese government continued to be firm in principles but flexible in diplomatic conduct.[52]

As a result, human rights incidents that once would have damaged Sino-U.S. relations now drew protest but did not derail efforts to improve relations. In fact, "the U.S. and China have reached a tacit agreement to put human rights in the margins so it doesn't become an irritant," noted Mike Jendrzejczyk, the Washington director of Human Rights Watch Asia.[53] Wang Dan, a student leader in the 1989 Tiananmen movement, was sentenced to 11 years in prison on October 30, 1996, after 17 months in detention without a hearing. This trial took place right before Christopher's visit to

Beijing. The Chinese government hoped to finish off the domestic dissident movement, which had been so badly crippled that it was virtually nonexistent. Equally important, it wanted to send a strong message to the Americans that human rights is China's internal affair. Upon his arrival in Beijing, Christopher told reporters that he would talk about human rights with the Chinese, but "no single" issue should be allowed to dominate the Sino-U.S. relationship. Accordingly, Shattuck, the highest U.S. human rights official, kept a low profile in the negotiations between Christopher and the Chinese. He did not hold separate talks with the Chinese.[54]

The two governments continued to confront each other over human rights issues in 1997.[55] As in previous years, Chinese diplomats were busy in the first half of the year, responding to ritualized American moves. In January, the 1997 State Department report on human rights concluded that the human rights situation in China had worsened in 1996. But no harsh policy toward China followed. Similarly, Beijing rebutted American criticism but announced progress in trade negotiations the same day the report was released. In March and April, the U.S. government wanted China to release some political prisoners, to resume talks with the International Red Cross on visits to Chinese prisons, and to sign the International Covenants on Civil and Political Rights and on Economic, Social, and Cultural Rights in exchange for not supporting a China resolution at the UN Human Rights Commission. Beijing made some gestures but no firm concessions. Thus, the United States went ahead and cosponsored a resolution on China. But China blocked debate on its rights record by winning a no-action vote on April 15. In May and June, Congress fought another annual battle over China's MFN trading status. In the end, the House approved China's MFN status again on June 24, by a vote 259 to 173. Moreover, Hong Kong was returned to China on July 1, which generated much U.S. scrutiny and criticism.[56]

Despite the disputes over human rights and other issues, the Clinton administration and the Chinese government pushed ahead to construct a strategic relationship. Albright visited Beijing in February 1997, the only Western leader to visit during a six-day mourning period for Deng Xiaoping. Vice President Al Gore visited Beijing in March 1997, the highest U.S. official to do so since 1989. Chinese Foreign Minister Qian Qichen visited the United States in April and National Security Adviser Berger visited China in August. More important, President Jiang Zemin paid his first state visit to the United States in October 1997. Right before Jiang's visit, on October 24, Clinton made his first speech exclusively on China. While critical of China's human rights record, Clinton defended his "pragmatic policy of engagement" as "the best way to advance our fundamental interests and values."

During Jiang's visit to the United States, he and Clinton agreed in a joint statement to "build toward a constructive strategic partnership between China and the United States through increasing cooperation to meet international challenges and promote peace and development in the world." But human rights was a major issue. Jiang encountered demonstrations by human rights activists and engaged in debates over human rights. The U.S. media also covered human rights issues extensively. While refusing to back down on human rights in his debate with American leaders, Jiang made some gestures by inviting three U.S. religious leaders to visit China. He also reaffirmed Beijing's intention to sign the International Covenant on Economic, Social, and Cultural Rights.

Jiang's successful visit allowed him to make further concessions. Wei Jingsheng was allowed to leave for America in November 1997, and some U.S. religious leaders visited China in early 1998. In response, the U.S. State Department's annual report for 1997 concluded that "there were positive steps in human rights [in China], although serious problems remained." The report then listed positive steps such as Beijing's signing of the International Covenant on Economic, Social, and Cultural Rights, its more tolerant response to dissent, its release of Wei Jingsheng and a few others, its progress in legal reform, and its more open society. This was in sharp contrast to the State Department report for 1996, which concluded that the Chinese government "stepped up efforts to cut off expressions of protest or criticism." Critics of China in the United States used the report to attack the Clinton administration's policy of engaging China. In public debates and editorials, they argued that the administration had failed to act upon its own conclusion that China's human rights situation had worsened and had sacrificed American values for commercial interests in China. Thus, Beijing's concessions allowed the State Department to offer a more positive assessment supportive of Clinton's cooperative approach toward Beijing.[57]

The Chinese government took another significant step in March 1998 when it decided to sign the International Covenant on Civil and Political Rights later in the year; China had already signed the International Covenant on Economic, Social, and Cultural Rights. As a reward, the Clinton administration decided not to seek censure of China at the UN Human Rights Commission.[58] Then Wang Dan was released from prison on medical parole and sent to the United States on April 19. Stanley Roth, Assistant Secretary of State for East Asia and Pacific Affairs called Wang's release "the direct outcome" of the Jiang-Clinton summit in the previous year and "a pre-summit deliverable" leading up to Clinton's June visit.[59] From the Chinese side, it was also a relief to see tensions reducing and cooperation increasing after several years of ups and downs.[60]

Clinton's and Jiang's efforts at creating a strategic partnership looked most promising with Clinton's nine-day state visit to China in June 1998. While few substantive results were anticipated and achieved from the trip, both sides won symbolic victories. The Clinton administration hoped to demonstrate the potential of the relationship and to change people's perceptions of China. Jiang cooperated by giving Clinton an unprecedented opportunity to talk directly and freely to the Chinese public about democracy and human rights as well as other issues, in a joint press conference with Jiang and a session with Beijing University students televised live on Chinese television, and in a radio call-in show in Shanghai. Clinton's performance won widespread praise in Washington.

On the Chinese side, Jiang hoped to present a more open China to the world, a more confident leader to the domestic audience, and a pledge from Clinton to discourage Taiwan's move toward independence. He performed well, appearing comfortable and confident. Clinton also gave a verbal pledge for a "three nos" policy on an informal occasion in Shanghai, meaning that the United States would not support an independent Taiwan, would not support Taiwan's entry into international organizations that require sovereignty, and would not support a policy of "one China, one Taiwan." But this expression was heavily criticized at home. As for Beijing's effort to convince the world that China had become more open, the result was mixed. On the one hand, the Chinese government's willingness to allow Clinton to discuss taboo issues directly with Chinese people won praise. On the other hand, the security apparatus harassed and arrested dissidents right before and during Clinton's visit, diverting much media attention away from Beijing's carefully orchestrated agenda.

The Sino-U.S. relationship deteriorated soon after Clinton returned to Washington. Ironically, Clinton and Jiang tried to elevate the bilateral dialogue to a strategic level to promote cooperation but only found significant strategic differences. Hard-liners in both countries attacked the engagement policy. Rather than hope for a better relationship, fear of each other's intentions has been driving the political dynamics in both countries, resulting in renewed tensions.

In the United States, critics of China, especially in Congress, argue strongly that the two countries cannot be partners when they differ so much in values. More significant, critics have seized every opportunity to embarrass the administration and undermine the strategic partnership. Congress has pursued allegations of the transfer of sensitive technologies to China by businessmen connected with the Democratic Party and allegations of Chinese influence in American elections. China's mounting trade surpluses with the United States and its continuous threat of force against Taiwan have also strained the relationship. The investigation of illegal technological transfers to China has led to allegations that some Chinese American scientists have stolen advanced nuclear secrets for Beijing and thus enhanced China's nuclear capabilities, directly threatening the United States. A special House committee headed by Christopher Cox, a Republican representative from California, concluded in late 1998 that China has been aggressively spying on the United States for the past twenty years and that the Clinton administration has not done anything about it. This report has had a chilling effect on the relationship and put defenders of a cooperative relationship on the defensive.

The Chinese government has given the United States plenty of reasons for continued criticism of its human rights record. Ironically, an improved Sino-U.S. relationship encouraged Chinese dissidents to seize the opportunity. On the day Clinton arrived in China, some dissidents in a number of cities tried to register the China Democracy Party, which claimed about 200 members in a dozen branches throughout China. Soon after Clinton left China, the government started harassing the members of the party. On December 22, 1998, three founders of the China Democracy Party received prison sentences ranging from 11 to 13 years. More activists were sentenced later. Beijing also intimidated and prosecuted some who had participated in lively discussions of political reform earlier in the year and imposed tighter control over internet discussions and access to the outside world.

Beijing's renewed repression reflected a familiar Chinese pattern of alternating relaxation and tightening of political control. The relaxation stage unleashes forces that prompt a frightened party leadership to impose new restrictions. The government, worried that a popular revolt could result from widespread public anger over official corruption, and from dissatisfaction with rising unemployment and the failure of state enterprises (conditions that had worsened during the Asian financial crisis), adopted resolute measures to nip in the bud any potential challenges to its authority, instead of adopting genuine reforms to remove the root causes of social unrest. In particular, the government wanted to ensure stability before the PRC's fifty-year anniversary in October 1999. In this context, international reaction was a minor consideration.

Not surprisingly, Congress strongly criticized Beijing. Right before the two countries resumed human rights dialogue on January 11–12, 1999, after four years' suspension, Congressional International Relations Committee Chairman Benjamin A. Gilman and four other House members sent a letter to Albright, protesting that "initiating a human rights dialogue at this time would be both inappropriate and fruitless, given the current Chinese attitude toward human rights and the current ongoing crackdown."[61] The administration also adjusted its assessment of the human rights situation in China while continuing to pursue a better bilateral relationship. The State Department report for 1998 concluded that "the [Chinese] government's human rights record deteriorated sharply beginning in the final months of the year with a crackdown against organized political dissent." The report stated that the Chinese government was trying to "nip in the bud" dissent beginning in the fall of 1998. The drastically different tone certainly reflected the realities in China but was also a product of American domestic politics. The "generous" assessment of China in the 1997 report was subject to severe criticism by Congress, the media, and human rights NGOs. Harold Hongju Koh, who replaced Shattuck as Assistant Secretary of State for Democracy, Human Rights, and Labor in November 1998, emphasized at the press conference on February 26 when the report was released that they pulled no punches when it came to China. To address particular Congressional concerns, the 1998 report emphasized China's poor record in religious freedom. Congress and NGOs were basically pleased with the report.

The Chinese government responded with its own report, "Human Rights Record in the United States," in March 1999. Referring to the U.S. report in its first sentence, the Chinese report was clearly a rebuttal. It listed America's problems with poverty, crime, money politics, racial discrimination, abuse of women and children, and neglect of international human rights conventions, selecting Western media stories to substantiate the charge that "the U.S., which often grades human rights records of other countries, gets low marks from its own people and the international community."

The United States also resumed its sponsorship of a UN resolution condemning China. The Senate voted 99–0 on February 25, 1999 to urge Clinton to sponsor a resolution. Albright, who was to visit China, indicated at the time that the administration had not made a decision whether to do so.[62] Once in Beijing she clashed with Chinese leaders on Beijing's crackdown on dissidents. But she made it clear that human rights disputes would not hinder progress on other issues such as China's WTO bid. In response, Chinese Foreign Minister Tang Jiaxuan objected to American criticism of China's human rights record and to UN resolutions criticizing China.[63] Albright's tough stance on human rights was partly due to increasing pressure on the administration from Capitol Hill.[64] The United States decided on March 26 to introduce a China resolution. EU members refused to be cosponsors. On April 23 China again succeeded in blocking discussion and a formal vote through a no-action motion, which was approved 22 to 17, with 14 abstentions. One day later, a Chinese foreign ministry spokesman declared that "the United States stands alone in this anti-China farce."[65] Determining that "China's human rights has continued to deteriorate," the U.S. State Department announced on January 11, 2000 that the United States would sponsor a China resolution at the UN Human Rights Commission meeting.[66] But Americans lost the battle at the commission again when the commission passed China's no-action resolution, 22–18, with 12 abstaining, on April 17.

What helped the Chinese government in this new round of human rights exchanges with the United States is that Western criticism does not resonate in Chinese society, as discussed in Chapter Two. Unlike in the early 1990s when Western criticism of the Chinese government was well received by a large segment of Chinese society, such condemnation has fed into rising nationalist sentiment for the past few years.[67] Such nationalist sentiment exploded when NATO planes accidentally bombed the Chinese embassy in Belgrade on May 7, 1999. This tragic incident hardened public and elite opposition to the idea of "humanitarian intervention" and human rights pressure. Some Chinese commentators asserted that the bombing revealed the hollowness of the American human rights crusade, a view shared widely.[68]

Many in the Chinese policy community now believe that the embassy bombing has handed the Chinese government a powerful tool to counter U.S. rights pressure and put Americans on the defensive for a change. The Chinese government promptly suspended military exchanges and bilateral dialogue on arms control, proliferation, and human rights. After a freeze of four months, Clinton and Jiang resumed high-level contacts with their summit at the APEC meeting in Auckland on September 11, 1999. The two leaders agreed on renewed bilateral negotiations on China's application to the WTO.[69] After tough negotiations over 13 years, the two governments reached a historic agreement on November 15. Deputy Assistant Defense Secretary Kurt Campbell went to Beijing on November 18 to discuss the renewal of military exchanges. In early December small groups of the People's Liberation Army, the U.S. Air Force, and Hong Kong's Civil Aviation Department mounted a joint civil rescue exercise. General Xiong Guangkai's visit to Washington in January 2000 fully resumed military exchanges. On December 16, 1999 the two governments also reached agreement on compensation for the damage to the Chinese embassy in Belgrade and the U.S. diplomatic mission in China, which essentially brought the incident to conclusion. On June 8, 2000, Beijing agreed to resume bilateral talks with the United States on proliferation and arms control. In contrast, bilateral talks on human rights remain suspended. While attending the ASEAN Regional Forum, Albright met with her Chinese counterpart Tang Jiaxuan on July 28, 2000. She urged Beijing to resume human rights dialogue with Washington, but Tang only agreed to study the issue.[70] The Chinese government clearly has no incentive to resume rights discussions.

With or without dialogue, the U.S. government continues to see human rights in China as its own concern. The State Department released its first annual report on international religious freedom on September 9, 1999, as mandated by the International Religious Freedom Act signed into law on October 27, 1998. China was a prominent target of criticism in the report. Four weeks later, the State Department identified China along with Afghanistan, Iran, Iraq, Burma, Serbia, and Sudan as responsible for "particularly severe" violations of religious freedom. Now the secretary of state is authorized to impose sanctions or waive them against these countries. Chinese Foreign Ministry Spokeswoman Zhang Qiyue promptly expressed Beijing's "indignation and firm opposition" on October 7. A major campaign against Falun Gong by the government since July has also invited U.S. criticism. The State Department report on human rights issued in February 2000 concluded that China's human rights situation worsened in 1999 as "the government intensified efforts to suppress dissent, particularly organized dissent."

However, the U.S. government is more focused on trade and security than human rights. Clinton's effort to grant China permanent normal trading relations (PNTR) status is a case in point. After Clinton formally called on Congress on March 8, 2000 to grant China PNTR, the China trade bill became one of the most contentious bills on Capitol Hill in the past decade. While Senate approval was virtually certain, the vote in the House was too close to call. Republican leadership and most Republicans were expected to support the China bill but Democratic leadership and two thirds of Democrats were opposed to it. Thus, the White House needed a solid majority of Republicans and a core of centrist Democrats to win the vote—at least 150 Republican votes and 70 Democrat votes, to be exact, as 218 votes were needed to pass or reject the bill.

The Clinton administration went all out to persuade Congress to grant China PNTR status. Seeing the vote as important to his legacy, Clinton started early, establishing a "war room" to coordinate lobbying efforts. On January 10, Clinton convened a special cabinet committee and named Commerce Secretary William M. Daley and Deputy White House Chief of Staff Steve Ricchetti to lead the lobbying campaign.[71] A report by the General Accounting Office showed that the Clinton administration used about 150 staffers, including 100 from the Agriculture Department, in its

China Trade Relations Working Group. Clinton himself was heavily involved, using the prestige of his office and his political skill to persuade wavering Democrats. He invited undecided House Democrats to the White House and met their requests for presidential favors.[72] He argued that Congress needed to grant China PNTR status for U.S. companies and farmers to benefit from market-opening concessions China had made to Washington in return for gaining entry into the WTO. He also argued that U.S. national security might be compromised if PNTR status was not granted, since Beijing would view a Congressional rejection of a trade bill with clear economic advantages to the United States as proof that the United States indeed intended to contain China. To build public support and put pressure on wavering members of Congress, the White House also invited former presidents and cabinet secretaries to speak up in support of the China trade bill.

The U.S. business community, which stands to gain from China's opening market, launched a well-organized and well-financed lobbying campaign on Capitol Hill and in electoral districts. The Business Roundtable, for example, targeted 88 districts and hired 50 full-time "trade organizers" for lobbying. The business group spent $9.2 million on the campaign, an amount larger than that it spent to lobby for Congressional approval of the North American Free Trade Agreement (NAFTA). The U.S. Chamber of Commerce spent $4 million on its campaign and mobilized local business leaders to lobby their legislators in 66 congressional districts. Moreover, corporate America committed more campaign money in the election cycle that was going on at the time.[73]

On the other side, organized labor, human rights activists, some religious groups, and Democratic leadership in the House were firmly opposed to giving PNTR status to China, arguing that free trade with a communist China would sacrifice American values and jobs. China's critics in Congress also argued that U.S. trade with China for the previous two decades had not moderated Beijing's behavior toward its citizens and Taiwan. Worried about losing jobs, and building on its successful demonstration to disrupt the WTO meeting in Seattle, the AFL-CIO turned the China trade vote into a litmus test for Democrats in Congress who needed labor support in their districts. But they weakened their case by giving a pass to Al Gore, who supported the China trade bill.

To find an alternative to annual reviews, Reps. Sander M. Levin

(D-Mich.) and Doug Bereuter (R-Neb.) introduced measures into the bill to create an independent commission to monitor China's human rights and compliance to trade agreements. Despite criticism that the mechanism was toothless, this companion bill became critical in persuading wavering Democrats to cast yes votes. Independently, Commerce Secretary William Daley announced a $22 million trade enforcement program to monitor China's trade performance, including the creation of a "rapid response team" led by a new deputy assistant commerce secretary for China. This move was also meant to influence undecided Democrats in the House.[74]

The China trade bill cleared major Congressional hurdles on May 17. The House Ways and Means Committee approved the bill by 34 to 4. The Senate Finance Committee voted 18 to 1 in favor. Neither side had secured enough votes on the eve of the vote, although the yes camp had gained momentum. According to Republican sources, 145 Republicans supported the bill, with 6 more leaning in favor and another 10 undecided. On the Democratic side, 68 had given firm support while 15 remained undecided.[75] But few insiders in Washington doubted that the bill would eventually pass. On May 24, the China bill passed in the House with surprising ease, with 237 (164 Republicans and 73 Democrats) in favor and 197 against. There were 19 more votes in favor than were needed to pass the bill. The approval margin of 40 votes for the China trade bill was larger than that for NAFTA, which passed 234 to 200 in 1993.

Although human rights concerns did not prevail over business interests, they were nevertheless important. It would not have been so difficult to pass the China trade bill if not for human rights concerns. It is amazing that there was such intense opposition to a trade bill when the country was experiencing a decade-long economic boom, the unemployment rate was at a historical low, and American business elites were so clearly in favor of a trade agreement with China that required Beijing to make one-sided market concessions.

Conclusion

The changing nature of the interaction between human rights and strategic and economic issues explains why human rights was not treated as a crucial issue in Sino-U.S. relations in the 1970s, why it became contentious after the Cold War ended, why the Clinton administration decided to delink human rights and MFN trade status for China in May 1994, and why the U.S. government has become largely muted over human rights in China since mid-1996.

Washington's high-pressure approach has been largely ineffective except for winning release for and better treatment of high-profile dissidents. The case of Sino-U.S. human rights exchanges shows how difficult it is, even for the world's most powerful country, to influence the domestic affairs of a major power like China if that major power is determined to resist such attempts. It also shows that the key reason Beijing has been able to fend off U.S. pressure lies in its demonstrated ability, so far, to maintain effective control over the country and promote economic growth. U.S. human rights policy at present receives little positive response from Chinese society, and even from reform-minded intellectuals.

Looking into the future, whether human rights tops the diplomatic agenda or falls somewhere down the list, it will remain an important issue in the Sino-U.S. relationship. China and the United States have different political systems and social values, a situation unlikely to change quickly. Due to the American public's strong negative view of the Chinese government, human rights groups in the United States have won "the rhetorical war," which sets the limits on U.S. policy toward China even though the actual policy influence of human rights groups is still limited.[76] As a result, advocates for deeper engagement and a strategic dialogue with China insist that human rights must remain important. In addition, Chinese domestic politics will have a pull on the United States. Chinese dissident individuals or groups operating in the United States may have a limited impact in China now, but supported by sympathetic media and scholars, they still influence public and congressional opinion in the United States. Furthermore, social forces such as the Falun Gong movement, unleashed by economic reform, will also catch American attention and complicate bilateral relations.

Chapter Four

Human Rights and Sino-European Relations

Non-Issue Through the 1980s

China formed diplomatic ties with Denmark in 1950, Britain and the Netherlands in 1954, and France in 1964, much earlier than with Japan and the United States. But China initially treated Europe as a low foreign policy priority due to Europe's declining influence, deference to Moscow's European policy, and a more urgent need to deal with its Asian neighbors. However, after splitting with the Soviet Union in the early 1960s, Beijing sought closer contact with Europe in order to seek allies against Moscow and advance its economic interests, but it compromised its efforts with the chaotic start of the Cultural Revolution. In the 1970s China actively promoted an anti-Soviet united front with Western Europe. Accordingly, Beijing reversed an earlier position and came to support European integration.[1] Once China adopted an independent foreign policy in 1982, Sino-Western European relations became based more on mutual economic and political interests and became less constrained by the superpower relationship.

Human rights was largely a non-issue in Sino-Western European relations through the 1980s. It is true that human rights in China became a concern for nongovernmental organizations in the late 1970s. Amnesty International, based in London, was the first to report on human rights abuses in China, issuing a report entitled "Political Imprisonment in the People's Republic of China" in 1978. But European governments did not treat China's human rights as a diplomatic issue. Despite appeals from Chinese dissidents and Amnesty International, Prime Minister Margaret Thatcher did not raise the issue of Wei Jingsheng and other jailed Chinese dissidents when meeting with Chinese leaders. Except for the French government, which raised some individual cases with the Chinese, Western European governments were silent about human rights in China. The European Community (EC) did not press the human rights issue with the Chinese government even though it had done so with other governments.[2]

Western Europe's neglect of human rights in China can be attributed, first of all, to the nature of its human rights foreign policy. Human rights became a central concern for Europeans after the Second World War because Europeans wished to prevent a repeat of the Nazi horrors in Europe. But they focused on building regional and global human rights institutions, accepting multilateral supervision of domestic practices and connecting rights concerns with European integration. They did not incorporate human rights into foreign policy until the late 1970s. The first European initiative was the adoption of a Joint Declaration on the Protection of Fundamental Freedoms by the European Commission, the Council of Ministers, and the European Parliament in 1977. Even then Western Europe targeted Spain, Greece, and Turkey, countries on the fringe of Europe, and their former colonies.[3] China was, therefore, off Europe's radar screen.

Like the United States, Western Europe exempted China because of inadequate information about that country's human rights situation, respect for its ancient civilization and bold socialist experiment, sensitivities about its century of humiliation, and lack of domestic lobbies.[4] In addition, starting in the early 1970s the West saw China as an important strategic check on the Soviet Union. While much more moderate on the Soviet Union than China was in the 1970s, Europeans did not hesitate to use a better relationship with Beijing as leverage with Moscow.[5]

Another reason was Western Europe's strong interest in supporting the Chinese economic reform and gaining access to the Chinese market.[6] Once NGOs started reporting on China's human rights situation in the late 1970s, this negative coverage was offset by a positive public image of Deng's daring economic reform that moved the country from a planned economy to a mixed economy incorporating market principles.

There were also unique reasons why some European governments avoided confronting China over human rights. Great Britain, for example, did not want to challenge China because Hong Kong's survival depended on Beijing's cooperation. Ironically, once China and Great Britain signed an agreement in 1984 on the reversion of Hong Kong to China based on a formula of "one country, two systems," human rights became a greater concern for the British government. London's later attempt at faster democratization in Hong Kong created tension with Beijing in the early 1990s.

Since the Chinese did not consider human rights to be an issue with Europeans, they did not take any diplomatic action to defend their human rights record. If anything, Chinese attacked Western colonialism and racism in the international arena.[7] Although the Chinese rarely used the term "human rights," their attack on the West was based on norms such as self-determination, racial equality, and justice, which gave them a powerful propaganda instrument.[8] Europeans did not enjoy a moral high ground over China in the 1960s when they were ending their colonial presence in the Third World. Then from 1975, when China established diplomatic ties with the EC, to June 1989, when the Tiananmen incident took place, the Chinese saw a steady improvement in political and economic ties with Western Europe, unlike in Sino-U.S. relations, which were plagued by periodic conflicts, and in Sino-Japanese relations, which were shadowed by history.[9]

Weathering the 1989 Storm

The 1989 Tiananmen incident and the European response to the incident sent Sino-Western European relations to a low point. Western Europe joined the United States to condemn the Chinese government. At the Madrid summit in June 1989 the EC imposed sanctions on China, including suspension of high-level official contact, a freeze on military cooperation, an embargo on arms trades with China, postponement of new requests for credit insurance and the examination of new loans by the World Bank, and restrictions on scientific, cultural, and technical cooperation. Particularly annoying to Beijing, the French government allowed prominent Chinese dissidents to gather in Paris to form an opposition group advocating overthrow of the government in China. At the G7 summit in Houston in July 1990, the French led the way arguing for maintaining a tough line on China, while the Japanese wanted a softer position.[10] Western Europeans also joined Americans in sponsoring resolutions criticizing China at the UN Human Rights Commission starting in 1990.

European economic sanctions inflicted immediate costs on China in development assistance and investment. But unlike the United States, Western Europe did not use China's Most Favored Nation (MFN) trade status for leverage even though it could technically have done so.[11] These costs were unpleasant but manageable for the Chinese. Deng stated in July 1990 that the impact of Western economic sanctions was limited.[12]

More significant, China suffered serious side costs due to its weakened bargaining position after Tiananmen. Following President Bush's decision to sell F-16 fighters to Taiwan, France agreed to sell 60 Mirage 2000-5 jet fighters and other advanced weapons to Taiwan in 1992. Also, the British government appointed Chris Patten as its last governor of Hong Kong. A former Conservative cabinet minister who was well connected with the prime minister and the foreign secretary and distrustful of the Chinese communist government, Patten complicated Beijing's takeover plan by accelerating democratization in Hong Kong.[13] In addition, European governments became more comfortable meeting with the Dalai Lama, the exiled Tibetan leader, thus further internationalizing the Tibetan issue. All these developments were detrimental to China's core national interest in territorial integrity.

In addition, China suffered a reputation loss. As economic sanctions hurt their own economic and commercial interests, Europeans increasingly resorted to public criticism as a less costly way to demonstrate their concerns over human rights in China. This symbolic pressure was costly because the Chinese government cared about its international image. As testimony to Chinese concerns, the Chinese government committed tremendous diplomatic resources to blocking anti-China resolutions at the UN Human Rights Commission.

Western Europe became assertive partly because of the shock effect of the Chinese government's brutal crackdown, which was broadcast on prime-time television. The end of the Cold War also turned Western Europe away from China. Western Europe no longer needed China as a strategic counterweight to the Soviet Union, and simultaneously became preoccupied with the democratization and economic restructuring of Eastern Europe and the former Soviet republics. More confident in the historical triumph of Western liberal democracy, Europe now saw China as a political laggard which under Western pressure could potentially follow the path of the European communist countries.

Furthermore, Western Europeans now better understood China's past and present human rights abuses. Ironically, when China started opening its door to the outside world in the late 1970s, the West became more critical of the country. An enhanced public awareness of human rights in China compelled Western governments to deal with the issue. Closer bilateral ties also offered Europe more leverage over China.

Western rights pressure and the collapse of China's fellow communist countries in Europe posed a severe challenge to the Chinese government. As discussed in Chapter One, Deng chose to continue China's economic reform while maintaining the communist party's political dominance. These two objectives explained China's combination of concessions and resistance when dealing with Western Europe over human rights disputes. The Chinese government adopted a measured approach, prioritizing its goals, making a distinction between Europe and the United States, and combining concessions and counterattacks.

China made no compromise over Taiwan and Tibet. The 1989 Tiananmen incident initially made it easier for Taiwan to expand its international space, given Beijing's weakened bargaining position and a growing international appreciation of Taipei's economic and political achievements. European nations such as France found it easier to sell advanced weapons to Taiwan. In retaliation, Beijing closed the French consulate in Guangzhou and did not allow French companies to participate in Guangzhou's subway project and in other areas. China "normalized" relations with France in 1994, only after the French government promised not to sell additional weapons to Taiwan. In fact, the Chinese position on France was much harsher than that on the United States, which had sold F-16s to Taiwan earlier. China did not want France to set a precedent in arms sale to Taiwan in Europe.[14]

By contrast, China did not retaliate against Western economic sanctions on human rights. But neither did Chinese leaders bend under pressure. Deng told former Canadian Prime Minister Pierre Trudeau in July 1990 that "we may not have other abilities, but we have proved ourselves in resisting sanctions." After all, the People's Republic of China "has developed under international sanctions for most of the more than forty years of its history." At the same time, Deng wanted to improve relations with the West.[15] Accordingly, the Chinese government strengthened human rights propaganda, focusing on the primacy of sovereignty and development rights, and criticism of the West's imperialist past and current shortcomings. At the same time, Beijing made opportune concessions to minimize conflicts with Western Europe, namely releasing prominent dissidents, starting a human rights dialogue, and joining international human rights conventions.

China did not criticize Western Europe as harshly as it did the United States. Except for France, which hosted some leading Chinese dissidents, Beijing did not blame Europe for trying to undermine the Chinese socialist system through peaceful evolution, an alleged U.S. conspiracy.[16] The Chinese media and government rarely named specific European nations when criticizing the West over human rights. Beijing was also more willing to engage in dialogue with Brussels. The Chinese were reacting to Europe's more moderate approach and hoping to divide the West to its advantage, by sending a message that dialogue was a more productive approach than confrontation.

Encouraging Pragmatic Dialogue Since the Early 1990s

Western Europe's Weakening Rights Pressure

Western Europe weakened human rights pressure on China in the 1990s. The European Community lifted most sanctions on China in October 1990.[17] From the Chinese perspective, 1993 was an important turning point in Sino-Western European relations. In contrast to previous years, the 1993 Tokyo G7 summit declaration did not mention China's human rights or sanctions on China.[18] In October the German government announced a new Asia policy that treated Asia as a new foreign policy focus; China was important in this context.[19] The French government also took action to improve relations with Beijing. Prime Minister Edouard Balladur visited Beijing to expand commercial ties with the Chinese in April 1994.

As Western European nations tried to improve their overall relations with China, human rights became less important in the scheme of things. The European Union (EU) adopted a "Long-Term Policy for China-Europe Relations" on July 15, 1995, which shifted the EU's human rights approach to China from confrontation to dialogue. The document concluded that it was dangerous to make frequent public denunciations of China because such denunciations would actually weaken one's intended message. The EU further developed a strategy to build a "Comprehensive Partnership with China" on March 25, 1998. These documents called for political and economic cooperation and human rights dialogue with China.

Human rights remains an issue. As the EU China policy document suggested, Western Europe engage in human rights dialogues with China twice a year. European leaders continue to raise human rights issues when meeting with their Chinese counterparts. As Premier Zhu Rongji commented at a press conference, when foreign guests meet Chinese leaders, they never fail to discuss rights issues and present lists of people they consider to be jailed dissidents, as if they cannot otherwise explain themselves on their return.[20] While Europeans have been serious in human rights dialogues,[21] such exchanges have become ritualistic, handled in a manner that is nonthreatening to the Chinese government.

The EU has also retreated at the UN Human Rights Commission. The 1995 EU China document emphasized the importance of dealing with China's human rights at the commission, using the 1995 conference to vindicate this new approach. At that meeting the West managed to defeat China's technical maneuver and came up short by only one vote in passing a China resolution. However, Western Europe was fighting a losing rear-guard action. The EU stopped sponsoring anti-China resolutions in 1997 due to the defection of France, Germany, Italy, and Spain. This caused a division among EU members. "If I were a political prisoner in China, I'd be a very disappointed political prisoner," Dutch Foreign Minister Hans van Mierlo complained after the EU meeting of foreign ministers ended.[22] Supported by the United States, Denmark introduced a China motion with several other European nations as cosponsors, including the Netherlands, Britain, Austria, and Portugal.[23]

To avoid repeating the public division among EU members, Britain, which was holding the EU presidency at the time, urged EU members to adopt a common position on China for the 1998 meeting. British Foreign Secretary Robin Cook told journalists before his trip to Beijing that "we are much more likely to get progress if we all speak with one voice and all press the same message." However, he was wearing two hats, one to represent the EU and the other to represent the new Labor government for a fresh start with the Chinese government.[24] A consensus on China was eventually formed. EU foreign ministers decided on February 23 that neither the union nor individual members would support a resolution on China. "We appreciated the EU's attitude of strengthening dialogue and cooperation and refraining from confrontation," Premier Li Peng told Irish Foreign Minister David Andrews on February 24.[25] The United States soon followed suit. As Human Rights Watch noted, "the EU led the way in capitulating on human rights."[26]

As the Chinese government cracked down on political activists in 1998, the EU was divided over whether it should sponsor a China motion at the 1999 conference. The EU sent a delegation to China before an EU foreign minister meeting at which the matter would be discussed. Chinese Deputy Foreign Minister Wang Yingfan met for three hours with diplomats from Germany, Austria, and Finland on March 16 and urged the EU not to criticize China at the human rights commission meeting. On March 22, EU foreign ministers decided not to criticize China and to continue human rights dialogue with Beijing instead.[27] As a compromise, German Foreign Minister Joschka Fischer, speaking on behalf of the EU and a group of Central and Eastern European countries, told the commission that China "does not comply with international standards" on human rights and that Beijing's actions against dissidents placed "a great strain" on the European-Chinese dialogue.[28] Washington decided to sponsor a China resolution and appealed for EU assistance. EU members refused to be cosponsors although they cast votes for the U.S. proposal. In the end, the commission voted 22 to 17, with 14 abstentions, in favor of a "no-action motion" on the U.S. proposal.[29] One day later, a Chinese foreign ministry spokesman declared that "the United States stands alone in this anti-China farce."[30]

Despite Beijing's crackdown on dissidents and Falun Gong, European governments are actively courting the Chinese government. Jiang Zemin paid a state visit to Britain, France, and Portugal in October 1999. Jiang was royally received in London in the first Chinese state visit to Britain. The British government used an old law to forbid demonstrations and protests in the royal parks along Jiang's route to Buckingham Palace, an act that prompted an *Economist* editorial to call Britain "a less liberal and more hypocritical place than is often claimed."[31] The French government formally received Jiang in Paris on the day when the Chinese government tried four democracy activists and formally charged the leaders of the Falun Gong movement with stealing state secrets. As in Britain, demonstrators in France were brushed aside. German Chancellor Gerhard Schröder visited China in early November 1999. During his talk with Zhu Rongji on November 4, they reportedly discussed human rights issues. Schröder indicated afterwards that Germany would not participate in actions harmful to China, due to the two countries' different opinions of democracy.[32]

Europeans still talk about human rights with the Chinese. In December 1999, a delegation of EU leaders, led by EU Commission President Romano Prodi, urged the Chinese government to ratify the two international human rights treaties it had signed earlier, abolish the death penalty, and resume a dialogue with the Dalai Lama. They also raised the issues of the recent Chinese crackdown on democracy activists and the Falun Gong spiritual movement. But Premier Zhu yielded little ground.[33] The EU delegation included Chris Patten, the last Hong Kong British governor, who promoted democratization and criticized "Asian values." Patten was appointed EU Commissioner for Foreign Relations in July 1999. On September 2, Patten promised a tougher stance on human rights in China at a confirmation hearing in the European Parliament, to the satisfaction of European parliamentarians.[34] But there were no reported clashes between Chinese officials and Patten.[35] It appears that Europeans are engaging in symbolic human rights diplomacy, largely for domestic audiences.

At the 2000 UN Human Rights Commission meeting, China again succeeded in a technical maneuver to block discussion of a U.S.-sponsored resolution on China, prevailing by a vote of 22 to 18, with 18 abstaining and one absent. EU members voted with the United States as they had done previously. However, France, Belgium, and Italy vetoed EU cosponsorship for the U.S. resolution.[36] Absence of strong European support has weakened U.S.-led efforts to censure Beijing.

Western Europe's weak position on human rights stands out against its tough position when its economic interests are at stake. After the Sino-U.S. market-opening agreement was signed in November 1999, the EU became the principal obstacle to China's entry into the WTO. As Europeans sought additional concessions from Beijing, difficult trade negotiations lasted for five months until May

19, the eve of the U.S. congressional vote on China's PNTR status. Europeans did not succeed in their key demand that Beijing allow foreign ownership of more than 49 percent of telecommunications ventures in China. But they received some additional concessions, namely a shorter timetable for implementation of the agreed market-opening measures, insurance licenses to at least seven European insurance companies upon accession, and reductions in tariffs on 150 products not covered in the Sino-U.S. agreement.[37]

Europe is also weak on human rights compared to the United States. My discussion of U.S. human rights policy in the previous chapter and my discussion of European policy bear out this fact. Europeans familiar with the subject have made similar observations. "When economic interests are at stake," commented Peter R. Baehr, a noted Dutch human rights scholar, "the Western Europeans have shown themselves more reluctant to act than their American colleagues."[38] Chris Patten, the last British governor of Hong Kong and now the EU Commissioner for External Relations, stated that

American power and leadership have been more responsible than most other factors in rescuing freedom in the second half of this century. . . . Now the United States has to continue, unthanked, to stand up for these values in Asia, not eschewing engagement with China and those in the authoritarian camp, but ensuring that the engagement is principled. Washington will have only spasmodic support from European countries, whose pretensions to a common and honorable global policy are, alas, regularly turned inside out by China's facility at playing off the uninformed greed of one against the unprincipled avarice of another.[39]

Moreover, the European Union has been more willing to punish small countries for human rights violations. For example, the EU imposed sanctions on Myanmar in 1998, including a visa ban for Myanmar officials, withdrawal of trade benefits, and an arms embargo. In its attempt to isolate the Myanmar military regime, the EU has recently canceled high-level meetings with ASEAN, which refuses to exclude Myanmar. On April 10, 2000, EU foreign ministers decided to toughen sanctions against Myanmar, for its military government's intensified repression of dissent, by banning equipment that might be used for repression and freezing overseas assets held by members of the military government.[40]

China's rapid economic development since the early 1990s is a major factor explaining Western Europe's shifting position. Western

Europe's adjustment of its China policy has been driven primarily by economic factors. In fact, Europeans took the initiative to establish a closer relationship with China and Asia in the 1990s, based on a general sense among European policy elites that Europe needs to turn to a rapidly growing Asia-Pacific region to enhance its bargaining position vis-à-vis the United States and Japan. Europeans launched a new strategy toward Asia in July 1994, a year before its new China policy. Consistent with this new emphasis on Asia, Asian and EU leaders held the first Asia-EU summit conference in March 1996. China is a key factor for European success in this.[41] The simple truth is that once Asia and China became more important, an economic rationale prevailed over human rights reservations.[42] There are good reasons for Europeans to be more interested in trade with China, a rising economic power and a growing trading partner. China ranked fourth among the EU's trading partners in 1999, with a trade volume of 68.8 billion euros or 4.5 percent of the EU's total, trailing only the United States (22.3 percent), Switzerland (7.5 percent), and Japan (6.9 percent).[43]

Western Europe also needs China's political support to expand its own influence. China occupies a permanent seat on the UN Security Council and plays an important political and security role in Asia. Former French Foreign Minister Hervé de Charette points out that it is important for France and China to engage in major international discussions. "It is not normal that dialogue with China should be the prerogative of the Russians and Americans, especially when Beijing's relations with Moscow and Washington have never been really smooth. This is why the Europeans, with France in the front rank, must engage in regular, intensive, and constructive dialogue with China. It is easy to see why some in the world are trying to prevent us from doing so—because they wish to conserve a monopoly."[44] It is not surprising that a senior French official made these remarks, since France has always demonstrated an independent streak in its foreign policy. As a recent example, French President Jacques Chirac warmly received Jiang and Iranian President Mohammed Khatemi back to back in October 1999, despite strong domestic criticism of the human rights records of the two countries.

Western Europeans are also deterred to some extent from taking a more activist stance by their own colonial past in Asia and Africa. As a result, it is easier for target countries to criticize Europe's historical record as a counterattack.[45] Recalling Britain's acquiring of

Hong Kong after the Opium War, and France's sacking of the Summer Palace in Beijing in 1860 and setting up a concession in Shanghai, Charette pointed out that "we should not forget the trauma caused by our predecessors. It explains also why the appeals for democracy and respect for human rights in China, which we make so readily, are sometimes very difficult for Chinese leaders to accept."[46] Chinese leaders certainly remind their European critics of Europe's own past.

Moreover, frustrated with past failures at pressuring China to change its behavior, pragmatic European politicians have needed to take a different course.[47] After announcing the French government's decision not to support a UN resolution criticizing China on March 28, 1997, the foreign ministry spokesman justified the decision by saying that "you have to choose between confrontation detached from reality and constructive dialogue."[48] One explanation for Jiang's warm reception in France in October 1999, called "degrading for France" by the daily *Le Monde*, is that realpolitik had prevailed over human rights.[49] To some extent, the U.S. administration feels the same way. But unlike the United States, Western Europe does not have strong anti-China lobbies exerting pressure on government. While the European Parliament continues to criticize Beijing, it is a far less important institution in Europe than Congress is in the United States. At the same time, European business communities are actively promoting a cooperative relationship with China.

China's Calculations and Responses

Two features stand out in China's calculations about its policy toward Western Europe. On the one hand, Beijing has confidence in its ability to manage European rights pressure, unlike in its human rights disputes with Washington. Human rights is not seen as an important issue in the bilateral relationship with Europe. In Chinese writings on Sino-European relations, human rights, as one of the last issues discussed, normally takes up little space.[50] By contrast, Chinese writings on Sino-U.S. relations always treat human rights as a central bilateral issue. There are even books on Sino-U.S. human rights confrontations.[51] Moreover, while China needs Europe's market, investment, and technologies, the Chinese are also aware of Western Europe's need for China's market and political influence.

Chinese analysts see Western Europe as borrowing China's strength to compete with the United States and Japan.[52] Chinese diplomats concur.[53] This understanding of European motives has enhanced Chinese confidence and strengthened its bargaining leverage with Western Europe.

On the other hand, the Chinese now understand that the idea of human rights is deeply entrenched in European political tradition. Most Chinese scholars see human rights as a persistent issue. Even strong advocates of the Chinese official view of human rights admit that China's publicity campaign has so far done little to change minds in Western Europe.[54] European public pressure ensures that Western European governments need to address the issue of human rights in China. Furthermore, as likeminded Westerners, Europeans are easily influenced by Americans.

Based on these assessments, the Chinese government has adopted a four-pronged strategy of propaganda, economic statecraft, concessions, and hardball diplomacy. First, Beijing has countered Western criticism with high principles of noninterference, rights to development, and a collective and relative notion of human rights. This propaganda campaign should not be dismissed simply because it does not resonate in the West. From the Chinese perspective, Chinese propaganda has contributed to an emerging consensus among likeminded developing nations whose support has been crucial for China's success in international arenas such as the UN Human Rights Commission.[55] More important, China's campaign has enhanced its legitimacy to its domestic audience. The Chinese public has increasingly come to share government views on human rights despite their frequent criticism of government corruption and other social and economic ills. This is important because Western criticism will not work unless it resonates among ordinary Chinese, as discussed in Chapter Two. Less concerned about the Chinese population cooperating with Western forces to undermine its authority, the government is more confident in dealing with the West, a crucial reason why Western pressure has become increasingly ineffective.

Second, based on its awareness of European economic interests, the Chinese government has adopted active economic statecraft, rewarding cooperative governments with lucrative commercial contracts while punishing those overly critical of China. In particular, visits between Chinese and European leaders are often accompanied by signing ceremonies for commercial contracts. Beijing's strategy has paid off in influencing European positions on China.[56] As an example, French President Jacques Chirac, during his visit to Beijing in May 1997, received a $1.5 billion airplane contract from the Chinese government, a contract worth more than twice what the Americans received during Vice President Gore's visit in March; this was an implicit reward for France's decision not to sponsor a China resolution at the UN Human Rights Commission meeting in March.[57] Chirac and Jiang agreed to settle human rights disputes peacefully and urged the EU to engage China in human rights "in a constructive manner on the basis of equality and mutual respect."[58] During Jiang's visit to France in October 1999, the two governments announced a $2.5 billion order for 28 Airbus jets.

It should be noted, however, that as China becomes more dependent on the EU market, with a trade balance heavily in its favor, Beijing is also becoming more vulnerable to European trade sanctions if the EU chooses to impose them. EU statistics show that the EU was China's third largest trading partner in 1998, accounting for 15.1 percent of China's total, closely following Japan (17.8 percent) and the United States (17.0 percent). More significant, China's exports to the EU increased from 26.3 billion euros in 1995 to 49.5 billion in 1999 and its trade surplus increased from 11.5 billion euros in 1995 to 30.1 billion in 1999.[59] According to China's statistics, the EU's trade with China totaled $55.7 billion, or 15.4 percent of China's total trade, and a close third to Japan (18.4 percent) and the United States (17.1 percent). China had a surplus of $4.7 billion.[60]

Third, Beijing has extended olive branches to Europeans, making calculated concessions such as releasing important dissidents at opportune times, agreeing to human rights exchanges, and signing international human rights treaties. While making these concessions to the United States as well as to Western Europe, China has been more conciliatory toward Europe. On the one hand, the Chinese appear more willing to talk and more comfortable talking to Europeans. On the other hand, while the Chinese media has been critical of Western pressure on China, the Chinese single out the United States by equating the West with the United States and seldom mentioning specific European nations, as is reflected in frequently used Chinese expressions such as the "U.S.-led West" or "the U.S. and a few other Western nations." Not even the accidental NATO bombing of the Chinese embassy in Belgrade has changed

China's nuanced approach. After the bombing, the Chinese government suspended all military and human rights dialogues with
the United States. Qiao Zonghuai, China's Ambassador to the UN
Office at Geneva, stated that "the U.S.-led NATO attack of the embassy . . . constitutes a gross violation of the sovereignty of China and
the human rights of the Chinese people." [61] By contrast, Beijing did
not suspend its human rights dialogue with Brussels. The Chinese
have focused heated criticism on the United States and "U.S.-led
NATO" while avoiding direct criticism of specific European nations,
with the exception of Great Britain. [62]

The Chinese strategy is meant to demonstrate its goodwill to
Europe and provide political cover for European politicians to improve the overall bilateral relationship. But this strategy is also an
implicit reward for Western Europe's more moderate human rights
approach to China and is meant to encourage further cooperation. [63] China rewarded Western Europe with "human rights dialogues" when major European nations ceased to cosponsor China
resolutions at the UN Human Rights Commission in 1997. Right
before the vote at the commission, Beijing indicated its willingness
to sign the International Covenant on Economic, Social, and Cultural Rights by the end of the year, allowed the International Red
Cross to visit prisoners, and invited the UN High Commissioner
for Human Rights to China. After the commission meeting in late
August 1997, a German parliamentary delegation visited detention
centers and monasteries in Tibet. In September, Chinese Foreign
Minister Qian Qichen met the foreign ministers of Great Britain,
the Netherlands, and Luxembourg in New York and agreed to resume the Sino-EU human rights dialogue. In January 1998 Qian
met Robin Cook, Foreign Secretary of Britain, which held the rotat-
ing EU Presidency from January to July. Qian agreed to allow a visit
by UN Human Rights High Commissioner Mary Robinson to China
and Tibet, to sign the International Covenant on Civil and Political
Rights, and to hold another Sino-EU human rights dialogue. [64] One
day after the EU decided not to sponsor a China resolution at the
1998 UN Human Rights Commission conference, European legal
experts and officials were allowed to tour a model Beijing prison on
February 24, 1998. [65]

Judicial cooperation has become an important form of cooperation and dialogue. In March 2000, the Chinese Ministry of Justice
and an EU consortium launched the China-EU Legal and Judicial

Cooperative Program, the largest Sino-EU cooperative program in China so far. With total funding of 13.5 million euros for four years, the program will fund study trips and visits by lawyers, judges, prosecutors, and other legal professionals from both sides.

China's conciliatory approach to Western Europe reflects its strong desire to improve its overall relations with Europe. This is indicated by frequent high-level visits to Europe. In 1998–99, President Jiang Zemin, National People's Congress Chairman Li Peng, and Premier Zhu Rongji, the three most powerful men in China, all visited Europe, along with other Chinese leaders. China wants to see Europe become more unified and stand on its own as a pole, which would contribute to the emergence of a multipolar world, a world order preferred by China.[66]

China also sees Western Europe as a nonthreatening partner to help them avoid excessive dependence on the United States and Japan. In a strategy of divide and rule, China wants to show Washington that it is more productive to engage in dialogue than confrontation. This does not mean that the Chinese believe that they can turn Western Europe against the United States. Rather, China is making a defensive move to prevent a Western united front against the country.[67]

Fourth, China has taken hard stands against individual European nations. Beijing treats the collective voice of the European Union seriously. But the Chinese are well aware that it is still EU members who decide their own foreign policy. From the Chinese perspective, Southern European nations Italy, Spain, and Portugal led Europe in restoring relations with China. The Italian prime minister visited China in 1991. Li Peng paid a return visit in 1992, the first visit by a Chinese premier to Europe since the Tiananmen incident. Spain and Portugal also engaged in active government visits and economic cooperation with China. By contrast, Germany and France started late but made rapid progress once they began mending their relationships with China. Northern and Central European countries took more initiative in improving relations with China than before. As an exception, Great Britain fell behind,[68] but the new Labor government of Great Britain also improved relations with Beijing after the Hong Kong handover in 1997.[69]

China has made much effort to improve relations with major European nations like France, Germany, and Italy as the key to closer ties with the EU. This strategy paid off when France's opposi-

tion led to the collapse of an EU cosponsorship of anti-China resolutions at the UN Human Rights Commission. While China retaliated against major European nations over issues such as arms sale to
Taiwan, it did not overreact to European human rights pressure.[70]

In sharp contrast, China has come down harshly on small European countries that have led the charge against China. As a primary example, Denmark, persuaded by the United States, led the
sponsorship of a China resolution at the 1997 UN Human Rights
Commission meeting after the EU decided not to do so. Beijing exhibited a rare show of anger over human rights disputes with Europeans. Until then, *People's Daily* commentaries and foreign ministry
spokesmen mainly talked about "a few Western nations" and sometimes mentioned the United States. The Chinese media now singled
out Denmark for criticism. "This anti-China resolution will, I think,
in the end become a rock that smashes on the Danish government's
head." Foreign Ministry Spokesman Shen Guofang warned at an
April 10 news briefing. "Denmark, the bird that pokes out its head,
will suffer the most."[71] Beijing also saw Holland, which was holding
the EU presidency at the time, as actively mobilizing forces against
China.[72] Beijing retaliated against Denmark, Holland, and other
smaller European nations that supported the China resolution. Examples of China's retaliation included cancellation of visits by the
Dutch economic minister to China and by Vice Premier Zhu Rongji
to Holland, Austria, Ireland, and Luxembourg, which was scheduled for May of that year; "the hundred boat project" to import 100
Dutch boats to dredge Chinese rivers and ports; and a joint project
with major Dutch supermarket chain Marco. As one senior Chinese
diplomat saw it, the Danes and Dutch panicked and sent people to
apologize and mend fences with Beijing.[73]

Beijing was particularly annoyed with these small European nations because their actions frustrated Chinese attempts to isolate
the United States after it succeeded in persuading major European
nations to shift their positions on China. By acting harshly, China
could send a strong signal to countries undecided about their policy
choice. Some Chinese diplomats use a cultural explanation for Denmark and Holland's action, seeing the Dutch and Danes as out-
spoken people, unlike the diplomatically skilled and calculating
British and French.[74] The Chinese government also appeared to believe that it was not diplomatically costly to play hardball with these

smaller countries. China's deterrence strategy has worked to some extent.

Beijing continues to watch what Europeans do regarding human rights in China. The Chinese government was worried that the 1999 Nobel Peace Prize might go to Wei Jingsheng or Wang Dan or both. Chinese Foreign Ministry officials reportedly called in Norway's envoy to urge the Norwegian government to pressure the Peace Prize Committee to choose another candidate.[75] In the end, the prize went to Doctors Without Borders, an international NGO. It is not clear whether Chinese pressure had any significant impact on the outcome but the episode shows the serious efforts made by the Chinese government. In a recent example, Beijing has protested to the Swedish and Danish governments their allowing the Dalai Lama to visit their countries in May 2000 and their arranging meetings for him with government leaders.

Through all the means listed above, the Chinese government has largely neutralized Western European criticism. As Human Rights Watch lamented, "China succeeded in convincing virtually all industrialized countries to substitute 'dialogue' for 'confrontation' and public criticism during 1998." And it is impossible to assess whether these dialogues, which lack transparency, will serve as sources of real pressure for change.[76] To China's satisfaction, there has also emerged since 1998 a consensus among European nations to adopt a unified, conciliatory, and pragmatic approach toward China, thanks both to Europe's common interest in strengthening economic cooperation with China and the leadership of major nations such as France and Germany.[77] China's confidence was vividly revealed during Jiang's visit to Europe in October 1999. On October 25, while Jiang was in France, the Chinese government put four organizers of the China Democratic Party on trial and charged some jailed leaders of the Falun Gong movement with the serious crime of stealing state secrets.

However, one should recognize that China's "diplomatic victory" entails high costs. On the one hand, Beijing has spent considerable diplomatic resources, which could have been used for other purposes. On the other hand, the Chinese government could have also made more genuine improvements in human rights, which would benefit the nation and the people as a whole and should take place independent of Western pressure.

Conclusion

As strategic, political, and economic considerations shaped Sino-Western European relations through the 1980s, human rights was a nonissue. The 1989 Tiananmen incident, the subsequent collapse of communism in the Soviet Union and Eastern Europe, and a better understanding of China's human rights situation helped shape an assertive European human rights policy toward China. Western Europe joined the United States in pressuring China in a public and confrontational fashion. Still, Western Europeans balanced human rights considerations with economic and political interests. Europeans adopted a more pragmatic and less confrontational China policy in the early 1990s, resulting in a gradual retreat in the human rights arena. Europeans have changed their position because of China's rapid economic growth, its greater market and political weight, and their own frustration with the failure of the previous approach. Despite symbolic discussions of human rights, human rights is now essentially sidelined in European relations with Beijing.

The Chinese government does not feel as threatened by Western Europe as by the United States. Western Europe is distant from China, no more powerful than China on the world stage, and more important, not apparently inclined to undermine the current Chinese political regime. The Chinese also believe that Europeans need the Chinese market and China's political influence to advance their interests. At the same time, Beijing needs European cooperation for its modernization drive and wants to prevent a united Western front against China. As a result, Beijing's largely successful strategy combines commercial incentives to encourage European cooperation, tough stances and retaliation against confrontation to demonstrate its costs, and symbolic concessions to provide political cover for European governments.

Looking into the future, human rights is likely to be managed within a framework of a distant but nonconfrontational Sino-EU relationship. China and Europe have strategic and economic incentives encouraging them to maintain stable relations. But China and Europe differ greatly in values and beliefs. Even though human rights may not be on the table at the moment, it will continue to fester, shaping a critical European view of China and influencing other policy issues between China and Western Europe.

Chapter Five
Human Rights and Sino-Japanese Relations

Non-Issue Through the 1980s

Among the major powers in the Asia-Pacific, Japan has had a long history of interaction with China, while the United States is a late-comer. The fates of Japan and China in the modern age have been intertwined. It was after having observed China's defeat by Great Britain in the Opium War of 1839–42 that Japan started a success-ful modernization following the Meiji Restoration of 1868. In the meantime, China disintegrated in the course of a series of painful transformations. In less than 30 years, Japan had become strong enough to defeat China in the Sino-Japanese War of 1894–95. Japan's actions toward China were an important reason for China's adoption of a different political system after WWII. The Japanese demand to inherit the German concessions in China after WWI touched off the May Fourth Movement of 1919, which contributed to the founding of the Chinese Communist Party (CCP) two years later. During the war that followed Japan's invasion of China proper in 1937, the CCP gained in legitimacy and strength. After WWII ended, the Communist forces won China within four years.

While Japan's actions helped to create favorable conditions for a communist China, they were also instrumental in the establishment of a democratic system in Japan itself. Japan's aggression ended in defeat and occupation by the Americans, who forced democracy on Japan. Although the U.S. occupation authorities adopted harsh measures against Japan initially, the CCP victory in mainland China made the United States reverse its Japan policy. China's interven-tion in the Korean War strengthened U.S. determination to help

Japan's economic recovery and development as part of the U.S. global strategy to confront the communist bloc.

This complicated history between China and Japan has been a crucial factor conditioning their relations in later years. The fact that Japan became a U.S. protectorate meant that Sino-U.S. relations conditioned Sino-Japanese relations through the early 1970s. Americans intervened strongly to prevent a closer economic and political relationship between China and Japan despite a persistent and strong interest and support in Japan for such ties.[1] Nevertheless, there was far more frequent contact between Tokyo and Beijing than there was between Washington and Beijing. The Japanese were eager to trade with China due to economic necessities, geographical proximity, historical ties, cultural affinity, and war guilt. Beijing used "unofficial trade" and "people's diplomacy" to satisfy its economic needs and manipulate Japanese domestic politics to its advantage.[2] Americans tolerated limited Japan-China trade as necessary for the economic survival and health of its key ally in the Far East. The Japanese government normalized diplomatic relations with China in 1972 only after President Nixon made a historic trip to China.

The fact that the United States imposed a democratic system on Japan did not have a significant impact on Japan-China relations in this stage. After all, powerful socialist and leftwing forces in Japan were sympathetic to the Chinese communist experiment, a fact which allowed Beijing to exercise influence by manipulating Japanese domestic politics. Through the 1960s, Japan's China policy, along with its security treaty with the United States, were serious domestic political issues that turned the country into "a house divided against itself."[3] This division aggravated the domestic Cold War raging in parallel to the international Cold War.[4] Furthermore, war guilt and cultural affinity widely shared by Japanese prevented them from criticizing China.

In this context, human rights was a nonissue in Sino-Japanese relations. Although this was similar to China's relations with the United States and Western Europe, there were important differences between Japan and the West in this period. First, Japan did not have a human rights foreign policy, unlike the United States and Western Europe, which started treating human rights explicitly as a foreign policy issue in the 1970s. As a result, Japan's neglect of China's human rights was a norm rather than an exception in its foreign policy. Second, there were no human rights incidents to complicate relations between Japan and China as there were between China and the West starting in the late 1970s. Japan did not have to take any action since emerging Chinese dissidents did not turn to Tokyo for assistance. Third, unlike the United States and Western Europe, Japan was on the defensive in its relations with China. In fact, China was the only country other than the United States that could use *gaiatsu*, or pressure on Japanese politics, due to Japanese respect for Chinese civilization and guilt for Japan's aggression.[5] It was China that frequently criticized Japan's policies and internal politics and often managed to win symbolic concessions from the Japanese government in the 1980s.[6] Beijing was thus on high moral ground while Tokyo kept a low profile.

Balancing Between China and the West in 1989–91

Japan became involved in human rights in China only after the 1989 Tiananmen incident and then only hesitantly. The 1989 Tiananmen incident put Japan in a difficult position.[7] On the one hand, Japan was worried about its image in the United States and other Western nations, an image which had already been tarnished due to Japan's relentless advance into the global market. With the end of the Cold War, the Japanese were concerned that Washington might replace the Soviet Union with Japan as its number one enemy and that the West might see Japan as "different" if the country took a different stance on China. Foreign Minister Mitsuzuka Hiroshi was thus dispatched to Washington on June 25 to demonstrate solidarity with its main ally. Tokyo eventually joined the Western camp in imposing economic sanctions on China by suspending yen loans. Japan did so more because of its desire to side with the West in appearance than because of its convictions about human rights.[8]

On the other hand, Japan wanted to maintain its special relationship with China. Japan thus showed its difference from Western nations by avoiding direct criticism of the Chinese government, particularly concerning human rights and democracy, and by dragging its feet. Also, unlike other industrial nations, the Japanese government refused to grant political asylum to Chinese dissidents and limited the freedom of expression, assembly, and association of Chinese students in Japan.[9] More significant, Japan led the way in easing China back into the international community. Japan saw a special role for itself when it came to China. "As relations between China and the West remain tied in a difficult knot," argued Tanino Sakutaro, director general of the foreign ministry's Asian Affairs Bureau, "the role of untangling it . . . naturally falls on Japan among the industrialized democracies."[10]

Sensitive to American views, the Japanese government waited cautiously to start normalizing relations with Beijing until it became known that Bush had sent National Security Advisor Brent Scowcroft and Under Secretary of State Lawrence Eagleburger to Beijing in early December 1989. In January 1990 Prime Minister Kaifu Taoshiki became the first leader of a major industrial country to receive an official Chinese delegation, which was led by State Councilor and Chairman of the State Planning Commission Zou Jiahua, and he emphasized the need to continue friendly ties between the two nations. Several Japanese private banks resumed loans to China in March 1990, loans which totaled around $20 million.[11] Encouraged by the White House's decision to grant MFN status to China in late May, Tokyo received Bush's "understanding" of its intention to renew its Third Yen Loan to China shortly before the G7 summit in Houston in July 1990, even though Kaifu did not receive support for his intention to lift sanctions.[12] A few days later, Kaifu sent a special emissary to Beijing to inform the Chinese government about the G7 summit and Japan's decision to resume aid to Beijing. Japan promptly resumed its aid to China after the summit. Kaifu's visit to Beijing in August 1991 fully restored normal relations between China and Japan, in contrast to the Sino-U.S. relationship.

Critics of Japan's balancing act believed that Japan was driven by commercial considerations. After Japan resumed aid to China in 1990, Nancy Pelosi, a Democratic House representative from California and a strong advocate of a tough line on the Chinese government, commented that Japanese "are basing their policy on deals, not ideals."[13] China was becoming important to the Japanese economy. China had become Japan's fifth largest trading partner, with total trade amounting to $19.3 billion in 1988. Japanese firms had invested more than $2 billion in over 567 projects in China.[14] Japan also provided large official and private loans to China. Japanese companies, which had made an impressive advance into the Chinese market since Deng opened China's door in 1978, wanted to further strengthen their positions by demonstrating to the Chinese government and their Chinese partners how reliable they were compared to their competitors.

However, it is equally important to recognize Japan's broader interests in regional stability, which the Japanese government often referred to in its policy statements. Japanese felt that assistance to China's modernization was necessary for stability in China and the region. If China's reform failed, Japan would suffer economically and face potential waves of Chinese refugees to its shores. Tokyo was concerned that isolating China would compromise the country's chances of economic reforms. Also, while democratization is important, few Japanese saw economic sanctions as the way to do it.[15] This view was really not that different from Bush's own opinion, but given different political environments, the Japanese government could do what the Bush administration could not. Besides, due to its past aggression, Japan was uncomfortable intervening in the internal affairs of its Asian neighbors and most of all in those of China. Foreign Minister Nakayama Taro told Zou Jiahua on January 23, 1990 that Japan was not interested in imposing its values on China, which has a different social system from Japan.[16]

Beijing was eager to use Japan as the weak link to break through diplomatic isolation. During his meeting on September 19, 1989 with Ito Masayoshi, the leader of the Parliamentarian League for Japan-China Friendship, Deng Xiaoping commented that the Chinese government noticed "some differences" between Japan and the West. He then emphasized that "Sino-Japanese friendship, important to both sides, is conducive to the interests of both peoples, and to world peace and development," a view Ito accepted.[17] Similarly, Party General Secretary Jiang Zemin told a Japanese journalist that while it is understandable that Japan emphasizes its relations with the United States, China and Japan are sovereign nations and should develop friendship and cooperation autonomously. He noticed Tokyo's positive attitude towards resuming economic cooperation with China.[18] Premier Li Peng told a delegation of Japanese senators that the Chinese government appreciated Kaifu's announcement that Japan would resume the Third Yen Loan to China.[19] Japan's efforts at bridging China and the West were also duly noted in the official Chinese media.[20]

As Kaifu was the first leader of a major industrial nation to visit China after the Tiananmen incident, Beijing saw his visit as an important step toward ending its diplomatic isolation. To demonstrate its appreciation, Beijing agreed in principle to sign the Non-Proliferation Treaty. In addition, China canceled memorial ceremonies for forced Chinese labor in Japan and the victims of the 1937 Nanjing massacre. And the Chinese officials did not comment on Japan's wartime acts when Kaifu made apologies for the war.[21] Although Beijing was not inhibited in voicing its opinion about Japan, its reaction was much more restrained than it could have been. For example, despite China's misgivings about Japan's sending mine sweepers to the Gulf at the end of the Gulf War, Japanese received China's "understanding."[22]

Japanese resources, to some extent, neutralized the effectiveness of U.S. efforts. Japan not only differed from the United States over human rights in China, it also helped shape southeast Asians' reactions to the Tiananmen incident in a much more modest way than the West wanted.[23] The American business community also used Japan as a weapon to put pressure on Congress not to impose sanctions against Asian nations.[24]

Did Japan gain special influence from its self-designated role as a bridge between China and the West? There is little evidence that Japan gained special leverage vis-à-vis the West based on its closer ties with China. The United States and other Western nations had their own channels to Beijing and did not have to go through Tokyo. If anything, Tokyo's straddling of the issue only increased Western suspicion that Japan had yet to converge with the West. In Beijing, however, Japan's distance from the West over the human rights issue did increase its bargaining leverage in the early 1990s. On November 14, 1989, in a sign of the importance China attached to Japan, Deng chose a Japanese delegation as the last foreign guests he would receive in his official capacity.

With a stronger bargaining position, Japan became somewhat more assertive than before. According to the sources close to Kaifu, the Japanese government considered changing its system of providing credits to China, from a multi-year to a single-year basis, after the expiration of the Third Yen Loan in 1995.[25] A single-year system would give the donor more influence. Kaifu raised arms control and other important issues with Chinese leaders, hinting that Japan would consider China's efforts at controlling its military development and weapons transfers when deciding on future government loans to China. However, he was cautious over the human rights issue.[26] This would be a trend in later years; Japanese became more and more concerned about China's military spending and environmental problems while remaining low key on human rights issues.

The China Exception in the Early 1990s

China's human rights was not an important bilateral issue even when Japan adopted a human rights foreign policy in the early 1990s. In fact, Beijing and Tokyo enjoyed a very warm relationship, in contrast to the big chill between China and the West. However, Tokyo continued to strike a balance between China and the United States. As Washington demanded a close linkage between human rights and MFN status, Tokyo actively mediated between the two sides behind the scene. Moreover, to demonstrate its identification with the Western camp, the Japanese supported Western attempts at criticizing China in the multilateral context.

Japan's Human Rights Policy

Japan became more concerned about human rights after 1991. On April 10, 1991, Kaifu announced in the House of Councilors Budget Committee that Japan would consider arms spending, the democratization process, market reform, and human rights in determining foreign aid to a country. These policy objectives were incorporated in the Official Development Assistance (ODA) Charter adopted by the Japanese cabinet on June 30, 1992. The Charter articulated, for the first time, a new approach to using Japan's ODA to improve human rights situations in recipient nations. It stressed four principles: (1) environment and development; (2) prevention of aid for military use; (3) military spending and arms production; and (4) democratization, market economy, and human rights.

Japan appeared ready for a more active human rights foreign policy in 1993. The Liberal Democratic Party (LDP), which had governed in Japan for 38 years, lost to a coalition of opposition parties in the general election. In the new coalition cabinet, Foreign Minister Hata Tsutomu had been active in human rights issues in the Diet. Prime Minister Hosokawa Morihiro had also made some promising remarks on human rights. Japan, indeed, became more active in some areas. The 1995 issue of *Japan's ODA*, an annual publication by the Ministry of Foreign Affairs to highlight Japan's ODA performance, listed a number of countries, mainly in Africa, that had been subjected to Japan's human rights pressure. In 1994, Japan suspended or cut off aid to Sudan, Sierra Leone, Malawi, Haiti (until President Aristide returned), and Nigeria over human rights issues.

In Asia, however, Japan did not follow the principle of democratization. In contrast to the United States, Japan preferred a low-key approach.[27] "Japan's criteria for giving aid, the so-called Four Principles, are not like U.S. laws," noted Japanese diplomat Okazaki Hisahiko: "They're not enforceable. It's just that we need to take into consideration the recipient country's behaviour under each of the four headings. That's certainly been done in China's case, but apparently they decided not to take any action."[28] Tokyo avoided using ODA to force China and other Asian nations to make immediate and issue-specific improvements on human rights, while it used ODA for other political objectives.[29] As a result, Human Rights Watch concluded in 1994 that despite the sea changes in Japan's domestic politics, "the impact on foreign policy, specifically in the area of human rights, was negligible."[30]

Japan's past aggression in Asia works against the nation. It is difficult for the Japanese to act assertively in Asia when they have not quite faced the past. Asians, Chinese in particular, would not react well if Japan chose to promote human rights and democracy in Asia. Simply put, few Asians see Japan as morally qualified to criticize other Asian nations.

Japan is further deterred by strong resistance to foreign intervention in human rights by some key Asian nations. Some Asian leaders, such as Singapore's Lee Kuan Yew and Malaysia's Mahamad Mahathir, advocate community-oriented "Asian values" as different from and even superior to the individually based Western conception of human rights.[31] It is not that easy to make a sharp distinction between the two systems and argue that Asians do not need individual rights. The advocates of Asian values often have their own political agenda, and use values to justify their political dominance and privilege. In addition, many Asians challenge so-called Asian values and champion universal values of human rights. As a boost to the human rights cause in the region, South Korea's long-time dissident, Kim Dae Jung, won the presidential election in December 1997. Kim supports the universality of human rights and rejects the myth of Asian values.

Nevertheless, most Asian governments have challenged the

moral authority of the West to criticize their human rights records based on Asian values, myth or not. They have largely ignored Western campaigns to isolate human rights violators. In fact, the United States is often isolated in human rights debates in the region. For example, the United States clashed with Asian nations over human rights at the annual ASEAN meeting in Kuala Lumpur in July 1997 when Myanmar joined the regional group. Few Asian participants shared U.S. Secretary of State Albright's concerns over human rights and individual freedom. Conversely, Asian governments generally welcome conciliatory U.S. measures. Clinton's decision to delink human rights and MFN status in 1994 for China, for example, was welcomed by Asians.[32]

This contentious situation between the West and Asia puts Japan in a difficult situation, as Japan has avoided confronting Asia since the end of the Second World War. Tokyo has adopted a two-track foreign policy, one for the West and the other for Asia. Japan has been less willing to accommodate the United States in Asia than in other regions.[33] Human rights is particularly sensitive. "Japan often found itself in an awkward position," as Ueki Yasuhiro points out. "Human rights constitute a pillar of democracy in the West, whereas they are often perceived as a threat to the regimes in power in non-democratic countries."[34] As a Japan specialist in China sees it, Japan would be isolated in Asia if it pushed Western values based on its economic power since Asian nations have different understandings of human rights and democracy than do the United States and Western Europe.[35] Given an emotional resistance to the West from nearly all key Asian nations and a lack of explicit U.S. pressure on Tokyo, Japan prefers to stay out of human rights controversies, especially when it comes to China, which it considers to be the most important country in the region.

Sino-Japanese Human Rights Relations

Sino-Japanese relations were normal in the early 1990s, in contrast to Sino-Western relations, which remained partially frozen as discussed in the previous two chapters. In fact, Beijing and Tokyo enjoyed one of the best periods in their often-troubled relations.[36] The two countries became closer economic partners. Tokyo continued to provide massive ODA to Beijing, totaling $6.3 billion (in 1988 dollars) in the Third Yen Loan (1990–95). Bilateral trade grew sharply, from $19.6 billion in 1989 to $57.9 billion in 1995, making China Japan's second largest trading partner and making Japan China's largest trading partner.[37] Despite the burst of the bubble economy in the early 1990s, Japanese companies invested $11.1 billion in China in 1989–95, compared to $2 billion in 1951–88.[38] Politically, the two governments engaged in frequent visits by leaders and high officials, in contrast to the United States, which refrained from high-level contacts with China.[39] Party General Secretary Jiang Zemin, Deng's chosen heir, visited Japan in April 1992 and Emperor Akihito made a historic visit to China in October of that year, marking the twentieth anniversary of the normalization of Sino-Japanese relations.

Human rights did add a new dimension to the bilateral relationship after the Tiananmen incident. For example, opponents of the emperor's visit to China cited China's poor human rights record and the 1989 Tiananmen crackdown as one of the reasons that the emperor should not go to China. However, the government supported the emperor's visit as crucial for a friendly relationship with Japan's enormous neighbor.[40] Unlike Western governments, the Japanese government did not treat human rights as important for its bilateral agenda with Beijing.[41]

The Chinese government continued to seek a stronger relationship with Japan. Beijing actively sought a high-profile visit by the Japanese emperor. Premier Li Peng extended the invitation to the emperor for the first time during his visit to Japan in April 1989. After the Tiananmen incident, Chinese leaders made repeated invitations for an imperial visit: Foreign Minister Qian Qichen in June 1991, Li Peng in August 1991, Qian again in January 1992, and Jiang in April 1992. Also, to encourage cooperation from the West, China adopted a warmer approach to Japan than to the West. A sharp contrast was made between China's treatment of Christopher's visit to Beijing in March 1994 and Prime Minister Hosokawa's visit shortly after, which reflected not only their different ranks but also Beijing's different attitudes toward them.[42] While praising Japan's cooperation, Beijing also wanted to keep Japan on the defensive by reminding the Japanese from time to time of their past aggression against China. The Chinese government continued to expect and ask for official Japanese apologies for Japanese aggression during the war.

Tokyo's awareness of actual or latent resentment against Japan deterred its pursuit of a proactive interventionist policy to improve human rights in China. Beijing was indeed ready to use history as a trump card against any potential Japanese criticism of China's human rights record. A Chinese diplomat responsible for human rights diplomacy pointed out that the Japanese never talk about human rights in bilateral talks with the Chinese. "We don't mind talking about human rights. We can talk about Nanjing and comfort women."[43] Ironically, a greater degree of democracy in China may unleash, at least in the short run, greater anti-Japanese sentiment. Such sentiment has been suppressed to a large extent by a Chinese government that seeks a good working relationship with Japan to realize economic modernization. As an example of such a linkage, the Global Alliance for Preserving the History of World War II in Asia, based in the United States, grew out of the 1989 prodemocracy movement in China. Inspired by its activities, Chinese American author Iris Chang published a highly publicized book, *The Rape of Nanking*, documenting the atrocities committed by the Japanese army in Nanjing.[44]

In contrast to its bilateral relationship, Japan was more active in multilateral arenas. Japan voiced different opinions about human rights from those by China, Burma, and Iran in the Asian regional human rights conference held in Bangkok in April 1993 before the World Conference on Human Rights to be held in June in Vienna. The Bangkok Declaration adopted by the 40 attending countries gave a strong voice to the "Asian views" of human rights. The Japanese delegation voiced strong opposition to the document even though it did sign on to it. The Japanese argued that international concerns about human rights do not count as interference in domestic affairs and that it is legitimate to link foreign aid to recipient countries' human rights records.[45]

More significant, Japan cosponsored resolutions criticizing China at the UN Human Rights Commission throughout this period. Japan's cosponsorship invited a formal protest from the Chinese ambassador in 1993.[46] Japanese officials gave somewhat different stories as to why Japan supported attempts to censure China at the commission. Some maintained that Japan really had no choice given the general international sentiment after the Tiananmen incident, and others suggested that Japan cared about human rights.[47] Both arguments have some validity, but it should be recognized that such a dichotomy between bilateral and multilateral approaches balances Japan's crucial relationships with the United States and

China. It is less costly to appease the West and criticize China in multilateral contexts. Given the importance of its relationship with China, Japan cannot afford to do too much, but given the importance of its relationship with the West, Japan cannot afford to do nothing.

Japan and Sino-U.S. Human Rights Relations

While Tokyo tried to and did improve its relations with China, it could not isolate its China policy from its relations with other countries, particularly the United States. Japan was concerned during 1989–94 when the U.S. Congress threatened to withdraw China's MFN trading status. Japan opposed the linkage between human rights and MFN status but had to support the United States publicly. Japan acted behind the scenes as a mediator. Tokyo wanted the removal of the MFN-human rights linkage, considering it an irritant in the Sino-U.S. relationship, and arguing that China was too important to isolate and that engagement with China would provide conditions for its eventual democratization. During his meetings with Secretary of State Christopher and President Clinton in February 1993, Foreign Minister Watanabe Michio wanted the Americans to take a "moderate approach" toward China and unconditionally renew MFN status for China. Prime Minister Miyazawa made the same pitch during his meeting with Clinton in April.

At the same time, Japanese officials tried to persuade the Chinese government to release some political prisoners and allow international organizations to visit Chinese prisons.[48] Japan played a crucial role in persuading the Chinese to talk to the International Red Cross. They also argued on the behalf of some Chinese dissidents, who were later released for health reasons. When Jiang Zemin met Clinton at the APEC meeting in Seattle in 1993, the Japanese wanted to make sure that the meeting would be successful.[49]

Japan's overtures were understood but not always welcomed by the United States. "Japanese tend to take the Chinese side more than we would like," a U.S. official observed.[50] Hosokawa's March 1994 visit to Beijing was a blow to the Americans. He espoused views that differed sharply from those of Secretary of State Christopher, who had clashed openly with the Chinese over human rights issues in Beijing earlier in the month. On his way home from Beijing, Hosokawa contradicted an earlier report that he had urged the Chinese government to improve its human rights record. He reported to the journalists, "I told [Li Peng] that it is not proper to force a Western- or European-type democracy onto others."[51] A U.S. official lamented, "China will get a lot of mileage out of this."[52]

Japan's lukewarm support for the United States in the human rights area certainly had to do with anticipated Chinese resistance, as discussed earlier. There are three other broad reasons, which exist to this day. First, Japan sees promoting human rights in Asia as a low priority due to its stakes in the region, its conception of human rights, and its weak human rights nongovernmental organizations. The Japanese value economic growth and political stability in the region and generally see a positive correlation between the two. As it is situated in Asia, Japan has a far greater stake in maintaining order and stability in the region than countries outside. The Japanese are particularly worried about an influx of Chinese refugees if chaos takes place in China.

Japan is a democracy that respects human rights at home, but Tokyo acts differently on human rights in other countries.[53] Few Japanese feel that Japan should promote democracy and human rights abroad. Japanese tend to see human rights as internal affairs. For example, Nakagawa Junji suggested that "the compatibility of the ODA guidelines with the principle of nonintervention is still not clear."[54] Japan's position on human rights has not escaped the attention of Chinese scholars. Liu Jiangyong, a Japan specialist in China, argued that there is no legal basis in Japanese laws for humanitarian intervention.[55] Japanese tend to believe that economic growth is necessary for democratization. Based on Japan's own experience and the experience of other East Asian countries, Japanese generally advocate patience and oppose intervention. In the case of China, Japanese focus on the tension between economic modernization and political liberalization rather than human rights. Modernization will lead to democracy but a strong hand is needed sometimes in the process to assure stability, which is key for economic success. Takashi Inoguchi argued that "East Asian leaders shrewdly recognize the potential for destabilization that political liberalization could bring. This explains . . . why Deng Xiaoping dealt with the Tiananmen Square demonstrators the way he did in 1989."[56]

Second, there is insufficient Japanese domestic pressure on the government to pursue a proactive human rights policy. The Japanese view of democratization and the importance of stability, as discussed earlier, is not really different from that of strategic thinkers in the United States.[57] In fact, President Bush himself did not feel too differently from the Japanese but was constrained by domestic politics. The Japanese and U.S. business communities also share similar views about human rights issues. The U.S. business community actively lobbies against economic sanctions on China, arguing that Western business activities in the region will promote capitalism and democracy in the long run. What makes Japan different from the United States is that Japan does not have a strong constituency for a proactive human rights foreign policy. NGOs play a limited role in shaping Japanese foreign policy. Opposition parties do not pressure the ruling party on the human rights issue. Even during the Tiananmen incident, no major opposition parties in Japan pressured the government to act strongly against the Chinese government. The powerful bureaucracy thus adopts a pro-business policy with little internal opposition.[58]

Few foreign dissident groups operate in Japan, unlike in the United States. Chinese dissidents and students in Japan have had little impact on Japanese policy. In contrast, Chinese dissidents and students in the United States have gained access to the administration and Congress. In the United States, human rights has its own momentum, entrenched in values and domestic politics, and as a result will remain an issue. In contrast, there are no powerful domestic players in Japan that can sustain pressure on the government to adopt a proactive human rights policy in cooperation with the United States.[59]

Third, the United States has not explicitly pressured Japan to support the U.S. human rights policy in China. Washington's political capital has mainly been used to resolve trade and security issues with Tokyo. This reflects the White House's priorities in Asia, with human rights as only one of the issues rather than the issue that commands high-level attention between American and Japanese leaders. American and Japanese officials certainly exchange views, and Japan keeps an eye on U.S. reaction to its dealings with China and other Asian nations, with the human rights issue included. In response to U.S. expectations and in anticipation of potential U.S. criticism, Japan has taken some modest measures in its bilateral relationships and a stronger stance in the multilateral context. Nevertheless, there is no explicit policy coordination between Japan and the United States regarding human rights in China and other Asian nations. Michael H. Armacost, the U.S. ambassador to Japan between May 1989 and July 1993, recalls that he was periodically instructed to ask the Japanese to discuss human rights issues with the Chinese leadership. "I generally encountered little resistance, and I have no doubt that our Japanese friends raised these matters as requested. Whether they did so in a determined manner, intending to achieve results, or in a perfunctory way, merely to mollify Washington, I cannot say." [60] A more persistent Washington would have gotten a stronger Japanese response, as is often the case in the relationship between the two nations.

The United States does not pressure Japan on human rights in part because it recognizes Japan's unique situation in Asia.[61] But more important, the United States itself is divided over human rights issues in Asia, torn between moral concerns and strategic and commercial interests, as discussed in Chapter Three. The U.S. and Japanese business communities use each other to avoid human rights issues. The American business community argued that unless the United States engaged China, Japanese firms would have a strong hold on the China market. Once the American business community succeeded in pressuring the White House to engage China, Japan enjoyed greater legitimacy in its own approach to China.

Sino-Japanese Human Rights Relations Since the Mid-1990s

Human rights remains an insignificant issue on the bilateral agenda. But unlike previously, Japan no longer stands out among industrial countries as the United States and Western Europe have softened their human rights approaches and normalized ties with China. Ironically though, tensions have arisen between China and Japan, which human rights issues have contributed to indirectly.

As in the early 1990s, Beijing and Tokyo have not addressed human rights in any serious fashion in their bilateral exchange. Tokyo welcomed Clinton's decision to delink trade and human rights in 1994, which made it less necessary for Japanese to raise the human rights issue with the Chinese. Since 1994, human rights has almost never come up in bilateral talks between China and Japan.[62] In fact, when Premier Li Peng visited Japan in November 1997, Prime Minister Hashimoto Ryutaro did not talk about human rights in China at all, not even in the pro forma discussions that Western leaders typically engage in.[63] As a reflection of the insignificant status of the human rights issue, works on Sino-Japanese relations by Chinese and Japanese scholars seldom mention the words "human rights," unlike writings on Sino-U.S. relations, which never fail to treat human rights as an important issue. It is also striking that few Chinese or Japanese officials and scholars initiate discussions of human rights when talking about the bilateral relationship, in sharp contrast to officials and scholars who talk about Sino-U.S. relations.

Japan has acted more assertively toward China since the mid-1990s over military spending, nuclear tests, and the environment.[64] In the Fourth Yen Loan agreed upon by China and Japan at the end of 1994, Japan emphasized the environment and assistance to China's interior regions.[65] In addition, Tokyo decided to offer the new loans in two phases (three years and two years) instead of its previous practice of determining loans for five years. In May 1995, Japan suspended grant aid to China after Beijing conducted a nuclear test immediately after the extension of the Nonproliferation Treaty and Prime Minister Murayama's visit to China.[66] When President Jiang visited Japan in November 1998, he apparently hoped to obtain a written apology from the Japanese government even though the two sides had not reached an agreement before his departure from Beijing.[67] As Japanese refused to do so, Jiang took his message to the Japanese public and made frequent references to the history issue wherever he went, which caused a backlash in Japan. From the Japanese perspective, this is a healthy development in Japan's relations with China; Tokyo no longer treats China as a special case and Japan says no when it should. But from the Chinese perspective, Japan is raising its profile compared to its past approach based on its economic power, a development that does not bode well for the bilateral relationship.[68]

Interestingly though, despite Tokyo's higher profile, Japan remains hesitant to pressure China on human rights issues. Logically, one may assume that Tokyo could use human rights as a card to counter the history card often used by the Chinese government. But Tokyo has not done so. While Chinese officials and analysts recognize a remote possibility that Tokyo might exploit human rights to put China down, they do not anticipate such a move by the Japanese government. As discussed earlier in the chapter, the Chinese are not really concerned about Japan's using the human rights card since they can raise the history issue even more forcibly. Japanese diplomats recognize this and do not see use of the human rights issue as a viable option, even after Jiang's frequent discussion of the history issue during his November 1998 trip.[69] Japan cannot really gain much by using the human rights card. After all, while the Chinese nation feels deeply about its past humiliation by Japan, Japanese public and policy elites do not consider human rights in China to be a top concern. Thus, by emphasizing the human rights issue Japan cannot hope to make substantive gains but will surely invite strong Chinese criticism of past Japanese aggression, which will arouse anti-Japanese sentiment in China and do real damage to the bilateral relationship.

In the multilateral arena, Japan continues to support the West. At the UN Human Rights Commission in Geneva, Japan cosponsored anti-China resolutions through 1997. But the Japanese privately expressed to the Chinese their reluctance to support the United States at the 1996 conference.[70] And Japan could hide itself among a bloc of countries criticizing China. While Japan's support for the West annoyed Beijing, the Chinese did not see Japan as the cause of their problems. Chinese discussions of Beijing's diplomatic endeavors to block China resolutions at the commission generally cast them as an extension of Sino-U.S. human rights relations. While Chinese scholars and officials also pay considerable attention to Western Europe, they treat Japan as they do other non-Western nations and rarely offer specific discussions of what Japan is doing at the commission. Importantly, the Chinese do not see Japan lobbying other countries to support resolutions criticizing China, as they see the United States and Western European countries doing.[71] When the European Union was divided over whether to cosponsor resolutions criticizing China in 1997, Japan had an opening. Foreign Minister Ikeda told his Chinese counterpart Qian Qichen in Beijing on March 29, the day after France had announced its decision not to be a cosponsor, that Japan was also considering discontinuing its own cosponsorship.[72] When Japan formally decided not to sponsor the motion to criticize China, the Chinese foreign ministry spokesman stated that "the Chinese government appreciates this attitude."[73]

In exchange for Japan's and Western nations' decisions not to be cosponsors, Beijing agreed to engage in human rights dialogues with them. Japan and China had their first formal human rights dialogue on October 21–23, 1997. The press secretary of the Japanese Foreign Ministry announced that Japan had recommended during the dialogue that the Chinese consider accession to the International Covenant on Civil and Political Rights.[74] Sino-Japanese human rights dialogues were held again in June 1998. Although some Japanese diplomats see these dialogues as serious endeavors,[75] these dialogues, which attract little media attention, are ritualized chat sessions in which two sides express different opinions. While agreeing to human rights dialogues, Beijing has no intention of being lectured on human rights and democracy. Unlike the Americans, the Japanese mainly talk about general principles rather than specific cases. Chinese officials normally respond that China cares about human rights but treats rights to survival and development as more important for the country and that it takes time to develop human rights, using Japan's own development over the past fifty years as an example. These arguments are familiar to Japanese diplomats involved in bilateral human rights discussions.[76]

Human rights in China is now a nonissue in Japan-U.S. relations. While Japanese diplomats and politicians often emphasize to American audiences Japan's sharing of fundamental values and democracy with the United States, Japan has not cooperated with the United States when it has come to human rights in China. The United States initiated discussion of cooperation with Japan on human rights after 1994 but, as the *Human Rights Watch World Report* concluded in 1996, there was "little demonstrable progress" in this area. For example, Japan insisted that human rights not be included in the "Common Agenda for Global Partnership" between the United States and Japan.[77] There has been little coordination between the U.S. and Japanese governments. The Clinton administration has really not pressured Tokyo over human rights in China partly because they know that the Japanese would listen but not yield on this issue.[78]

Sino-Japanese relations have become tense since the mid-1990s mainly for security reasons. The United States and Japan have increased security cooperation since 1995, partly to counterbalance a rising China. The two countries reaffirmed their security arrangements in April 1996 and concluded an agreement on new defense guidelines in September 1997. The Japanese Diet approved laws related to the new defense guidelines in May 1999. As the new defense guidelines require Japan to offer greater assistance to the United

States in hostilities in areas surrounding Japan, Beijing sees this en-hanced Japan-U.S. security cooperation as a threat to its national security and particularly its claim to Taiwan. Moreover, Japan is now actively involved in the research and development of a Theater Mis-sile Defense (TMD) system. Although Tokyo names North Korea's missile program as the reason for its strong interest in TMD, an effective missile defense system will negate China's advantage in missiles, the only effective offense weapon in its arsenal. Beijing be-comes particularly alarmed when Taiwan wants to join the TMD sys-tem and some members in the U.S. Congress support such an ar-rangement for the island. In addition, Beijing and Tokyo continue to spar over the history issue and the territorial dispute over Diao-yudao/Senkaku.

The bilateral relationship has stabilized since Prime Minister Obuchi Keizo's visit to China in July 1999. Beijing adjusted its policy toward Japan when its relations with the United States were strained after the NATO bombing of the Chinese embassy in May. But the two countries are headed toward a more wary relationship. Beijing does not accept repeated explanations by the Japanese side about the nature of enhanced Japan-U.S. security cooperation, and China is speeding up the modernization of its military, setting the stage for a long- term rivalry with the United States and Japan.

As argued earlier, human rights is not a significant issue on the bilateral agenda and human rights is not a direct reason people cite for the recent tensions in the relationship. However, human rights is an important indirect factor underlying Sino-Japanese tensions. First, human rights has contributed to a rising distrust of China in Japan. The brutal crackdown in Tiananmen in June 1989 had a pro-found impact on Japanese public opinion of China. Although the public did not strongly urge the government to impose sanctions they were dissatisfied with its weak response.[79] More important, the year 1989 marked a watershed in Japanese opinions about China. According to the polls published by the Prime Minister's Office, while around seventy percent of the respondents consistently ex-pressed some or more affinity with China in 1978–88, only around half of the polled felt close to China in 1989–93.[80] Tiananmen has also had a major negative impact on Japanese policy elites' view of the Chinese government.[81]

Moreover, the 1989 incident removed a major inhibition among Japanese journalists regarding China. The Japanese media coverage of China has become clearly more negative in the 1990s. It is true that the Japanese government is still in control of policy making, which explains why sensitive issues such as human rights are discussed in Japan but not with the Chinese government. The Japanese government still wants to improve relations with China despite criticism of China by some members of the Diet and the media.[82] However, growing negative Japanese public opinion of China and a generational change mean that Beijing can no longer take advantage of divisive Japanese politics to its advantage as it used to at times in the past.[83]

Second, China's human rights has complicated its relations with the United States and Taiwan, which in turn have had a profound impact on its relations with Japan. China's poor human rights record and its rule by the Communist Party are key reasons for U.S. distrust of the country, particularly in Congress. Conversely, Taiwan, which has achieved democracy, has found it easier to win American sympathy and support. As we know, the Taiwan issue is at the root of China's military expansion and Japan's growing concerns about the intentions and capabilities of its neighbor. As Japan colonized Taiwan for fifty years until 1945, Beijing deeply distrusts Japan's intentions regarding the island. What complicates the cross-strait relationship is that Taiwan does not trust a nondemocratic mainland while Beijing is determined to prevent Taiwan from moving toward independence and to use force if necessary to achieve national unification. If Beijing uses force, however, the United States is most likely to be involved, which will drag Japan into direct military confrontation with China.

Conclusion

In a balance between China and the West, Japan has avoided confrontation with China over human rights and has acted as either a mediator or a concerned third party in Sino-U.S. disputes in human rights. But Japan has been supportive of the West in the multilateral context, especially at the UN Human Rights Commission. Japan's approach is explained by its lack of interest in promoting human rights in Asia, its past aggression in China, absence of explicit U.S. pressure on Japan, and the deterrent effect of strong Chinese opposition to foreign intervention on human rights. Also, Japan is interested mainly in facilitating economic prosperity and political stability in East Asia, conditions which are crucial for its own economic and strategic interests.

Aware of Japanese calculations, Beijing cultivated relations with Tokyo in the early 1990s, a strategy that helped break through the Western isolation of China. China has a trump card it is ready to use if and when the Japanese discuss human rights issues: as Japan committed atrocities in its aggressive war in China in 1931–45 it is not qualified to criticize China. Unlike in its relations with the West, the Chinese government does not have to defend its human rights record in its relations with Japan since the latter rarely raises the issue in the bilateral context.

However, while open clashes over human rights between China and Japan are rare, human rights is an important underlying factor shaping Sino-Japanese relations. From a bilateral perspective, a sharp decline in China's popularity among Japanese citizens and policy elites since the 1989 Tiananmen incident means that Beijing can no longer manipulate Japanese domestic politics to its advantage. From a regional perspective, the human rights issue strains the relationship between China and the United States, which complicates Sino-Japanese relations. In addition, Taiwan's democratization and China's lack of political reform have contributed to increasing tensions across the Taiwan Strait, a situation that may draw Japan into a potential military conflict between China and the United States. China's military expansion aimed at national unification and Japan's hedging strategy against a rising China explain the growing mutual suspicion and distrust between the two sides.

Looking into the future, human rights will remain a nonissue in the official agenda between China and Japan. As the United States and Western Europe have also retreated from their previous confrontational approach toward China, Japan does not now have to worry about alienating its Western allies by taking a soft stand on Beijing. However, human rights will remain an indirect issue shaping the relationship between the two Asian giants. As Japan continues to see its alliance with the United States as the foundation of its foreign policy, human rights in China will affect Japan's China policy as long as Americans pursue the issue and judge China negatively on account of its human rights violations.

Chapter Six

Human Rights and Sino-UN Relations

This chapter examines Beijing's multilateral human rights policy. The three previous chapters include discussions of the country's diplomatic efforts at the UN Human Rights Commission to fend off Western criticism since 1990. But the subject deserves a separate chapter to provide a more focused analysis. Moreover, China's multilateral human rights relations involve countries not discussed in the previous chapters.

The theoretical issue in this chapter is how the international human rights regime has affected China's domestic politics and foreign policy behavior.[1] The international human rights regime emerged with the founding of the United Nations. The UN Charter and the Universal Declaration of Human Rights laid the foundation for international human rights laws. The UN human rights regime includes an expanding body of laws such as the International Covenant on Civil and Political Rights, the International Covenant on Economic, Social, and Cultural Rights and other rights treaties. The regime also includes institutions dealing with human rights such as the UN Commission on Human Rights, which drafts international human rights treaties, monitors and reviews human rights violations, and the UN Sub-Commission on Prevention of Discrimination and Protection of Minorities, which is composed of 26 experts elected on a regional basis.

Cautious Exploration in the 1970s

After joining the United Nations in 1971, China took a system-reformist approach in the 1970s, supporting a new international economic order and treating the UN as a forum to advance the causes of developing countries. By contrast, Beijing did not take an active interest in UN functional activities, joining only eight specialized institutions in the UN system by the end of the decade.[2]

Consistent with its general approach and revolutionary rhetoric at this time, Beijing placed itself on a moral high ground. The Chinese government did not hesitate to criticize imperialism, colonialism, and racism. China joined the Commission on the Status of Women, a functional committee under the Economic and Social Council and the Social, Humanitarian, and Cultural Committee of the General Assembly. It supported UN sanctions against South Africa but not Cuba. The Chinese also criticized the Soviet Union for their human rights abuses.[3] However, Beijing did not participate in the activities of the UN Human Rights Commission nor did it sign any international human rights conventions.

China's chaotic domestic politics was the principal reason for its hesitation. The Chinese government could not fully engage internationally given the intense power struggle before and after Mao's death in 1976. Shortly after China joined the UN, Mao criticized Zhou Enlai, who was in charge of foreign affairs, as leaning "right," a serious charge at a time when leftists dominated. In July 1973 Mao termed the analysis of the international situation by the Foreign Ministry as having "rightist tendency." Informed by Wang Hairong and Tang Wensheng, two rising young diplomats who served as Mao's liaison with the Politburo until late 1975, Mao ordered Politburo meetings to criticize Zhou's "rightist" mistakes allegedly committed when meeting with Henry Kissinger in November 1973. After Zhou was hospitalized in June 1974, Deng Xiaoping took over Zhou's responsibilities until Mao purged Deng in April 1976 for reversing the verdict of the Cultural Revolution.[4] China became more fully engaged in UN operations only after Deng adopted economic reforms and the open-door policy in 1978.

Another important reason for China's passive stance in the UN is that China had to learn how the UN worked. In fact, Beijing did not anticipate winning admission in 1971. As a result, when China was invited by the UN secretary general to send a delegation to New York immediately, Chinese officials felt unprepared and could not decide what to do. Mao decided to send a delegation, arguing that the Chinese government should not disappoint African friends who "carried China on their shoulders" into the UN. At the time, "China was not familiar with the procedures and inner working of the UN," commented a Chinese diplomat specializing in UN affairs. "China was, in a sense, a student learning to be an influential permanent member."[5] With regard to the UN human rights regime, Chinese diplomats saw human rights as a complicated issue involving politics, economics, social systems, and ideologies. Furthermore, as existing international human rights documents had been adopted before China took its UN seat, Beijing needed to study them before making any commitment.[6]

Human rights could have become an issue for China. After all, even though Beijing did not join any international human rights treaties or any human rights institutions, it became a party to the UN Charter, which embodies basic human rights principles. But fortunately for the Chinese government and unfortunately for Chinese dissidents, the West did not press China on the human rights issue. As discussed in the previous chapters, the West did not treat human rights in China as an important diplomatic issue. The United States and its Western allies were interested in Chinese assistance in resisting the Soviet Union. Moreover, the United Nations as a whole did not work well due to the Cold War rivalry between the two superpowers.

Controlled Participation in the 1980s

Deng launched economic reform in 1978. This shift in China's basic strategy encouraged a more pragmatic foreign policy. China began to participate more fully in UN activities in the 1980s, joining virtually all specialized institutions in the UN system. There was also a clear shift in China's focus from system-reforming to system-maintaining in that Beijing was now more interested in taking advantage of what the UN could do to help its modernization drive than in reforming the global institution.[7]

Consistent with its general approach toward the United Nations, China became more engaged in the UN human rights regime. The Chinese government made statements in support of the UN human rights regime. For example, in commemoration of the forty-year anniversary of the Universal Declaration on Human Rights, at a speech given at the UN General Assembly on September 28, 1988, Chinese Foreign Minister Qian Qichen gave high praise to the document, suggesting that it had had a positive impact on the development of international human rights in the postwar era.

More important, China became institutionally involved in the human rights regime. The PRC sent observers to the human rights commission in 1979–81 and was elected a member in 1981. Since 1982 Beijing has been sending delegations to the commission. Since 1984 Beijing has also had its recommended experts elected in the UN Sub-Commission on Human Rights. Once in the institution, China became more active in dealing with human rights issues in other countries. In 1984 Beijing supported the appointment of a rapporteur to study the human rights situation in Afghanistan despite the protests of the Soviet Union and Eastern Europe. In 1985 China supported a UN Human Rights Commission resolution to examine the human rights situation in Chile.

China also made itself a party to seven human rights conventions and one protocol between 1980 to 1989: Convention on the Elimination of All Forms of Discrimination Against Women (1980); International Convention on the Elimination of All Forms of Racial Discrimination (1981); Protocol Relating to the Status of Refugees (1982); Convention Relating to the Status of Refugees (1982); Convention on the Prevention and Punishment of the Crime of Genocide (1983); International Convention on the Suppression and Punishment of the Crime of Apartheid (1983); International Convention Against Apartheid in Sports (1987) (not yet ratified); Convention Against Torture and Other Cruel, Inhuman, or Degrading Treatment or Punishment (1988). Thus, the Chinese government took on obligations to abide by these conventions.

While one can understand why Beijing was interested in financial institutions such as the World Bank and the IMF, one may wonder why China was willing to take part in an international regime that deals with human rights, a weak spot in the country. Three factors explain why China has accepted the UN human rights regime. First, China accepts the United Nations. The Chinese communist government saw itself as a founding member of the United Nations because the Nationalist Government's delegation to the UN founding conference included a renowned communist member and because the PRC is now the ruling government in China.[8] It would be strange for a permanent member of the UN Security Council not to accept the basic principles of the UN.

Second, Beijing came to appreciate the importance of participating in the UN human rights regime to advance its own interests. One key reason for China's decision to send an observer to the human rights commission in 1979 was to defend the Khmer Rouge, which was ousted after Vietnam invaded Cambodia in December 1978. To support the Khmer Rouge, China fought a brief border war with Vietnam in early 1979. China felt that the Western focus on the massive human rights violations by the Khmer Rouge in the UN would benefit Hanoi. At the 1979 commission conference, the Chinese observer charged that any discussion of the Cambodian question without condemnation of Vietnam as the principal culprit in human rights violations in Cambodia would equal tolerance of aggression. As ASEAN members and some other third world members voiced similar opinions, the conference passed a resolution sponsored by Yugoslavia and others to postpone discussion of human rights in Cambodia.[9] The Chinese observer also condemned the Soviet invasion of Afghanistan at the 1980 commission conference, which passed a resolution demanding immediate Soviet withdrawal, the first ever resolution criticizing a superpower.

Third, China does not see the UN as belonging to the West. Chinese scholars emphasize the participation of socialist countries and newly independent third world countries in the creation and development of global institutions. In fact, the UN is often the forum in which developing nations criticize the West. Moreover, the Chinese government does not see the UN as a fundamental constraint on its actions.

Beijing had good reason to be confident in its ability to manage the international human rights regime in the 1980s. China enjoyed a good image in the West in the decade, first as a strategic ally against the Soviet Union and then as a pioneer leading the reform movement among communist countries. China was thus on "the right side of the history," a development that the West wanted to encourage. As a result, China could participate cautiously in criticism of other countries without being a target itself. In fact, the country had not faced the consequences of its domestic practices. And there was no reason to believe that this favorable environment for China would not continue into the future. Furthermore, the international human rights regime has weak enforcement mechanisms and countries often evade legal obligations.

China on the Defensive in the Early 1990s

The television coverage of People's Liberation Army soldiers shooting their way into the center of Beijing in June 1989 severely tarnished the image of the Chinese government. In a sharp turn of fortune, China found itself on the defensive in the UN system. Naturally, international human rights institutions such as the UN Human Rights Commission and the Sub-Commission on Human Rights came to play a crucial role in shaping international response to human rights in China.

China in the UN Human Rights Commission and Sub-Commission

As a striking example of China's declining international prestige due to the brutal crackdown, China lost a major battle in the UN Sub-Commission on Human Rights meeting in August 1989. As the sub-commission met shortly after the incident, the China issue took center stage. Despite intense lobbying efforts by the Chinese expert serving on the sub-commission and the Chinese observer delegation, the sub-commission passed a resolution on "Situation in China" by 15 votes to 9. The resolution was mildly worded, indicating mainly concerns over the recent events in China, requesting information for the UN Human Rights Commission, and appealing for clemency for people detained in the democracy movement. It did not even mention Tiananmen. Nevertheless, China became the first permanent member of the UN Security Council to receive censure on human rights in its own country.

Since Western nations and advocates of human rights intended to use public shame to pressure China to improve its human rights, we need to ask how China's loss at the sub-commission affected human rights in China. The 1989 resolution is a good test case since China was censured only twice in the sub-commission in the 1990s, with the other occasion coming in 1991. From the perspective of Chinese society, the sub-commission resolution encouraged dissidents in exile, who were actively organizing and agitating against the government at that point. But there is little evidence that this event had any profound impact on the Chinese public's view of the government.

The Chinese government promptly pronounced the resolution to be "null and void" and having no effect on China. This is not surprising since Beijing seldom backs down in rhetoric. But international public criticism did embarrass the Chinese. Chinese human rights literature gives scant attention to this vote, in sharp contrast to the lengthy and glowing discussions of Chinese victories at the UN Human Rights Commission since 1990. A few scholars mentioned the two resolutions in passing and attributed China's loss to the Western manipulation of an abnormal, secret voting procedure.[10] However, the fact that the Chinese were embarrassed did not mean that Beijing would make changes in response to Western criticism. Rather, the loss put pressure on Chinese diplomats to try harder to prevent more humiliation.

China's diplomatic difficulties increased further when Eastern European communist governments collapsed in 1989 and the Soviet Union disintegrated in 1991.[11] The end of the Cold War had a profound impact on China's multilateral diplomacy. The West became more confident about the eventual triumph of democracy and freedom while it found little strategic value in close ties with China. Also, China was now seen as a political laggard rather than a pioneer for reform. As a result, the West intensified pressure on the Chinese government. Furthermore, some of the former communist countries were eager to demonstrate their democratic credentials by criticizing countries like China that had refused to democratize.

After losing the sub-commission vote in August 1989, the Chinese government sent a large delegation to the human rights commission conference in February and March 1990. The Western nations were strongly in favor of a resolution against China. Australia, Canada, and Sweden composed the text of the resolution. While supporting the Western position, the Japanese representative managed to water down the tone of the resolution.[12] The resolution was sponsored by 11 member countries (Belgium, France, Germany, Italy, Portugal, Spain, Britain, the U.S., Japan, Sweden, and Canada) and 7 nonmember countries (Denmark, Greece, Holland, Ireland, Luxembourg, Australia, and Norway). In response, China's friend Pakistan proposed a no-action procedural resolution, which passed by a narrow margin, with 17 in favor, 15 against, and 11 abstaining. All ten Western nations voted against China's procedural maneuver. China did not receive solid support from the third world except for Asian members. While Japan voted against the no-action resolution and the Philippines abstained, the other seven members supported China. Latin America largely abstained. Only half of the African members supported China. Bulgaria and Hungary sided with the West while the Soviet Union, Ukraine, and Yugoslavia supported China.

Thanks to the Iraqi invasion of Kuwait in August 1990, China could use its veto power in the UN Security Council to its advantage. The 1990 sub-commission session started four days after the invasion. The sub-commission did not introduce a resolution on Tibet in exchange for Beijing's agreement not to oppose a resolution on Iraq.[13] Similarly, Washington did not propose any resolution on China at the 1991 human rights commission meeting to prevent a Chinese veto of UN authorization of use of force against Iraq. This episode was a reminder that China has considerable influence in the UN, a fact which would become a more important deterrent to the West in the following years. Still, the sub-commission passed a resolution on Tibet in August 1991, with 9 votes in favor, 7 against, and 4 abstaining. The resolution called on the Chinese government to "fully respect the fundamental rights and freedoms of the Tibetan people." According to the procedures, the resolution that passed at the sub-commission would be discussed at the next human rights commission meeting. The Chinese government declared again that it considered the resolution to be "null and void."

The 1992 human rights commission conference saw a sea change. The Soviet Union had collapsed and the Cold War was over. As a result, Russia, Czechoslovakia, and Hungary sided with the West. As the sponsors of the China draft resolution were all Western nations in 1990, Western nations initially encouraged Costa Rica to be the lead sponsor for a resolution on the situation in Tibet. However, under pressure from China, Costa Rica decided not to take the lead.[14] In the end, China scored an easy victory, with 27 votes in favor of a no-action resolution, 15 against, and 10 abstaining.

The main reason for China's success at the 1992 conference was the expansion of the commission from 43 to 53 members in 1991, at the urging of developing nations. The 10 additional seats were divided among Africa (4), Asia (3) and Latin America (3) after developing nation members passed a resolution over the opposition of Western and Eastern European members. Not surprisingly, China supported giving all additional seats to developing nations[15] because that would boost its support base in the commission. In the 1992 vote, China won 11 votes from Africa and 10 from Asia while the West received only one developing nation vote, from Latin

America. Beijing was working hard to win support from Asian and African countries to avoid international isolation. China adopted a more friendly peripheral policy toward its Asian neighbors in the early 1990s and significantly improved diplomatic relations with them.[16] Beijing also renewed its diplomatic efforts in Africa after neglecting the continent to some extent in the 1980s. Africans had consistently supported China's positions on human rights, the "one-China principle," and other important international issues.[17]

Moreover, the West was divided initially. The European Union was interested in a Tibetan resolution based on the Tibetan resolution that had passed in the 1991 sub-commission. By contrast, the United States, Australia, and Japan opposed the Tibetan resolution because it contradicted their one-China policy. After long debates, the Europeans accepted the American proposal for a resolution on China and Tibet. The division among Western nations cost them much valuable lobbying time.[18]

In the next two annual meetings, China also succeeded in preventing discussion of China resolutions. However, the margin of China's support shrank from 12 in 1992 to 5 in 1993 and 4 in 1994. The support for the West actually remained unchanged. But the number of countries taking a neutral position increased from 10 in 1992 to 17 in 1994. This was not due to a lack of effort on the Chinese part. In fact, the Chinese delegation became more vocal in refuting Western criticism and publicizing the country's improvement in broadly defined human rights. However, the U.S. delegation that had been sent by the new Clinton administration vigorously lobbied other countries against China. The head of the American delegation in 1993 was Richard Schifter, who had served as the assistant secretary of state for human rights in the Reagan and Bush administrations and had resigned during the Bush administration partly to protest the Bush policy toward China. European Union members were also active in the commission. In addition, several countries that had supported China at the 1992 meeting were no longer commission members in 1993, which reduced China's support base.[19]

China was severely tested in 1995. For the first time since 1990, China did not receive enough votes to pass its no-action resolution, with 22 in favor, 22 against, and 9 abstaining. Both the United States and China lobbied hard in Geneva and in capitals of member countries. In the vote on the U.S. draft resolution, China won a narrow victory, with 21 against, 20 in favor, and 12 abstaining. In this round,

Russia switched sides and cast a decisive vote in favor of China due to heavy Chinese lobbying.[20] Ethiopia and Egypt, which had supported China in the procedural vote, and the Philippines, which had voted against China, chose to abstain in the substantive vote.

The main reason for the near victory for the West was the committed and organized lobbying of the United States. Since Clinton had delinked human rights and MFN status in 1994, the U.S. government now saw the UN Human Rights Commission as an important venue to pressure China and demonstrate its commitment to human rights in foreign policy. From early on, the American delegation engaged in intense lobbying efforts and succeeded in changing some countries' positions. To attract more votes, the U.S. government adopted more moderate language in the draft resolution. The European Union also actively lobbied developing nation members to support a resolution on China. The West gained votes from Latin American and Eastern European members. In addition, due to its recent territorial disputes with China, the Philippines supported the West in the procedural vote.

China and the UN World Conference on Human Rights

In addition to its actions at the UN Human Rights Commission and the UN Sub-Commission on Human Rights, Beijing also engaged in active human rights diplomacy before and during the UN World Conference on Human Rights, which was held in Vienna in June 1993. The idea of a world human rights conference had floated around since 1988 and became a reality in December 1990 when the UN General Assembly adopted Resolution 45/155 to authorize the conference. Before the Vienna conference, the Preparatory Committee (PrepCom) that was created by the UN General Assembly met four times and Africans, Latin Americans and Asians held regional preparatory meetings in Tunis, San Jose, and Bangkok. China played an active role in influencing the process and outcome of this world conference as a vice chairman of the First PrepCom, the Bangkok regional meeting, and the Vienna conference.

From the Chinese perspective, the United States and other Western nations, encouraged by the success of a "peaceful evolution" strategy in Eastern Europe, were trying to spread a universal standard of human rights to the rest of the world. The Western initiative thus kicked off a major debate between North and South.

However, since the Western initiative was supported by the former Soviet Union, Eastern European countries and some developing countries, there was no choice but to prepare for such a meeting as dictated by UN practice. The Chinese delegation recommended two specific amendments to the draft of Resolution 45/155. One called for examining the relationship between development and human rights and the other called for convening regional preparatory meetings by 1992. For the second amendment, the Chinese had the following considerations. It normally takes five or six years to prepare for world conferences dealing with social issues in the UN. More important, the West and Eastern Europe had already reached a consensus on human rights and were thus fully prepared for a world human rights conference. By contrast, most developing nations were not at all mentally prepared for the meeting. Therefore, their views would not be fully expressed at the world conference unless they discussed and coordinated their views and strategies in regional meetings in advance. Despite opposition from the West, the Chinese amendments were written into the draft resolution.[21]

The Chinese position on the conference became more explicit over time. At a speech at the 47th session of the UN Human Rights Commission in 1991, Ambassador Fan Guoxiang emphasized the importance of cooperation and warned against turning the conference into a "cold war" environment in which some countries interfere in others' internal affairs. He wanted to see the conference to be "held in the spirit of seeking common ground while putting aside differences, of mutual respect and better mutual understanding." He emphasized economic rights and the need to prevent massive violations of human rights associated with racism and colonialism.[22]

Ambassador Li Daoyu's speech at the Third Committee of the 47th Session of the UN General Assembly on December 2, 1992 spelled out China's five priorities for the Vienna conference: (1) combating racism, colonialism, foreign aggression, and foreign occupation, (2) reaffirming the right to development and introducing effective measures to realize this right, (3) emphasizing the indivisibility and interdependence of different rights, (4) reiterating the principle of state sovereignty, and (5) promoting international cooperation based on the UN Charter and equality and mutual respect. Li gave particular attention to the right to development. He also emphasized China's willingness to support UN efforts for promoting universal human rights. He announced that Beijing would contribute $11,000 to help the least developed nations send delegates to the UN Conference and its preparatory meetings.[23]

At the Bangkok regional preparatory meeting held from March 29 to April 2, 1993, the Chinese delegation appealed for Asian solidarity at the Vienna conference. Ambassador Jin Yongjian, head of the Chinese delegation, told Asian delegates:

> In our view, the Asian countries should first demonstrate solidarity among themselves through this meeting. They should, under the guidance of the UN Charter, proceed from the reality and overall interests of raising the standard of enjoyment of human rights and fundamental freedoms by the Asian peoples, seek common ground while preserving differences so as to reach common understanding, and identify the problems concerning most Asian countries and peoples, especially those that have great influence on the universal and full enjoyment of human rights by the world people, clearing up obstacles to the full enjoyment of various human rights.[24]

Jin identified six priorities for the meeting, which were similar to the five priorities cited by Ambassador Li three months earlier. Jin added respecting the right of all countries to choose their own systems and development paths as the third priority. He also moved state sovereignty to number two in the priority list. Jin pointed out specifically that the meeting should "avoid provoking ideological debates, exerting political pressure, and turning the UN into a forum for one country to launch a political attack against other countries in the name of promoting human rights."

The Bangkok meeting demonstrated that there was no single Asian voice on human rights. Japan, Thailand, Nepal, South Korea, and the Philippines adopted more liberal views of human rights while China, Indonesia, Iran, and Burma took a hard-line position. In addition, many Asian human rights NGOs who also met in Bangkok differed from their governments regarding universality of human rights. As a result, the Bangkok Declaration contained references to universality of rights and was more enlightened than the Chinese position.[25] Nevertheless, it was recognized that Asians largely differed from the West in attitudes toward human rights and democracy.[26] And the document was a disappointment for international human rights NGOs.

China has high praise for the Bangkok Declaration. A summary commentary on the declaration by Chinese analysts sees the document as "stating the basic position on human rights by Asian and other developing nations in the post-Cold War era" and "in a sense, marking the beginning of a converging view on human rights." The Chinese commentary emphasized six basic contributions of the document to human rights discourse. First, while recognizing the universality of human rights, one needs to take into consideration unique national and regional conditions. Second, the document calls for balance between different types of rights. Third, self-determination is a universal right. Fourth, the right to development is a universal and basic right. Fifth, promotion of human rights should be based on respect for state sovereignty and territorial integrity, noninterference in internal affairs, and nonuse of rights for political pressure. Sixth, countries should promote human rights by cooperative means.[27]

It is true that if it were up to the Chinese, they would have written a very different declaration for the Bangkok meeting. However, China was not trying to win other Asian nations over to its view, an attempt which would have been unlikely to succeed. For example, Luo Yanhua, a Beijing University professor, noted that East Asian nations have very diverse views of human rights due to their different cultures, traditions, and religions, and that not even ASEAN nations found it easy to forge a common view on human rights. But she emphasized that East Asian nations do often "naturally stand together in international forums on human rights, sharing same or similar views, especially where they differ from the Western notion."[28] This line of reasoning explains why China saw the Bangkok Declaration as a major success. As quoted earlier, Ambassador Jin urged Asians to "seek common ground while preserving differences so as to reach common understanding, and identify the problems concerning most Asian countries and peoples." China did not mind different views on human rights as long as Asians reached a consensus on resisting Western attempts to force universal values on unwilling Asians. The main objective of Chinese diplomacy in Bangkok was not to make others think like Beijing but to prevent external interference in its domestic affairs.

The Bangkok regional meeting and the other two regional meetings enhanced Beijing's confidence in countering the Western human rights offensive at the Vienna conference. The Chinese government sent a large delegation led by Vice Foreign Minister Liu Huaqiu, one of the ablest Chinese diplomats. As a vice chairman

of the Vienna conference, China played a central role in setting
the agenda and procedures of the meeting. In particular, the Chinese delegation asserted itself by preventing the Dalai Lama, invited by the host government, from appearing at the opening cere-
mony, and preventing any involvement of NGOs in the drafting of
the final declaration.[29] Beijing took a hard-line position at the beginning of the meeting, but made concessions later. Chinese writings on the conference emphasize Beijing's firm principles but flexible and cooperative moves to make the final document possible.[30]
However, China's behavior in the Vienna Conference reflects its
diplomatic negotiating style; it starts strong with firm principles but
makes "concessions" at the end to conclude the negotiation once it
tests the position of the opposing side and finds its interests served.[31]

The Vienna Declaration was a product of compromise among
conference participants, particularly between developed and developing nations. Beijing accepts the Vienna Declaration, which "reflects the strong concerns for human rights issues of developing
nations, which have a majority of world population." Specifically,
the document recognizes the special conditions of countries, the
inseparability of different types of rights, and rights to development.[32] Furthermore, the meeting demonstrated that China is not
alone in the world regarding human rights. In fact, Beijing was a
vocal leader in the meeting, supported by many developing nations,
particularly the so-called "Asian group" including Syria, Iran, Iraq,
Burma, Vietnam, North Korea, Malaysia, Bangladesh, Singapore,
Indonesia, and others. As a result, Beijing felt that the developing
countries had regained some ground in the human rights debate
with the West.[33]

China's Multilateral Human Rights Diplomacy in 1989–95

Looking at China's multilateral human rights diplomacy in 1989–
95, what stood out the most is actually what Beijing chose not do,
that is, pulling itself out of a forum in which China was a constant
and often the principal target. Rather, the Sino-Chinese government
doggedly engaged in UN human rights proceedings.

The main reason for China's continuous engagement is that the
Chinese government under Deng's guidance remained committed
to a policy of economic reform and the open door policy. Self-
isolation from the international community was thus a nonoption

politically for Beijing. At the same time, Beijing was confident that China would not be isolated in the world. Beijing did not see debate in the UN forum as international concern for the rights of Chinese citizens but as a U.S.-led effort to interfere in China's internal affairs. Most Chinese analysis of the Chinese efforts at the UN focused on the United States, seeing U.S. designs behind everything. In contrast, the Chinese saw themselves as leading the progressive forces in the international community to resist Western pressure. A March 6, 1992 *Renmin Ribao* commentary noted that "the rejection [of an anti-China resolution] helped protect the reputation and prestige of all international organizations including the UN." It promised that "China is willing to work together with all other nations and people who defend justice to uphold the UN purpose and principles and the basic norms of international law."[34] Moreover, Beijing largely succeeded in fending off Western criticism. It was thus possible to see more benefit inside the group than outside it.

Such a Chinese assessment did not allow much room for self-reflection about human rights performance. In fact, whether the West succeeded in passing anti-China resolutions or not, it would not have had much impact on the actual situation in China. Although such resolutions may cause public embarrassment for Beijing and encourage international human rights NGOs and Chinese dissidents to continue exerting pressure on Beijing, it is unlikely that Beijing would make any serious domestic adjustments solely because of human rights commission resolutions, which are vague in terms of what Beijing is supposed to do. When asked specifically about the impact of a successful China resolution on the Chinese government, a senior Chinese diplomat at the UN Human Rights Division of the Chinese Foreign Ministry insisted that such a situation would not be a big deal but would be harmful for Sino-U.S. relations as the American intention of undermining the Chinese government would then be in full display.[35]

The official Chinese media attributed their success at the UN to China's improvements in the economic and political realm, its growing importance, and support from developing nations.[36] Furthermore, the Chinese view that economic development must take precedence over political and civil rights struck a chord among developing nations. Merle Goldman, a China specialist who joined the 1993 American delegation, found it difficult to counter the argument made by the non-Western delegates who contrasted China's rapid economic growth, which was based on a model of economic reform without corresponding political reform, with Russia's economic difficulties after its hasty move toward democracy. In addition, Beijing made some opportune concessions to sway international opinion. Just when the 1993 UN Human Rights Commission meeting started, CNN replayed Chinese television coverage of the early release of Wang Dan, a principal Tiananmen student leader, and China's better treatment of other political prisoners. The CNN story had a positive impact on the non-Western delegates, who argued that China should be encouraged to improve its human rights gradually.[37]

Another important reason for China's success was spirited lobbying by Chinese diplomats. Goldman observed how the 19-member Chinese delegation singlemindedly lobbied the non-Western delegates and saw defeating a China resolution as its sole purpose.[38] Even though China's failure at the UN would not have had a serious impact on its domestic practice, it would have had a negative impact on the careers and pride of Chinese diplomats engaged in human rights. The Chinese diplomats also became more convinced of their mission based on their growing nationalism and developmentalist views of human rights. Moreover, Chinese human rights diplomats, highly specialized in the area, had learned the workings of the UN human rights regime and become more effective in influencing the political agenda and procedures of the UN Human Rights Commission.

Turning the Tide Since the Mid-1990s

Building on its efforts in the early 1990s, China had turned the tide by the mid-1990s. "By the end of 1995, Beijing had successfully insulated its economic and political relations and ambitions from being seriously affected by its human rights record," concluded Human Rights Watch, an NGO that closely monitors the international community's role in human rights in China.[39] Since the mid-1990s, Beijing has become more assertive and has had more comfortable margins of victory in the human rights commission.

After the close call at the 1995 meeting, the Chinese government was determined not to lose the vote at the 1996 meeting. Beijing continued to court African and Asian members that had been its consistent supporters. The Chinese also worked on the swing voters among Eastern European and Latin American countries. Unlike in the early 1990s, China also started active lobbying among Western nations.[40] In particular, major European members such as France, Germany, Italy, and Spain lost their resolve for continuous confrontation with China over human rights and delayed the tabling of a resolution. In addition, Europeans did not lobby developing nation members as actively as they had before, which made Beijing's lobbying efforts easier.[41] A senior Chinese diplomat who attended the conference commented shortly afterwards that while still supportive of the Americans, European delegates privately told the Chinese about their unwillingness to isolate China and said that the June 4 incident was already behind them.[42] As a result, China's margin of support in no-action resolutions increased from 0 in 1995 to 7 in 1996.

China won a major victory at the 1997 meeting. France, Germany, Italy, and Spain announced their decisions not to be cosponsors, which made it impossible for the consensus-based European Union to be a cosponsor. Shortly afterward, Japan, Australia, Greece, Canada, and others also indicated their unwillingness to continue sponsoring China resolutions. The American delegation managed to persuade Denmark to take the lead in tabling a resolution almost at the end of the conference. Emboldened by such a favorable development, Chinese delegates took offense and repeatedly interrupted the speeches by Swedish, Dutch, and American speakers.[43] In the end, China won the no-action vote easily, with 27 in favor, 17 against, and 9 abstaining.

Beijing had also helped neutralize the UN Sub-Commission on Human Rights by the mid-1990s. The sub-commission ceased to consider country-specific human rights issues that the UN Human Rights Commission had already taken up. In August 1997, Chinese expert Fan Guoxiang, who had served as a human rights ambassador, succeeded in passing a sub-commission resolution to avoid "politicization" of the sub-commission and to promote human rights dialogue.[44]

In 1998, the United States stopped sponsoring anti-China resolutions. Some Chinese observers apparently felt that they had just seen the conclusion of a long struggle between China and the United States at the UN Human Rights Commission.[45] However, as the Chinese government stepped up repression of dissidents in the second half of 1998, the United States again proposed a draft China resolution at the 1999 commission meeting. Beijing tried in vain to persuade Washington not to sponsor a resolution on China. Premier Zhu Rongji stated at a joint press conference with President Clinton on April 8, 1999 that "I'm firmly opposed to the U.S. tabling of a draft resolution directed at China at the Human Rights Commission session. I not only regard that as unfair, but also take it as an interference in China's internal affairs." To emphasize his point, he raised his voice and paused after the sentence. In fact, in an interview with a *Wall Street Journal* reporter before his trip, he had indicated that there was strong resistance to his visit to the United States. He listed three reasons: NATO's bombing of Serbia, which China opposed; Washington's tabling of China resolutions at the UN Human Rights Commission; and excessive U.S. demands for Chinese concessions in exchange for WTO membership.[46] In the end, China won a no-action motion, with 22 in favor, 17 against, and 14 abstaining. At the 2000 commission meeting, China again succeeded in defeating a U.S.-sponsored China resolution with a "no-action" resolution, passed with 22 in favor, 18 against, 12 abstaining, and 1 absent.

The most important reason for China's success at the UN is its rapid economic growth and relative political stability. China's economic success, in particular, has great appeal among developing nations. "Western pundits have been filled with loathing as they survey China's human rights record," Walden Bello, a professor of sociology at the University of the Philippines, commented. "But I would wager that for most of us in the South, China—warts and all—is still one of the success stories of the century." Besides China's economic performance, he also cites its ability to stand up to the international business community.[47] Such sentiment is shared by decision-makers. Hishammuddin Hussein, Malaysia's deputy minister of primary industries and the alternate leader of the Malaysian delegation to the 1997 UN Commission on Human Rights meeting, commented that "the nations of the North and South have in fact diverged." He defended China. "The North's persistent attacks on China, for example, have ignored the fact that the nation's gross domestic product has grown from $215 billion in 1986 to $817 billion in 1996. The number of people below the poverty line has come down from 250 million in 1975 to 65 million in 1996. Possibly, never before in the field of human affairs has so much been done for so many in so short a time."[48]

China is not really isolated in the international community on the issue of human rights. In fact, the United States sometimes finds itself isolated. For example, U.S. and Asian diplomats clashed openly over Asian values and universal values at a news conference after a meeting of the Association of Southeast Asian Nations in July 1997. The United States found itself isolated from Asian countries over how to deal with Burma and whether to give aid to Cambodia.[49] When Secretary of State Madeleine K. Albright visited Africa in December 1997, she emphasized a partnership with the continent while refraining from lecturing Africans on human rights and democracy.[50] A confrontational approach over human rights would have caused significant resentment among her African hosts.

China's rising power has also influenced Western behavior. On the one hand, Western governments value their commercial interests in the expanding China market, spurred on by their business communities. This is particularly the case for major Western European nations, which have high unemployment rates and weak anti-China constituencies. On the other hand, China's rising power means that the country is an important player in a wide range of areas. As a result, the United States and its Western partners cannot afford to focus only on human rights issues.

Moreover, China has waged an effective lobbying campaign, which is grudgingly acknowledged even by critics of China.[51] Beijing has intensified high-level exchanges with member nations in all continents. Although there are other important issues at stake, such as denying Taiwan international recognition, China resolutions at the UN Human Rights Commission are an important issue for Chinese diplomacy. China continues to cultivate good relations with developing nations and to seek allies on human rights and other contentious issues with the West.

For critics of China, Beijing uses both sticks and carrots. On the one hand, Beijing can be firm in both principles and tactics. The Chinese have threatened—and at times used—retaliatory measures against countries censuring China. Also, Chinese delegates have become more assertive. This tough stance is meant to demonstrate to critics of China that their position entails high costs and "unproductive" confrontations with Beijing.

On the other hand, Beijing has made "concessions" to demonstrate its willingness to cooperate and the potential gains for others who are cooperative as well. Beijing has released dissidents at opportune times to manipulate international opinion to its advantage. After giving strong indications earlier, Beijing signed the International Covenant on Economic, Social, and Cultural Rights in October 1997 and the International Covenant on Civil and Political Rights in October 1998. Beijing is yet to ratify the two covenants. In October 1997 the UN Working Group on Arbitrary Detention visited China. The group reported to the commission on its visit in April 1998 and strongly criticized the "vague and imprecise" offenses in the Chinese criminal code, particularly ones concerning state security. The Chinese government invited UN Human Rights Commissioner Mary Robinson to visit China and Tibet in September 1998. The two sides signed a Memorandum of Intent on a technical cooperation program. But earlier in the year China had blocked her briefing at the Security Council in February and June by arguing that human rights issues should be dealt with only in the UN Economic and Social Council. Beijing was concerned that the Security Council might follow the precedent and discuss sensitive issues such as Tibet.[52] Then in 1999, China invited an expert group from the Office of the UN High Commissioner for Human Rights to visit China. In particular, as a key form of cooperation, the Chinese government has rewarded the West by holding governmental and nongovernmental talks on human rights with Norway, Britain, France, Australia, Canada, Sweden, Brazil, Japan, the United States, and the European Union.

Chinese concessions are not really meaningful. Bilateral human rights dialogues are ceremonial and do not threaten the political regime. There is no question that China's signing of the two international human rights covenants is a significant event that may have an important impact on the country's future political development. However, with or without external pressure, the Chinese government would have had no choice but to join at some point. Most UN member nations had already done so. It would be embarrassing for a UN Security Council permanent member to be a laggard.

China's diplomatic success entails high costs. First, Beijing could have used international concerns about human rights in China to help address serious rights abuses in the country. Chinese citizens are the big losers when the government refuses to live up to international human rights standards. Second, Beijing has spent consider-able diplomatic capital to seek allies and discourage critics. Thus, continuous external pressure on human rights weakens Beijing's bargaining leverage in other issue areas. To cite one example, a Chi-nese military expert argues that some Southeast Asian nations such as Vietnam, Malaysia, and the Philippines took advantage of China's effort to improve relations after Tiananmen to accelerate "invasion and plunging of resources in our Nansha islands [Spratly]" and that the Chinese government took a low-key stance and made com-promises to stabilize recently restored or established relations with these countries.[53]

How much has China learned from its participation in the UN human rights institutions? Or put another way, how much has the international human rights regime affected Chinese behavior? After an exhaustive study of China and the UN human rights insti-tutions, Kent argues that China has indeed gradually accepted and begun to implement some international human rights standards, but she recognizes that for China, "the human rights regime repre-sents an intervening, rather than an autonomous, causal variable."[54] A central question here is whether China has had a change of heart through its participation in the United Nations. Despite signs indi-cating cognitive learning among some individuals and for certain issues, I see little evidence supporting the notion that there has been systematic learning on China's part. If anything, Chinese writ-ings on China and UN human rights institutions and actual Chi-nese behavior indicate tactical learning by which highly special-ized Chinese human rights diplomats have learned how to work the UN system to China's advantage. Such learning certainly does not preclude concessions, which China, like any other nation, makes frequently in its bilateral dealings with other nations as well as in multilateral arenas. Ironically, the Chinese have also learned the importance of bargaining from strength in the UN institutions, see-ing their human rights disputes with the West from a perspective of power politics, which makes it harder to accept the noble idea of human rights behind Western criticism of China. And China's power moves to defend itself and advance its interests in the UN human rights institutions have also weakened, to some extent, the institutions themselves.

Conclusion

China has become more integrated in the international human rights regime since the late 1970s. Ironically, China has had to fight off strong criticism since the late 1980s after a decade of increased activism. The 1989 Tiananmen incident put China on the defensive in the UN Commission on Human Rights and the UN Sub-Commission on Prevention of Discrimination and Protection of Minorities in the early 1990s. China became the first permanent member of the UN Security Council to be censured by the sub-commission in 1989. More significant, to bring collective power and international opinion to bear on China, the United States and its allies have sponsored resolutions on China's human rights situation at the UN Human Rights Commission every year except 1991 and 1998. And Beijing sees its human rights diplomacy at the UN mainly as an extension of its rights exchange with the West. But unlike in their bilateral relations, the United States and China compete in the multilateral arena mainly by lobbying non-Western member states to pass or defeat China resolutions.

Beijing has succeeded in preventing the West from passing resolutions on its human rights situation thanks to its considerable political influence in the United Nations, its impressive economic growth and relative stability, its traditional friendship with Asian and African nations, its intense lobbying efforts, and by playing economic cards. But Beijing's diplomatic victory means a lost opportunity to make genuine improvements in human rights for Chinese citizens and a weakened international human rights regime. Moreover, what stands out in China's multilateral human rights diplomacy is that its participation has so far only led to adaptive learning about how to defend its sovereignty and national interests, rather than a change of heart about the importance of safeguarding human rights at home.

Despite Beijing's successes in recent years, its human rights record will remain an issue in the UN human rights institutions. The most important reason for this is that while making further improvements in a broad range of areas, the Chinese government continues to repress political dissidents and any organized group outside its direct control. Moreover, Beijing's human rights violations will continue to concern international human rights groups, who will then lobby the U.S. government and other Western governments to exert bilateral and multilateral pressure on Beijing. However, it will be difficult for the UN human rights institutions to censure Beijing as long as developing nations account for a majority of the membership and China continues to exercise its considerable political and economic influence.

Chapter Seven
Conclusion

The previous chapters have offered a broad survey of China's bilateral and multilateral human rights relations with the United States, Western Europe, and Japan, analyzing these countries' motives and calculations, and the reasons for their policy successes or failures on a case-by-case basis. This chapter summarizes Western human rights approaches toward China and Chinese human rights foreign policy on a comparative basis. In addition, the chapter further explores several theoretical issues that have emerged in the book, namely the role of ideas and power in international relations and the impact of the international human rights regime on state behavior.

Western Human Rights Policy Toward China

Human Rights and Western Policy Toward China

Two features stand out in Western human rights approaches to China. First, the idea of human rights matters in Western policy toward China. Human rights in China has been a persistent issue between China and the West since the Chinese government brutally repressed demonstrators in June 1989, an event that was carried on live television around the globe. If human rights did not matter in international relations, we would not see human rights diplomacy between China and the West at all.

Second, when push comes to shove, the idea of rights has seldom prevailed over traditional power calculations. Western governments have not committed as many policy resources to pressuring China on human rights as they have on other issues. Moreover, there is clear variation among major industrial democracies in their degree of commitment to the cause of human rights, and each country's policy varies over time. From the beginning, Americans, Europeans, and Japanese differed in their objectives and preferred tools. Moreover, human rights has come to play a less prominent role in shaping foreign policy toward China for all these countries over time.

Human rights became a decisive factor in Western policy toward Beijing immediately following the June 1989 Tiananmen incident. In fact, human rights in China became virtually a universal issue. The international community united in condemning the Chinese government. Equally important, ordinary Chinese citizens welcomed international criticism, still shocked as they were by the brutality of the government crackdown.

In the wake of Tiananmen, the United States and Western Europe imposed sanctions on China, suspending military sales, military exchanges, high-level official exchanges, and multilateral development aid. They also accepted Chinese dissidents in exile and extended visas for Chinese students and scholars studying in their countries.

The tough Western position stemmed from widespread public pressure to punish Beijing in the name of freedom and democracy. But it also reflected drastic changes brewing in the world at this time, the fall of the Berlin Wall, the end of the Cold War, and the disintegration of the Soviet Union. After winning the Cold War, the West became more convinced of the values of human rights and democracy while it simultaneously saw China's strategic value as a counterweight to the Soviet Union decreased in world politics. In addition, a strategy of pressuring the Chinese government to democratize would also enhance Western security based on the notion that democracies do not fight each other. Under these circumstances, human rights activists and conservatives could agree on pressure tactics against Beijing.

Would the West have reacted as powerfully to Tiananmen during the Cold War? Probably not, judging by Washington's tolerant attitudes toward anti-communist dictatorships during the Cold War. In fact, given its strategic value, China was exempted from Western human rights policy in the 1970s and the 1980s. Even in the dark weeks of the summer of 1989, President Bush kept contact with Beijing and did not sever trade relations, as advocated by human rights activists and some members of Congress, because Bush wanted to encourage China's cooperation and avoid cornering its leaders.

Japan sided with the West, suspending yen loans to China and halting official exchanges with Beijing. As China's largest foreign aid donor and a major trading partner, Japan could have hurt China economically. But Tokyo dragged its feet and avoided explicit references to human rights and democracy. Japan's lukewarm support for the West was consistent with its foreign policy at this time, which did not incorporate human rights concerns. Unlike the Americans, the Japanese pursued a strategic objective of promoting stability and economic reform. China's geographic proximity made the prospect of widespread instability a greater threat to Japan's own security and prosperity than did the communist party clampdown on demonstrators. Japan's past aggression in Asia also deterred its activism on rights. Tokyo would not have taken any punitive actions against Beijing but for the strategic need to avoid the perception of divergence from its Western allies. This was particularly important at a time when the West was attacking Japan for its seemingly unstoppable economic advance in the world.

The variation in commitment to human rights foreign policy and the importance of rights relative to other considerations explain why Japan, Western Europe, and the United States, in that order, gradually retreated from confronting Beijing. Japan led the way in easing sanctions. Within a year of Tiananmen, Japan began to normalize relations with China by resuming yen loans and meeting with Chinese leaders. Prime Minister Kaifu visited China in August 1991, and was the first leader of a major industrial country to do so. In contrast to its Western allies, Japan has chosen a nonconfrontational, behind-the-scenes approach to dealing with human rights in China, balancing between the West and China. Unlike Americans and Europeans, Japanese officials discuss human rights in general terms and refrain from criticizing Chinese policy when they meet with the Chinese. However, Tokyo has sided with the West at the UN Human Rights Commission. Given the importance of its relationship with the West, Japan cannot afford to do nothing, but given the importance of its relationship with China, Japan cannot afford to do too much.

Western Europeans, as assertive as Americans initially, adopted similar sanctions on China. The French government in particular took a hard-line position on Beijing. The French honored Chinese exiles and allowed them to gather in Paris to form an opposition group, which advocated overthrowing the ruling Chinese government. At the G7 summit in Houston in July 1990, the French camp championed a tough position on China while the Japanese preferred moderate measures. Similar to the Americans, Western Europeans demanded that Beijing improve human rights in general and release political prisoners in particular. They also cosponsored and actively lobbied for resolutions on China at the UN Human Rights Commission.

Western Europe began improving relations with China after 1993. Major European nations such as France and Germany adjusted their policy, replacing confrontation with dialogue. This change was rooted in China's rapid economic growth and growing market and political weight as well as Europe's own frustration with the failure of the previous approach. Western Europe also retreated at the UN Human Rights Commission, ceasing cosponsorship of China resolutions in 1997. Europeans continue to raise human rights issues with Chinese leaders in bilateral talks, but such purely symbolic discussions are mainly intended for a domestic audience, not for improving the human rights situation in China.

The United States led in exerting external pressure on China and adopted a highly confrontational approach focused on human rights issues in the early 1990s. The U.S. government explicitly linked China's human rights record and its MFN trading status until 1994. Washington maintained military sanctions and refrained from high-level official exchanges with Beijing. The State Department issued annual reports on China's human rights situation, and the United States sponsored China resolutions at the United Nations Human Rights Commission. However, as a litmus test, commercial interests prevailed over human rights concerns in annual battles over MFN/NTR status in Congress.

Trailing Japan and Western Europe, the U.S. government relaxed human rights pressure on China in late 1996 by declaring its intention not to let bilateral relations be held hostage to human rights concerns and, instead, to forge a strategic partnership with China. While the Clinton administration argued that engagement was the best way to promote human rights and democracy in the long run, its new approach was also due to strategic concerns. Washington's preoccupation with human rights disputes with China was seen to have contributed to a serious deterioration in bilateral relations, demonstrated most glaringly when the two powers came to the brink of military conflict over Taiwan in March 1996.

While continuing to raise human rights issues with Beijing and to criticize China at the UN Human Rights Commission, the Clinton administration adopted a strategy of increasing cooperation and reducing conflicts, which effectively sidelined rights issues in the scheme of things. Clinton and Jiang paid highly publicized state visits to each other's countries in 1997 and 1998. Still, the U.S. Congress continuously attacks Clinton's China policy, thus keeping human rights a central issue between the two countries.

Except for about two years after Tiananmen, the United States, Western Europe, and Japan have committed far fewer policy resources to the human rights cause than to other issues. To protect U.S. security interests in Asia and warn Beijing not to miscalculate, Clinton sent two carrier battle groups to the Taiwan area in the largest show of U.S. force in East Asia since the end of the Vietnam War. The U.S. government has also played hardball with Beijing over intellectual property rights, arms proliferation, and entry into the World Trade Organization, combining threats with incentives. In fact, the White House has put as much, if not more, effort into persuading Congress to accept its engagement policy with China as it has into persuading Beijing to improve human rights.

Compared with the United States, Western Europe and Japan have been even less willing to commit policy resources to human rights in China. Western Europe has not hesitated to defend its trade interests in negotiating with China and has not taken costly measures for the sake of human rights in China. In fact, Europeans have made concerted efforts in recent years to improve their ties with China to advance their economic and political interests. The Japanese have invested still more resources to improving relations with China. And compared to its efforts to influence Chinese policy on military spending and environmental protection, Tokyo's efforts on human rights have been minimal. The Japanese government suspended grant aid to China in 1995 in protest of Beijing's continual nuclear tests, a daring move hitherto unheard-of in the bilateral relationship. Tokyo has also adopted a cautious hedging strategy against China, but mainly due to Beijing's military expansion, not its human rights record.

Assessing Western Human Rights Strategies

How one evaluates Western human rights approaches toward China depends on one's preferences. Human rights activists want Western governments to take resolute actions against Beijing and do not believe that these governments have done nearly enough. But the Chinese government does not want the West to do anything regarding human rights, which it considers an internal affair. How one evaluates Western human rights approaches also depends on one's expectations. If one does not believe that the West can realistically overcome Beijing's resistance to change, one will not be overly critical of weak Western efforts. But if one believes that the West can indeed force the Chinese government to alter its ways, an assessment that the West has been "kowtowing" to China is more likely.

My own assessment of Western approaches is based on two assumptions. One is that human rights is indeed desirable for China. The other is that it will not be easy for China to democratize. The first assumption means that external pressure should be an important condition for realizing democracy in China. But the second assumption means that any external intervention has to be nuanced and well timed.

Western human rights diplomacy has largely failed if judged by its declared objective of changing Chinese behavior. There surely have been some successes, namely the release and better treatment of known dissidents, permission for occasional visits to Chinese prisons—even Beijing's agreement to talk about human rights at all. The Chinese government has signed on to international human rights treaties sooner than it would have without international pressure. However, the U.S. government itself has repeatedly admitted that China's human rights situation has not really improved, judged by State Department annual reports on human rights.

Interestingly, both advocates and critics of human rights pressure on Beijing agree that Western approaches have not worked, though they differ on what Western failure means. Activists believe that Western governments could have achieved better results with greater commitment. As a starter, denying China MFN/NTR status would have gotten Beijing's attention. Chinese analysts argue, on the other hand, that misguided Western human rights policy had little chance to succeed in the first place.

On a broader level, I argue that the engagement approach, advocated by many in the West throughout the decade and adopted as an official policy by the Japanese government right after Tiananmen, by European governments in the early 1990s, and by the U.S. government since the mid-1990s, has been largely successful—if one considers the absence of viable alternatives, the fact that China has indeed become more open economically and socially, and the fact that citizens now enjoy far greater freedom in making decisions about their own lives. In fact, Chinese peasants now choose their leaders in contested village elections. All these improvements make democracy in China more likely if not necessarily inevitable.

Could and should the West have acted differently concerning human rights in China? After examining diplomatic exchanges between the West and China for the past decade, and domestic politics in each country, this book concludes that there is actually little room for a different path. The West could not and should not ignore what the Chinese government did to its citizens in June 1989. That would have sent a bad signal about what kind of world order one wanted and about what governments could get away with. The West could not and should not have continued to isolate China once Beijing lifted marshal law and proceeded with economic reform. That would have encouraged hard-liners in China and undermined the position of reformers, thus risking reversion to pre-reform ways and heightened hostility to the West. The West can and should engage China since the country is furthering economic reform, which can potentially lead to a pluralistic society and a more open political system. The West cannot realistically turn China into a democratic country overnight if the current leadership has a sufficient hold on power to resist such pressure.

How do we assess the different approaches adopted by the United States and Japan, the two countries most important for China? Some Japanese view the difference as positive, arguing that it gives China a safety valve, Japan as a good cop and the United States as a bad cop. Such an arrangement, however, being good for Japan and detrimental to the United States, is more justification than motive.

Tokyo has been largely successful if judged by its own objectives regarding China's human rights disputes with the West. On the one hand, Japan helped China avoid international isolation, which contributed to Beijing's decision to continue reform. China did not collapse, as some Japanese analysts had feared in the early 1990s, which would have damaged crucial Japanese security and commercial interests. Japan became a major economic partner with China in the 1990s. Tokyo achieved all this while also preventing Sino-U.S. human rights disputes from damaging its crucial relationship with Washington.

However, compared with high-pressure U.S. tactics, a softer Japanese approach would have yielded even fewer direct results in human rights in China. In fact, the Chinese government welcomed Japan's low-profile approach and used Japan as the weak link in the Western front to break through diplomatic isolation in the early 1990s. Japanese resources, to some extent, neutralized the effectiveness of U.S. efforts. The Western business community also used Japan as a weapon to put pressure on governments not to impose sanctions against China.

What policy implications does this assessment of Western approaches offer? This book shows that Western governments have limited ability to change Beijing's general behavior in human rights when the Chinese government rigorously resists external pressure. And ultimately a high-pressure or a low-key approach does not make much difference if judged by actual behavior changes in China. This means, while it is important to express clear opinions on human rights and democracy, one also needs a good dose of political realism. There is no quick fix to human rights in China. One just has to let the country's domestic evolution take its due course while trying to nudge the Chinese government to further open itself to the outside world. Moreover, excessive pressure may backfire and contribute to rising nationalist sentiment. This risk is heightened if one fails to understand the dynamic relationship between the state and society in China and how responsive to external pressure a majority of Chinese is at a given moment.

China's Human Rights Foreign Policy

High Costs for China

Western sanctions after Tiananmen inflicted direct costs on China in terms of trade, investments, dual-use technologies, development assistance, tourist income, and a mass defection of elite students and scholars. Beijing has also had to commit valuable policy resources to fend off Western human rights pressure; for example, offering financial incentives to developing nations to support it in its human rights disputes with the West. Beijing's need for support among developing nations in the early 1990s also weakened its bargaining leverage and restrained its diplomacy in areas such as territorial disputes.

More important, China has faced an indirect linkage of human rights and other issues. In the United States, human rights NGOs have had success in rhetorical debates over an appropriate policy toward China, setting limits as to how far foreign policy-makers can move toward normal ties with Beijing. The U.S. government has to justify an engagement policy with Beijing and fend off Congressional and media criticism. Also, those opposed to free trade with China have used China's poor human rights record as a weapon to pressure the U.S. government. In addition, human rights has complicated U.S.-China security relations. China, a nondemocratic nation that has grown strong economically and militarily, is perceived by many in the U.S. security community as a potential or present threat to the United States. Taiwan's successful transition to democracy has allowed the Taiwanese government to make persuasive appeals to Congress and others based on comparisons with the authoritarian mainland regime. This new political reality has led to greater American support for Taiwan and has undermined America's traditional "one China policy."

While human rights is a non-issue on the bilateral diplomatic agenda between Japan and China, the issue has been an important indirect causal factor in recent tensions between the two nations. The brutal crackdown in Tiananmen and the subsequent decade of reports on China's human rights abuses have contributed to a growing distrust of China among Japanese citizens and officials. As a result, the Chinese can no longer influence Japanese domestic politics as much as they used to. This explains in part Tokyo's growing assertiveness vis-à-vis Beijing. Moreover, human rights-related strains in the Sino-U.S. relationship complicate Sino-Japanese relations. While China and Japan may move closer to each other in the short run, as they did in the early 1990s, Japan will ultimately side with the United States, which offers it military protection, the world's largest market, and its most important source of technology.

As for Western Europe, media coverage of China's human rights abuses has tarnished Beijing's reputation and allowed European governments to adopt policies detrimental to vital Chinese interests. France and others exported advanced weapons to Taiwan and

stopped doing so only after intense Chinese protests and retaliation. In addition, the Dalai Lama has won greater popular support
in Europe, thus internationalizing the issue of Tibet, which China
considers to be threatening to its territorial integrity.

We should also recognize even more important opportunity costs
for Chinese citizens. It goes without saying that Chinese citizens
have been denied civil and political rights when the government
has refused to improve its human rights record. And their loss is
the nation's loss; it is hard to imagine how the nation can realize its
full potential and gain international respect without the voluntary
participation of free citizens.

Yet, what stands out in China's human rights foreign policy is that
Beijing has stood its ground, without retreating to isolation or yielding to external pressure. Despite Western rights criticism, Beijing
continues to seek a better relationship with the West, but Beijing
has not redefined its national interest in the face of Western pressure. While there has been subtle change in the tone and focus of
Chinese propaganda, this is more a reflection of Beijing's efforts to
find a better pitch than of a change of mind. Beijing's main objective in human rights foreign policy has remained the same: to fend
off and neutralize Western human rights pressure, which is seen as
detrimental to its national interests of ensuring regime survival and
social stability.

Why does the Chinese government not accept Western criticism
as beneficial for the country? An obvious reason is that the communist party leadership has no incentive to yield to Western rights
pressure, which really aims at ending its political monopoly. At the
same time, the Chinese feel that they can survive the costs of external pressure. Chinese analysts recognize that human rights disputes
with the West do entail costs for China but generally believe that
they are manageable. While the Chinese have an incentive to dis-
miss external pressure, the earlier discussion of Western pressure
suggests that the West did not go all out to inflict costs on China.

This portrait of Chinese calculations is not the full picture of what
has driven Chinese human rights diplomacy. To understand Beijing's behavior, we need to have a more nuanced understanding of
the government's definition of national priorities and the dynamic
relationship between the state and society.

Setting National Priorities

Deng charted a new course for China in 1978, deepening and widening economic reform while maintaining the leadership of the Communist Party. He reasoned that party leadership is necessary for social stability and economic growth and that, conversely, rising living standards and greater national strength would justify party rule. This basic party line meant that China needed to integrate with the global economy while building firewalls against Western cultural and political values. Full of contradictions, this line was challenged from different directions, but Deng largely prevailed in policy debates and guided the country according to his vision. The current leadership has essentially carried on Deng's policy. Reflected in China's human rights foreign policy, Beijing has made calculated moves to maintain ties with the West to facilitate economic reform while resisting the kind of Western demands that could undermine party rule.

How Beijing defines its national interests determines how it defends them. What has emerged in the government is a developmentalist consensus, which sees fast economic development as China's number one priority and social stability as a necessary condition for realizing this cherished national objective. Chinese officials see China's rapid economic growth and Russia's current difficulties as testimony to Deng's wisdom. Western human rights pressure is increasingly perceived by the Chinese government to be cover for keeping China weak and advancing Western interests in other areas. For all these reasons, the Chinese government has become more confident in its human rights exchange with the West.

This book shows the importance of examining the views of Chinese society and its dynamic relations with the government. One may suggest correctly that the Chinese government was defending the interests of the party rather than the nation after Tiananmen. It was hard to imagine then how the government could ever regain the trust of Chinese citizens. However, the government has regained popular support, particularly for its foreign policy. Currently, a majority of Chinese side with the government in human rights disputes with the West, doubting Western motives and criticizing Western tactics.

Most Chinese support the government based on cynical calculations. They see the party-state as an evil necessary for making the

nation strong and the people prosperous. There is an implicit social contract between citizens and the government: the party maintains its power in exchange for ensuring continuing economic success. As long as the economy grows and citizens are content with
improvement in their personal circumstances, the government will
enjoy popular support. In this context, foreign pressure over human rights and other issues has contributed to rising nationalist
sentiment among Chinese citizens as well as officials.

Defending National Interests

Beijing did not have a master plan for its response to Western
human rights pressure. Rather, guided by Deng's central policy line,
and adjusting for evolving bargaining situations and for different
actors, Chinese diplomats searched for an appropriate combination of tools to fend off Western pressure, learning from their successes and failures. Over the past decade the Chinese have used
propaganda, opportune concessions, confrontation and tough bargaining, intense lobbying, and economic statecraft. They have also
searched for weak links among industrial countries, using a strategy
of divide-and-conquer.

The Chinese government faced its toughest challenge after Tiananmen, and its initial response to Western pressure set the tone
for its later exchanges with the West. In a sense, the fact that the
Chinese government took the West's best punches without being
knocked out gave confidence and valuable experience to Chinese
officials dealing with human rights issues.

Deng's decision to continue economic reform was a key factor for
China's success in human rights diplomacy. Though driven mainly
by China's domestic considerations, the decision also had important foreign policy implications, as recognized by Deng and others
in China. Deng's continuing reforms created a dilemma for Western
policy-makers: how far could they push Beijing to improve human
rights and accept democracy without undermining Deng's ability
to proceed with his reform program, which was also desirable for
the West and promised possible liberalization down the road? Excessive sanctions, it was feared, would create the worst-case outcome of an isolated and hostile country controlled by hard-liners.
China's decision to continue reform also meant that the country
would offer an expanding market for Western companies. Similarly,

Beijing would need to demonstrate willingness to cooperate with the West, all compelling reasons to support engagement.

As human rights was a central factor in Western policy toward China in the first two years after Tiananmen, Beijing also adopted a comprehensive strategy in response. The Chinese government redoubled its efforts to improve relations with its Asian neighbors and other Third World countries to avoid international isolation. At the same time, China avoided frictions with the West and demonstrated willingness to cooperate on other issues.

In the human rights arena, Beijing resorted to its typical negotiating style of "firm in principles but flexible in tactics." The government mobilized its propaganda machine to defend China's record and portray Western rights pressure as interference in China's internal affairs. However, despite its declaration to the contrary, the Chinese government made compromises when intense foreign pressure threatened its core economic and political interests. Compared to its policy toward Western Europe and Japan, China was more responsive to U.S. demands because Washington held more cards than anybody else. In particular, to ensure its MFN trading status, China met some demands of the Bush administration. But the Chinese made it clear that there was a limit to what they were willing to do, and whatever concessions Americans received came only after exhausting negotiations.

Recognizing the different strategic calculations and commitments among industrial nations, China focused on improving relations with Japan, seeing Japan as a weak link in the Western consensus, to break through isolation by industrial nations. Chinese leaders emphasized reform and business opportunities and reminded the Japanese of their past aggression in China. This strategy paid off. Beijing also used diplomacy and economic statecraft to sway major European nations. In particular, the Chinese offered commercial incentives to those European leaders willing to improve relations with China. By normalizing relations with the Japanese and Europeans, Beijing undercut Washington's ability to rally international support for rights pressure on China.

The Chinese government recognized that the United States took the lead on Western rights pressure on China and often saw Western human rights pressure simply as an American crusade. Beijing mobilized its propaganda machine to counter American criticism, both defending the Chinese record and revealing American sins.

The Chinese also used economic statecraft, rewarding European or Japanese competitors with lucrative contracts to pressure American firms to lobby the U.S. government, and sending shopping delegations to the United States. Chinese negotiators also tried to frustrate the Americans with difficult negotiations. And Beijing released a few prominent dissidents at times to influence American opinion before Congressional debate on MFN status, UN Human Rights Commission meetings, or votes on the site of the 2000 Olympics. Beijing achieved a major victory when the Clinton administration delinked China's human rights record with MFN status in 1994.

By the mid-1990s, the Chinese government had largely succeeded in fending off Western human rights pressure. China had essentially removed human rights as a diplomatic issue with Japan and neutralized the issue with Western Europe. Since 1996 Beijing has also marginalized the human rights issue with the U.S. government. Chinese officials and analysts have come to realize that human rights is not going away as a bilateral issue due to American political culture and domestic politics, and have learned to live with human rights disputes as long as they do not compromise China's vital interests.

Chinese diplomats have made great lobbying efforts at the UN Human Rights Commission to defeat Western attempts to pass resolutions on China's human rights that were intended to bring public shame on Beijing. The Chinese have seen the annual fights at the commission as a test of strength with the United States. Beijing has used everything in its tool box—propaganda, commercial incentives, threats, and persuasion—to sway the position of member states, and it has succeeded in that no Western-sponsored resolutions on China have ever passed at the UN Human Rights Commission.

Implications for International Relations Theories

The main implication of the book for international relations theories is that while ideas matter in contemporary international relations, they do so in a dynamic interplay with power. First, the idea of human rights becomes effective in shaping foreign policy only when it is perceived to enhance rather than hurt traditional power-based interests. Second, traditional power is needed to implement human rights foreign policy, which ironically obscures the difference between value-driven human rights diplomacy and interest-driven traditional diplomacy, thus making it difficult for target countries like China to accept Western rights pressure. Third, by successfully resisting external rights pressure, powerful target nations like China weaken the importance of human rights in the foreign policy deliberations of the Western countries that initiate pressure.

This book shows that the idea of human rights matters in contemporary international relations, justifying critical analysis of human rights diplomacy in the first place. The constructivist approach explains why human rights has become an important factor in foreign policy making in the West. As deeply internalized values, human rights and democracy shape Western governments' views of the world and standards of conduct. The western media focuses on human rights issues in the world, thus highlighting problems and influencing public opinion, something which governments cannot ignore. Human rights activists also play a crucial role in keeping human rights in China on the agenda of Western governments. Human rights in China has become internationalized in part because outside human rights observers have become more aware of the situation in the country and because some Chinese human rights advocates have reached out to make transnational connections with foreign supporters.

Not surprisingly, how much importance a country attaches to human rights explains in part how much effort it makes in pursuing human rights goals in dealing with China. The United States and Western Europe, which are more committed than Japan to human rights, have indeed adopted a stronger human rights policy than the latter. Tokyo would adopt a tougher human rights policy if it came to define human rights as an important national interest and if Japanese human rights groups became more powerful players in domestic politics. As for China, as a target of Western rights pressure, if the government decided to embrace human rights values its foreign policy would be fundamentally different.

However, this book shows that enlightened ideas embraced by activists alone are not enough to produce a committed human rights policy. The United States and its Western allies took strong measures immediately after Tiananmen mainly because of a convergence of ideals and interests. The subsequent collapse of Eastern Europe and the Soviet Union demonstrated the power of the idea of human rights and democracy in helping the West win the Cold

War. Human rights activists and liberals supported a tough China policy because morally this was the right thing to do. Pragmatists and conservatives also believed that an active human rights policy would facilitate realization of traditional national interests in security and trade. A China that is more democratic and respectful of human rights would be a more peaceful and trustworthy country. A more open and democratic China would also make a better trading partner. However, as soon as it was realized that pressure for immediate improvements in human rights in China would compromise trade interests, the U.S. business community and their supporters mobilized to prevent a linkage between trade and human rights. When pragmatists realized that a China policy dominated by human rights had compromised U.S. strategic interests and might lead to a dangerous showdown with China over Taiwan, they immediately pushed the Clinton administration to engage China as a strategic partner and to treat human rights as only one of the issues on the table.

The Japanese saw human rights pressure have a negative impact on their security and trade interests earlier than the Americans did, an important reason that they were not keen on pressuring the Chinese. Tokyo believed that China's stability was important for regional security and that an isolation of China would compromise its commercial interests. And engagement with China was the only pragmatic way to ensure that China would be stable and would continue to open up to the outside world. While the Japanese government stood out as an outlier in the early 1990s, the Japanese position has largely become the norm among Western governments. Now Western public opinion and human rights advocacy constrain but do not determine Western policy toward China. In other words, the idea of human rights has become less influential in policy-making.

The importance of human rights in Western foreign policy has diminished due to the power play with China. On the one hand, there is a structural conundrum in human rights policy. The more committed a country is to human rights, the more it needs to use traditional power to change the behavior of target nations, power ranging from political isolation to economic sanctions, and even to use of military force, as in the case of Kosovo. Such power play is meant to hurt the target's national interests and is generally perceived as such in these countries. This explains why target governments tend to resist external rights pressure rather than make change in light of the enlightened ideas underpinning it. The fact that countries that initiate rights pressure also adopt policies to advance their own national interests in security, trade, and other issue areas further creates the impression that human rights is part of the Western design to bully others for their own benefit. This has been the case for China. Its human rights exchanges with the West have mainly led to adaptive learning about how to fend off Western pressure rather than to cognitive learning about the importance of rights.

On the other hand, what instruments Western nations use also depends on the power of target nations. China's major power status means that the West cannot and will not use military force for humanitarian reasons the way they did against Serbia over Kosovo. China's growing economic power and expanding market mean that the West would also suffer from a trade war, though Beijing would suffer more. China's political influence and geostrategic weight mean that the West cannot isolate the country easily in the world and that the West itself needs China's cooperation in important issue areas. Beijing's ability to mobilize resources in defense of its national interests has frustrated Western governments and weakened their resolve to push the human rights issue with the Chinese.

Besides showing the importance of the interplay of ideas and power, this book also shows that the institutionalist approach explains part of China's human rights relations with the West. The international human rights regime, broadly defined as principles, norms, and rules, has created universal standards and legitimized international concerns over the domestic practices of individual countries. The West thus feels justified in pressuring the Chinese government about its domestic practices. Furthermore, the regime provides an alternative to bilateral diplomacy. Washington decided to try harder to get a China resolution passed in 1995 to compensate for its decision to delink human rights and trade in its bilateral relations with China. Japan found it easier to balance between China and the West by siding with the West in a multilateral context.

The international human rights regime has also affected Chinese behavior. Rather than challenging the regime head on, Beijing accepts the regime's legitimacy while finding ways to minimize China's obligations. It is also conceivable that by joining the international human rights regime and signing the international human rights covenants, China will gradually modify its behavior in the human rights area.

However, a power struggle with the West dominates China's multilateral human rights policy. Without U.S. and Western initiatives, it is hard to imagine that the UN Human Rights Commission will ever act on its own to criticize China. The UN Human Rights Commission, as it is structured now, has a weak enforcement mechanism and thus places few constraints on sovereign nations, particularly powerful ones.

In short, power still plays a central role in international relations. While the idea of human rights explains why Beijing has to engage in human rights diplomacy with the West, power and bargaining explain the process and outcome of human rights exchanges between China and the West. Realists can explain much of what has happened in this new issue area. Nevertheless, this book also shows that power itself evolves in meaning and content depending on the prevailing ideas and institutional context.

Notes

Chapter 1

1. See Hungdah Chiu, "Chinese Attitudes Toward International Law of Human Rights in the Post-Mao Era," in Victor C. Falkenheim, ed., *Chinese Politics from Mao to Deng* (New York: Paragon House, 1989), pp. 237–70.

2. For early Chinese dissident writings, see James D. Seymour, ed., *The Fifth Modernization: China's Human Rights Movement, 1978–1979* (Sanfordville, N.Y.: Human Rights Publishing Group, 1980).

3. For academic writing, see Merle Goldman, "Human Rights in the People's Republic of China," *Daedalus* 112, 4 (Fall 1983): 111–38; R. Randle Edwards, Louis Henkin, and Andrew J. Nathan, *Human Rights in China* (New York: Columbia University Press, 1986); Yuan-li Wu et al., *Human Rights in the People's Republic of China* (Boulder, Colo.: Westview Press, 1988); Andrew J. Nathan, *China's Crisis: Dilemmas of Reform and Prospects for Democracy* (New York: Columbia University Press, 1991) and *China's Transition* (New York: Columbia University Press, 1997); Michael C. Davis, ed., *Human Rights and Chinese Values: Legal, Philosophical, and Political Perspectives* (Hong Kong: Oxford University Press, 1995); and Ann Kent, *Between Freedom and Subsistence: China and Human Rights* (Hong Kong: Oxford University Press, 1993).

4. Andrew J. Nathan, "Human Rights in Chinese Foreign Policy," *China Quarterly* 139 (September 1994): 622–43 and "China and the International Human Rights Regime," in Elizabeth Economy and Michel Oksenberg, eds., *China Joins the World: Progress and Prospects* (New York: Council on Foreign Relations Press, 1999), pp. 136–60; and James D. Seymour, "Human Rights in Chinese Foreign Relations," in Samuel S. Kim, ed., *China and the World: Chinese Foreign Policy Faces the New Millennium* (Boulder, Colo.: Westview, 1998), pp. 217–38.

5. Ann Kent, *China, the United Nations, and Human Rights: The Limits of Compliance* (Philadelphia: University of Pennsylvania Press, 1999).

6. Roberta Cohen, "People's Republic of China: The Human Rights Exception," *Human Rights Quarterly* 9, 4 (November 1987): 447–549.

7. Ibid.

8. For examples, see Li Yunlong, *Zhongmei guanxi zhong de renquan wenti* [Human rights issues in Sino-U.S. relations] (Beijing: Xinhua chubanshe, 1998), pp. 1–5; and Robert S. Ross, Foreword, in Ross, ed., *After the Cold War: Domestic Factors and U.S.-China Relations* (Armonk, N.Y.: E.M. Sharpe, 1998), pp. vii–x.

9. Robert F. Drinan and Teresa T. Kuo, "The 1991 Battle for Human Rights in China," *Human Rights Quarterly* 14, 1 (February 1992): 21–42; Peter Van Ness, "Addressing the Human Rights Issue in Sino-American Relations," *Journal of International Affairs* 49, 2 (Winter 1996): 309–31; Ming Wan, "Human Rights and Sino-U.S. Relations: Policies and Changing Realities," *Pacific Review* 10, 2 (1997): 237–55; and Quansheng Zhao with Barry Press, "The U.S. Promotion of Human Rights and China's Response," *Issues and Studies* 34, 8 (August 1998): 30–62.

10. For exceptions, see Seiichiro Takagi, "Human Rights in Japanese Foreign Policy: Japan's Policy Towards China After Tiananmen," in James T. H. Tang, ed., *Human Rights and International Relations in the Asia-Pacific Region* (London: Pinter, 1995), pp. 97–111; Ann Kent, "Australia-China Relations, 1966–1996: A Critical Overview," *Australian Journal of Politics and History* 42, 3 (1996): 365–84; and Ming Wan, "Policies, Resource Commitments, and Values: A Comparison of U.S. and Japanese Approaches to Human Rights in China," in John D. Montgomery, ed., *Human Rights: Positive Policies in Asia and the Pacific Rim* (Hollis, N.H.: Hollis Publishing Company, 1998), pp. 43–70.

11. See Li, *Zhongmei guanxi zhong de renquan wenti*; Dong Yunhu, ed., *Renquan zhongmei jiaoliang beiwanglu* [Human rights: memorandum on Sino-U.S. contest] (Chengdu: Sichuan renmin chubanshe, 1998); and Jiang Haiyang, *Shuishi yingjia zhongmei renquan jiaoliang jishi* [Who is the winner? report on Sino-U.S. human rights contest] (Beijing: Dangdai shijie chubanshe, 1998).

12. For an exception, see Liu Jiangyong, "Renquan wenti yu riben de lichang jiqi duihua taidu" [Human rights issues, Japan's position and its attitude toward China], *Riben wenti* 32 (August 1990): 1–15.

13. For Chinese perceptions of the United States, see David Shambaugh, *Beautiful Imperialist: China Perceives America, 1972–1990* (Princeton, N.J.: Princeton University Press, 1991); and Jianwei Wang, *Limited Adversaries: Post-Cold War U.S.-China Mutual Images* (Hong Kong: Oxford University Press, 1999).

14. For surveys of the field of Chinese foreign policy, see Bin Yu, "The Study of Chinese Foreign Policy: Problems and Prospect," *World Politics* 46, 2 (January 1994): 235–61; David Shambaugh, "A Bibliographical Essay on New Sources for the Study of China's Foreign Relations and National Security," in Thomas W. Robinson and David Shambaugh, eds., *Chinese Foreign Policy: Theory and Practice* (Oxford: Clarendon Press, 1994), pp. 603–18; Quansheng Zhao, *Interpreting Chinese Foreign Policy* (Hong Kong: Oxford University Press, 1996); and Samuel S. Kim, "Chinese Foreign Policy in Theory and Practice," in Samuel S. Kim, ed., *China and the World: Chinese Foreign Policy Faces the New Millennium*, 4th ed. (Boulder, Colo.: Westview Press, 1998), pp. 3–33.

15. Some Chinese scholars are pushing for the government to be more explicit and bold in pursuing national interests. See Yan Xuetong, *Zhongguo guojia liyi fenxi* [Analysis of China's national interests] (Tianjin: Tianjin renmin chubanshe, 1997).

16. See Thomas Christensen, "Chinese Realpolitik," *Foreign Affairs* 75, 5 (September/October 1996): 37–52; and Yong Deng and Fei-Ling Wang, eds., *In the Eyes of the Dragon: China Views the World* (Lanham, Md.: Rowman and Littlefield, 1999).

17. R. J. Vincent, *Human Rights and International Relations* (New York: Cambridge University Press, 1986); Jack Donnelly, *Universal Human Rights in Theory and Practice* (Ithaca, N.Y.: Cornell University Press, 1989) and *International Human Rights*, 2nd ed. (Boulder, Colo.: Westview Press, 1998); David P. Forsythe, *The Internationalization of Human Rights* (Lexington, Mass.: Lexington Books, 1991); James T. H. Tang, *Human Rights and International Relations in the Asia-Pacific Region* (London: Pinter, 1995); and Frances V. Harbour, *Thinking About International Ethics: Moral Theory and Cases from American Foreign Policy* (Boulder, Colo.: Westview Press, 1998).

18. Kenneth N. Waltz, *Theory of International Politics* (Reading, Mass.: Addison-Wesley, 1979), p. 200.

19. Jack Donnelly, "International Human Rights: A Regime Analysis," *International Organization* 40, 3 (Summer 1986): 599–642.

20. Kathryn Sikkink, "The Power of Principled Ideas: Human Rights Policies in the United States and Western Europe," in Judith Goldstein and Robert O. Keohane, eds., *Ideas and Foreign Policy: Beliefs, Institutions and Political Change* (Ithaca, N.Y.: Cornell University Press, 1993), pp. 139–70; Martha Finnemore and Kathryn Sikkink, "International Norm Dynamics and Political Change," *International Organization* 52, 4 (Autumn 1998): 887–917; and Margaret E. Keck and Kathryn Sikkink, *Activists Beyond Borders: Advocacy Networks in International Politics* (Ithaca, N.Y.: Cornell University Press, 1998).

Chapter 2

1. Chiu, "Chinese Attitudes Toward International Law of Human Rights in the Post-Mao Era," p. 239.

2. Interview with a senior official of the China Society for Human Rights Studies. Beijing, May 1999.

3. Human Rights Watch, *Human Rights Watch World Report 1994* (New York: Human Rights Watch, 1994), p. 155; and *Human Rights Watch World Report 1995*, p. 145.

4. For Chinese studies of human rights, see Kent, *Between Freedom and Subsistence*; Seymour, "Human Rights in Chinese Foreign Relations"; Robert Weatherley, *The Discourse of Human Rights in China: Historical and Ideological Perspectives* (New York: St. Martin's Press, 1999); Zhou Wei, "The Study of Human Rights in the People's Republic of China," in James T. H. Tang, ed., *Human Rights and International Relations in the Asia-Pacific Region* (London: Pinter, 1995), pp. 83–96; and Chih-yu Shih, "Contending Theories

of 'Human Rights with Chinese Characteristics,'" *Issues and Studies* 29, 11 (November 1993): 42–64.

5. "China Hits Condition of Children in U.S.," *Washington Post*, February 23, 1996.

6. Huang Nansen, "Rendaozhuyi ganyu de shizhi" [The essence of "humanitarian intervention"], *Renmin ribao*, June 3, 1999, p. 9. For a more recent article, see Zhu Muzhi, "U.S. Theory of Human Rights Being Superior to Sovereignty Is Ridiculous," *Beijing Review*, March 20, 2000, *Beijing Review* online.

7. Zhen Yan, "Rendaozhuyi ganshe yufaburong" ["Humanitarian intervention" is illegal], *Renmin ribao*, June 21, 1999, p. 6.

8. "Jiandingbuyi di baochi shehui wending" [Maintain social stability unswervingly], *Renmin ribao*, June 2, 1999, p. 1.

9. For instance, see Dong Yunhu, ed., *Renquan jiben wenxian yaolan* [Collection of basic human rights documents] (Shenyang: Liaoning renmin chubanshe, 1994).

10. For instance, see Xia Yong, *Renquan gainian qiyuan* [The origin of the concept of human rights] (Beijing: Zhongguo zhengfa daxue chubanshe, 1992); and Xia Yong, ed., *Zouxiang quanli de shidai zhongguo gongmin quanli fazhan yanjiu* [Toward an era of rights: research on the development of civil rights in China] (Beijing: Zhongguo zhengfa daxue chubanshe, 1995).

11. For a discussion of the Chinese *xitongs*, see Kenneth Lieberthal, *Governing China: From Revolution Through Reform* (New York: W.W. Norton, 1995), pp. 192–207. In addition to the foreign affairs and propaganda *xitongs*, the political and legal affairs (*zhengfa*) *xitong* controls China's courts, prisons, and "reeducation through labor" camps. Its practices toward political dissidents, Christian priests, and Tibetan monks create international issues that the propaganda *xitong* has to defend and the foreign policy *xitong* has to resolve. But this chapter does not discuss China's judiciary system.

12. The Information Office of the State Council, set up in June 1991, is under the dual leadership of the State Council and the Central Propaganda Department. The officials in the office are from the propaganda *xitong*.

13. For a good study of the Chinese Foreign Ministry, see Lu Ning, *The Dynamics of Foreign-Policy Decisionmaking in China* (Boulder, Colo.: Westview Press, 1997).

14. In fact, Chinese diplomats sometimes complain that the propaganda agencies have performed poorly in creating a positive image for China, especially regarding Tibet. Discussion with a senior official of the Chinese Foreign Ministry, Washington, D.C., December 1997.

15. Interview with a senior official of the UN Human Rights Division of the Chinese Foreign Ministry, Beijing, May 1996.

16. When talking with veterans in the Chinese propaganda apparatus, one also hears the suggestion that earlier Chinese leaders like Mao Zedong emphasized human rights although they did not use the term human rights. However, Mao's implicit reference to democracy and human rights has little practical significance in China now.

17. Deng Xiaoping, *Deng Xiaoping Wenxuan* [Deng's selected works], vol. 3

(Beijing: Renmin chubanshe, 1993). For Chinese discussions of Deng's human rights theory, see Wang Xigen, "Lun deng xiaoping de renquanguan" [On Deng Xiaoping's view of human rights], *Xiandai guoji guanxi* 4 (1997): 29–33.

18. There has been much research done on China's *guoqing*. For example, see China Social Investigation Institute, *Zhongguo guoqing baogao* [Report on China's conditions] (Shenyang: Liaoning renmin chubanshe, 1998).

19. Interview, Washington, D.C., November 9, 1996.

20. Ma Licheng and Ling Zhijun, *Jiaofeng dangdai zhongguo sanci sixiang jiefang shilu* [Clash: records of the three thought liberations in modern China] (Beijing: Jinri zhongguo chubanshe, 1998).

21. For example, former government official Fang Jue issued a liberal document in November 1997, which was translated and published in the United States. See Fang Jue, "A Program for Democratic Reform," *Journal of Democracy* 9, 4 (October 1998): 9–19. The same issue also included another liberal paper by Mao Yushi, entitled "Liberalism, Equal Status, and Human Rights": 20–23.

22. Li Shenzhi, "Fengyu canghuang wushinian guoqingye duyu" [Weathering fifty years: solitary words in the night of the national day], *Dangdai zhongguo yanjiu* 68 (March 2000): 74–83. He has recently been criticized by the party for the article.

23. One such government official, Wang Zhenyao of the Ministry of Civil Affairs, has caught Western media attention for his devoted work to promote village elections. Wang was reassigned to a disaster relief job in the ministry in 1997. See a long feature story by Steven Mufson, "A Quiet Bureaucrat, Promoting the Vote One Village at a Time," *Washington Post*, June 14, 1998, A1.

24. For an interesting analysis, see Ling Zhijun and Ma Licheng, *Huhan dangjin zhongguo de wuzhong shengyin* [Shouts: five voices in present China] (Guangzhou: Guangzhou chubanshe, 1998).

25. Interviews in Beijing and Shanghai, June 1999.

26. Xiao Qiang, "Let Freedom Ring in Beijing," *Washington Post*, October 29, 1997, A23.

27. Yang Zhong, Jie Chen, and John M. Scheb II, "Political Views from Below: A Survey of Beijing Residents," *PS: Political Science and Politics* 30, 3 (September 1997): 476. The survey was conducted in cooperation with the Public Opinion Research Institute of People's University. A total of 700 Beijing permanent residents were selected through random sampling procedures (response rate at 97 percent). Answers were anonymous.

28. Paul Mooney, "China's Elite," *Far Eastern Economic Review*, October 21, 1999, pp. 42, 46.

29. Andrew J. Nathan and Tianjian Shi, "Cultural Requisites for Democracy in China: Findings from a Survey," in Tu Wei-ming, ed., *China in Transition* (Cambridge, Mass.: Harvard University Press, 1994), pp. 115–16.

30. Yongnian Zheng, "Development and Democracy: Are They Compatible in China?" *Political Science Quarterly* 109, 2 (Summer 1994): 241–42. He cites a survey conducted in China that was originally published in Shang

Xiaoyuan, *Zhongguoren de ziwo yizhixing renge* [The Chinese self-controlling personality] (Kunming: Yunnan renmin chubanshe, 1989).

31. This was a national poll conducted entirely by Gallup staff based on over 3700 hour-long, in-home interviews in every province, municipality, and autonomous region of the country. "1997 Survey: The People's Republic of China Consumer Attitudes and Lifestyle Trends" (Princeton, N.J.: Gallup, October 27, 1997).

32. Shi Xiuyin, "Zhongguo shehui zhuanxing shiqi de quanli yu quanli" [Public power and rights during the transformational period in China], in Xia Yong, ed., *Zouxiang quanli de shidai zhongguo gongmin quanli fazhan yanjiu*, pp. 108–14.

33. Xia, *Zouxiang quanli de shidai zhongguo gongmin quanli fazhan yanjiu*. The research team conducted a survey in six provinces, with a sample of 6,000 (5,461 valid returns). The team also conducted field research in 10 Chinese provinces and cities, with over 230 interviews.

34. Gao Hongjun, "Zhongguo gongmin quanli yishi de yanjin" [The awakening of consciousness of rights among Chinese citizens], in Xia, ed., *Zouxiang quanli de shidai zhongguo gongmin quanli fazhan yanjiu*, p. 44.

35. For a comparison of similarities and differences between China and Taiwan, see Harry Harding, "The Halting Advance of Pluralism," *Journal of Democracy* 9, 1 (January 1998): 11–17. For a broad survey of East Asian experiences in democratization, see Edward Friedman, ed., *The Politics of Democratization: Generalizing East Asian Experiences* (Boulder, Colo.: Westview Press, 1994).

36. Gao, "Zhongguo gongmin quanli yishi de yanjin," pp. 46–47.

37. Mooney, "China's Elite," p. 42.

38. Lu Jiang, "Fanxifangzhuyi huichao" [The return of anti-Westernism], *China Times Weekly*, January 2, 1994, pp. 16–19.

39. Based on my trips to China and my exchange with Chinese in China.

40. Jie Chen, Yang Zhong, and Jan William Hillard, "The Level and Sources of Popular Support for China's Current Political Regime," *Communist and Post-Communist Studies* 30, 1 (1997): 45–64. The survey used for this article is the same as that discussed in note 27.

41. Cited in Alfred L. Chan and Paul Nesbitt-Larking, "Critical Citizenship and Civil Society in Contemporary China," *Canadian Journal of Political Science* 28, 2 (June/July 1995): 293–309.

42. This was no secret among Chinese students and scholars in the U.S. Dissidents' bitter rivalry has also become the subject of interest in the Western media. For example, see "Infighting Among Exiles," *Wall Street Journal*, May 12, 1999, A18.

43. Lei Guang, "Elusive Democracy: Conceptual Change and the Chinese Democracy Movement, 1978–79 to 1989," *Modern China* 22, 4 (October 1996): 437–38; Andrew G. Walder and Gong Xiaoxia, "Workers in the Tiananmen Protest: The Politics of the Beijing Workers 'Autonomous Federation,'" *Australian Journal of China Affairs* 29 (January 1993): 1–29; Daniel Kelliher, "Keeping Democracy Safe from the Masses: Intellectuals and Elitism in the Chinese Protest Movement," *Comparative Politics* 25, 4 (July 1993): 379–96.

44. Joanna Slater, "Wrong Answer, China's Limits on Surveys Upset Market-Researchers," *Far Eastern Economic Review*, October 28, 1999, pp. 66–68.

45. For news stories, see George Wehfritz, "Beijing Spring," *Newsweek*, April 13, 1998, pp. 38–40.

46. See Merle Goldman, Perry Link, and Su Wei, "China's Intellectuals in the Deng Era," in Lowell Dittmer and Samuel S. Kim, eds., *China's Quest for National Identity* (Ithaca, N.Y.: Cornell University Press, 1993): 125–53; and Merle Goldman, "Politically Engaged Intellectuals in the Deng-Jiang Era: A Changing Relationship with the Party-State," *China Quarterly* 145 (March 1996): 35–52.

47. See Kate Xiao Zhou, *How the Farmers Changed China: Power of the People* (Boulder, Colo.: Westview Press, 1996); and Edward Friedman, Paul Pickowicz, and Mark Selden, *Chinese Village, Socialist State* (New Haven, Conn.: Yale University Press, 1991).

48. Chen, Zhong, and Hillard, "The Level and Sources of Popular Support," p. 51.

49. Chan and Nesbitt-Larking, "Critical Citizenship," p. 306.

50. Zheng, "Development and Democracy," p. 244. He cites the same poll as Chan and Nesbitt-Larking.

51. Tianjian Shi, *Political Participation in Beijing* (Cambridge, Mass.: Harvard University Press, 1997).

52. John Pomfret, "Chinese Workers Are Showing Disenchantment," *Washington Post*, April 23, 2000, A23.

53. For the impact of an economic slowdown on China's economic reform agenda and the broad political implications of the Asian economic crisis for China, see Avery Goldstein, "Political Implications of a Slowdown," *Orbis* 43, 2 (Spring 1999): 203–22.

Chapter 3

1. See Cohen, "People's Republic of China: The Human Rights Exception."

2. Chiu, "Chinese Attitudes Toward International Law of Human Rights in the Post-Mao Era," pp. 238–39.

3. Quoted in Harry Harding, *A Fragile Relationship: The United States and China Since 1972* (Washington, D.C.: Brookings Institution, 1992), p. 198.

4. Ibid., pp. 198–200.

5. China had high hopes for Bush. Before his visit, an editorial in the *Beijing Review* noticed that the White House announced Bush's visit five days after he took office. "The Chinese people are waiting for Bush, an old friend of Beijing, and his government to do something worthwhile to drive the friendly Sino-U.S. Express in the right direction." "Let Friendly Sino-U.S. Train Roll On," *Beijing Review*, February 28, 1989, p. 7.

6. Fang Lizhi is a famous Chinese dissident who was invited by the U.S. embassy to the dinner in honor of Bush, but was prevented from attending by the Chinese police.

7. Quoted in George Bush and Brent Scowcroft, *A World Transformed* (New York: Vintage Books, 1998), p. 176.

8. Robert S. Ross, "National Security, Human Rights, and Domestic Politics: The Bush Administration and China," in Kenneth A. Oye, Robert J. Lieber, and Donald Rothchild, eds., *Eagle in a New World: American Grand Strategy in the Post-Cold War Era* (New York: HarperCollins, 1992), pp. 287–89. For views of China held by Bush and Scowcroft, see Bush and Scowcroft, *A World Transformed*, Chapter Four.

9. The Harris Poll, released, June 11, 1989, was conducted by telephone with a nationwide cross section of 1,006. Interestingly, although the public gave a 48 percent negative and 41 percent positive rating to the way Bush responded, they basically agreed with the administration's decision to maintain communication with the Chinese government.

10. See Bush and Scowcroft, *A World Transformed*, Chapter Four. Also see Robert G. Sutter, *U.S. Policy Toward China: An Introduction to the Role of Interest Groups* (Lanham, Md.: Rowman and Littlefield, 1998), pp. 26–35. Also see Rosemary Foot, *The Practice of Power: U.S. Relations with China Since 1949* (Oxford: Clarendon Press, 1997), pp. 242–57.

11. The Chinese side also believed that it was the United States that should take action to improve the relationship since the U.S. was in China's view interfering in China's internal affairs. For example, see "U.S. Must Take Steps to Patch Up Sino-U.S. Rift," *Beijing Review*, November 13, 1989, pp. 9–11.

12. For example, right before the review, China allowed Fang Lizhi to leave the U.S. embassy and go abroad. Fang had been staying in the U.S. embassy since the Tiananmen incident, a situation which was a thorn in Sino-U.S. relations.

13. Nathan, "Human Rights in Chinese Foreign Policy," pp. 633–34.

14. Earlier in the summer, the Clinton administration had started worrying that U.S. human rights policy toward China was leading toward "a train wreck." Susumu Awanohara, "Collision Course: Pragmatists and Idealists Set to Clash over Asian Policy," *Far Eastern Economic Review*, February 3, 1994, p. 19.

15. Charles Krauthammer, "The Pushover Presidency," *Washington Post*, May 12, 1995, A25.

16. Nathan, "Human Rights in Chinese Foreign Policy." Also see Chapter Two.

17. An improved relationship with neighboring countries was an important goal in Chinese foreign policy after the Tiananmen incident as a response to Western pressure. See Zhu Qizhen, "China's Foreign Policy and China-U.S. Relations," *Beijing Review*, March 30, 1992, pp. 31–33; Takagi Seiichiro, "Posuto reisen kozo to chugoku gaiko no 'shinkaidan'" [The post-Cold War structure and the 'the new stage' in Chinese foreign policy], *Kokusai mondai* 394 (January 1993): 18–32; and Chen Jie, "Human Rights: ASEAN's New Importance to China," *Pacific Review* 6, 3 (1993): 227–37.

18. For discussions of Asian views of human rights, see James C. Hsiung, ed., *Human Rights in East Asia: A Cultural Perspective* (New York: Paragon House, 1986); Kishore Mahbubani, "The West and the Rest," *National Inter-*

est 28 (Summer 1992): 3–13; Tang, *Human Rights and International Relations in the Asia-Pacific Region*; Luo Yanhua, *Dongfangren kan renquan* [Orientals view human rights] (Beijing: Xinhua chubanshe, 1998); William Theodore de Bary and Tu Weiming, eds., *Confucianism and Human Rights* (New York: Columbia University Press, 1997); William Theodore de Bary, *Asian Values and Human Rights: A Confucian Communitarian Perspective* (Cambridge, Mass.: Harvard University Press, 2000); Joanne R. Bauer and Daniel A. Bell, eds., *The East Asian Challenge for Human Rights* (New York: Cambridge University Press, 1999); and Peter Van Ness and Nikhil Aziz, eds., *Debating Human Rights: Critical Essays from the United States and Asia* (London: Routledge, 1999). For China's appeal for an Asian perspective of human rights, see Ambassador Jin Yongjian's speech at the Asian Regional preparatory meeting in Bangkok in March 1993. "Asia's Major Human Rights Concerns," *Beijing Review,* April 19, 1993, pp. 10–11.

19. Awanohara, "Collision course," pp. 18–20.

20. *Human Rights Watch World Report 1995*, p. 146.

21. Interviews in Beijing on March 17 and March 22, 1994.

22. Very few Chinese students wanted the U.S. to withdraw MFN status from China. The debate was mainly between "conditional granting" and "nonconditional granting." See Yang Manke, "Zuihuiguo wenti de lixiang jieju" [An ideal outcome of the MFN issue], *China Spring* 9 (1991): 33–35.

23. David M. Lampton, "America's China Policy in the Age of the Finance Minister: Clinton Ends Linkage," *China Quarterly* 139 (September 1994): 597–621.

24. William Branigin, "Asians Welcome China Decision," *Washington Post,* May 29, 1994, A49.

25. Human Rights Watch/Asia, *Human Rights in the APEC Region: 1994* (New York: Human Rights Watch, November 1994), p. 16.

26. Clay Chandler, " 'Code of Conduct' Draft Assailed," *Washington Post,* March 28, 1995, D4.

27. Interview with a staff member of Amnesty International, Washington, D.C., May 8, 1995.

28. Except for a few firms such as Sears, Roebuck & Co., Timberland Co., and Levi Strauss & Co., no American businesses are willing to do anything about human rights in China. Steven Mufson, "The Beijing Duck: What U.S. Firms in China Don't Do for Human Rights," *Washington Post,* April 9, 1995, Cl, C4.

29. *Boston Globe,* March 7, 1996, p. 2.

30. John Shattuck's testimony to the International Operations and Human Rights Subcommittee of the House of Representatives, March 26, 1996.

31. Ibid.

32. Kent, *China, the United Nations, and Human Rights*, p. 73.

33. Shattuck's testimony, March 26, 1996.

34. Agence France Presse, April 23, 1996. Countries that supported the resolution included European Union members, the U.S., Australia, Brazil, Britain, Canada, and Japan. Countries that objected to the resolution included Bangladesh, Bhutan, Cuba, Egypt, India, Indonesia, Malaysia,

Nepal, Pakistan, and Sri Lanka. South Korea, the Philippines, and Russia abstained.

35. Interview with a senior official of the UN Human Rights Division, Chinese Foreign Ministry, Beijing, May 1996.

36. Interview with a Chinese scholar familiar with China's human rights diplomacy, Beijing, May 27, 1996.

37. Shattuck's testimony, March 26, 1996.

38. Agence France Presse, April 23, 1996.

39. Interview with a senior official of the UN Human Rights Division, Chinese Foreign Ministry, Beijing, May 1996.

40. Statement by Mike Jendrzejczyk, Washington Director of Human Rights Watch/Asia before the International Relations Subcommittees on Asia and the Pacific, International Operations and Human Rights, U.S. House of Representatives on March 16, 1995.

41. *Boston Globe*, October 1, 1995, p. 9.

42. *Economist*, June 8, 1996, p. 28.

43. Interview, Beijing, May 22, 1996.

44. This was based on my extensive interviews in Beijing in May 1996. There has also been much written along this line. For example, see Liu Shulin et al., *Dangdai zhongguo renquan zhuangkuang baogao* [Report on the human rights situation in China] (Shenyang: Liaoning remnin chubanshe, 1994), p. 5.

45. For a detailed two-part front page news story about how tension over Taiwan led to efforts to repair ties, see Barton Cellman, "U.S. and China Nearly Came to Blows in 1996" and "Reappraisal Led to New China Policy," *Washington Post*, June 21–22, 1998.

46. John F. Harris, "Clinton Waxes Idyllic on Pacific Rim's Future," *Washington Post*, November 21, 1996, A28.

47. R. Jeffrey Smith, "China Sold Nuclear Items Before Now," *Washington Post*, October 10, 1996, A38; "China May Cancel Proposed Sale of Nuclear Facility to Iran," *Washington Post*, November 6, 1996, A9; and Michael Dobbs and Steve Mufson, "Christopher cites 'progress' in China," *Washington Post*, November 21, 1996, A28.

48. Thomas W. Lippman, "Albright to 'Tell It Like It Is' on Human Rights," *Washington Post*, January 25, 1997, A4.

49. *Washington Post*, January 18, 1997, A10.

50. Based on my discussions with Chinese scholars and officials over the past few years, virtually no one has any illusion that the U.S. will stop human rights pressure on China.

51. Discussion with a top Chinese diplomat, December 1997.

52. For China's negotiating style, see Richard H. Solomon, *Chinese Negotiating Behavior: Pursuing Interests Through "Old Friends"* (Washington, D.C.: U.S. Institute of Peace Press, 1999).

53. Laura Myers, "Albright Eyes Challenge of China," Associated Press, January 29, 1997.

54. Michael Dobbs, "Human Rights Issue To Be Muted in China Talks," *Washington Post*, November 20, 1996, A27; and "Aide's Low Profile in Bei-

jing Signals White House Shift," *Washington Post*, November 25, 1996, A18. Direct human rights dialogues between the United States and China had not been held since 1995 when the Chinese broke off negotiations due to the U.S. attempt to condemn China at the UN Human Rights Commission.

55. See Ming Wan, "Human Rights in China 1997: Domestic Politics and Foreign Policy," in Joseph Y. S. Cheng, ed., *China Review 1998* (Hong Kong: Chinese University Press, 1998), pp. 209–33.

56. Interestingly, as Hong Kong's reversion to China went smoothly, two journalists from *Far Eastern Economic Review* suggested that "in a mere five months Hong Kong has changed from being a potential thorn in China's relations with the West to an unexpected force for reconciliation." Bruce Gilley and Nigel Holloway, "No Thorns: Territory Helps to Smooth Sino-U.S. Ties," *Far Eastern Economic Review*, September 25, 1997, p. 16.

57. The connection between the report and the administration's desire for an improved relationship was highlighted in the *Washington Post*. See Thomas W. Lippman, "China's Rights Record Improves in U.S. Report," *Washington Post*, January 31, 1998, A18.

58. There was also concern that the U.S. would be isolated, as the European Union had decided against sponsoring an anti-China resolution.

59. Stanley Roth's talk at the American Enterprise Institute, May 12, 1998.

60. See Chu Shulong, "Zhongmei hezuo yu fenqi" [Cooperation and differences between China and the U.S.], *Xiandai guoji guanxi* 6 (1998): 2–6.

61. *CQ Weekly*, January 16, 1999, p. 153.

62. Tom Raum, "Clinton Asked to Condemn China," Associated Press, February 25, 1999.

63. Michael Laris, "Albright 'Deplores' Beijing Crackdown," *Washington Post*, March 1, 1999, A13.

64. Miles A. Pomper and Chuck McCutcheon, "State Department Talks Tough to Beijing as GOP Assails 'Failed Policy,' " *CQ Weekly*, March 6, 1999, pp. 560–61.

65. "China Exults after U.S. Plan Fails," Associated Press, April 24, 1999.

66. Steven Mufson, "U.S. to Sponsor Rights Measure Critical of China," *Washington Post*, January 12, 2000, A14.

67. My extensive interviews in China in 1994, 1996, and 1999 clearly indicated such a trend.

68. This is based on my own observation in various cities in China in May 1999. For Western news stories about this Chinese mood, see John Leicester, "Bombing Changes Chinese View of U.S.," Associated Press, May 13, 1999.

69. For discussions of how intense and involved top-level leaders and officials in both China and the U.S. were in WTO negotiations, see Joseph Fewsmith, "China and the WTO: The Politics behind the Agreement," National Bureau of Asian Research, *NBR Report*, 1999; and Helene Cooper, Bob Davis, and Ian Johnson, "To Brink and Back: In Historic Pact, U.S. Opens Way for China to Finally Join the WTO," *Wall Street Journal*, November 16, 1999, A1.

70. *World Journal*, July 29, 2000, A2.

71. John Burgess, "Clinton to Press Hill to Back China Deal," *Washington Post*, January 11, 2000, E8.

72. Charles Babington, "China Softens Push for China Trade Bill," *Washington Post*, May 21, 2000, A6.

73. Charles Babington and Matthew Vita, "President Begins China Trade Push," *Washington Post*, March 9, 2000, A1; John Burgess, "A Winning Combination: Money, Message, and Clout," *Washington Post*, May 25, 2000, A4; and Matthew Vita and Juliet Eliperin, "House Passes China Trade Bill," *Washington Post*, May 25, 2000, A1.

74. Matthew Vita, "U.S. to Track Compliance by China," *Washington Post*, May 4, 2000, A4.

75. Matthew Vita and Juliet Eliperin, "China Trade Bill Gains Supporters," *Washington Post*, May 24, 2000, A1.

76. Steven M. Teles, "Public Opinion and Interest Groups in the Making of U.S.-China Policy," in Robert S. Ross, ed., *After the Cold War: Domestic Factors and U.S.-China Relations* (Armonk, N.Y.: M.E. Sharpe, 1998), pp. 40–69.

Chapter 4

1. Harish Kapur, *China and the European Economic Community: The New Connection* (Dordrecht: Martinus Nijhoff, 1986).

2. Cohen, "People's Republic of China," pp. 485–89.

3. Sikkink, "Power of Principled Ideas"; and Peter R. Baehr, *The Role of Human Rights in Foreign Policy* (New York: St. Martin's Press, 1994), pp. 105–24.

4. Cohen, "People's Republic of China," pp. 447–549.

5. For example, the EC established diplomatic relations with China but not the Council for Mutual Economic Assistance, in part to let the Soviet Union know that it was a force in world politics. Roy H. Ginsberg, *Foreign Policy Actions of the European Community: The Politics of Scale* (Boulder, Colo.: Lynne Rienner, 1989), pp. 68–69.

6. For Sino-European economic cooperation, see Hu Yuanxiang, *Legal and Policy Issues of the Trade and Economic Relations Between China and the EEC: A Comparative Study* (Deventer, Netherlands: Kluwer Law and Taxation, 1991).

7. Nathan, "Human Rights in Chinese Foreign Policy," pp. 624–28; Tian Jin et al., *Zhongguo zai lianheguo* [China in the UN] (Beijing: Shijie zhishi chubanshe, 1999), pp. 200–206.

8. A senior researcher at the China Society for Human Rights Studies argued that the Chinese Communist Party was always fighting for human rights although the party did not use the term explicitly. Interview, Beijing, May 26, 1999.

9. Dai Bingran, "Lengzhanhou shiqi zhongou guanxi zhanlue jichu chutan" [The strategic basis of Sino-European relations in the post Cold War era], in Song Xinning and Zhang Xiaojin, eds., *Zouxiang ershiyi shiji de zhongguo yu ouzhou* [China and Europe toward the twenty-first century] (Hong Kong: Xianggang shehuikexue chubanshe, 1997), pp. 98–99.

10. Roberto Suro, "Aid Accord Eludes Leaders at Summit," *New York Times*, July 11, 1990, A4.

11. The EC granted MFN status to China in the April 1978 Sino-EC trade agreement, which was replaced by the 1985 Trade and Economic Cooperation Agreement. Since the 1985 agreement expired in 1995, China's MFN status is now renewable every year automatically unless notice to the contrary is given. Xiao Zhi Yue, *Current EC Legal Developments: The EC and China* (London: Butterworths, 1993), p. 27.

12. *Deng Xiaoping Wenxuan*, p. 359.

13. For Patten's own take on the issue, see Christopher Patten, *East and West: China, Power, and the Future of Asia* (New York: Times Books, 1999).

14. Interview with a leading European specialist from the Institute for Western European Studies of the Chinese Academy of Social Sciences, Beijing, March 17, 1994. By contrast, the U.S. had a history of arms sales to the island.

15. *Deng Xiaoping Wenxuan*, p. 359. His words are translated by the author.

16. David Shambaugh, "China and Europe," *Annals of the American Academy of Political and Social Science* 519 (1992): 111.

17. This decision did not immediately improve the bilateral relationship, in part because Western Europe had now turned its attention to Eastern Europe, and EC-China economic relations did not look as promising as in the late 1970s. Xiao, *Current EC Legal Developments*, p. 1.

18. Liu Jiangyong and Wang Hongjun, "Cong dongjing huiyi kan xifang qiguo de xietiao yu maodun" [Coordination and divisions of the Tokyo G7 summit], *Xiandai guoji guanxi* 8 (1993): 19.

19. Wu Jiuyi, "Deguo xinyazhou zhengce chuxi" [Germany's new Asian policy], *Xiandai guoji guanxi* 12 (1993): 29–31.

20. *World Journal*, March 16, 1999, A7. He indicated that he would normally agree to look into the list of political activists.

21. Interview with a senior diplomat specializing in Western European affairs in the Chinese Foreign Ministry, Beijing, May 1999. He also confirmed that in every meeting, Western Europeans would discuss human rights and produce lists of jailed political activists.

22. "EU Mulls China Rights Issues," Associated Press, April 7, 1997.

23. Among non-European industrial countries, Australia, Canada, and Japan decided not to be cosponsors.

24. David Buchan and James Kynge, "China: United EU Line Urged on Human Rights," *Financial Times*, January 16, 1998.

25. Chen Yanni, "Li: Nation Welcomes EU's Wise Decision," *China Daily*, February 25, 1998.

26. Human Rights Watch, *Human Rights Watch World Report 1999*, p. 181.

27. *World Journal*, March 15, 1999, A7; "China Asks EU Not to Criticize It," Associated Press, March 16, 1999.

28. "EU Decries China's Rights Policies," Associated Press, March 23, 1999.

29. Stephanie Nebehay, "China Derails U.S. Proposal for UN Rebuke on Abuses," *Washington Post*, April 24, 1999, A14.

30. "China Exults after U.S. Plan Fails," Associated Press, April 24, 1999.

31. "China's British Friends," *Economist*, October 23, 1999, p.18.

32. *World Journal*, November 5, 1999, A7.

33. John Leicester, "China, EU Talk Trade, Human Rights," Associated Press, December 21, 1999.

34. *Far Eastern Economic Review*, September 16, 1999, p. 17.

35. After meeting with Chinese leaders, Patten commented that the Chinese "were as civil and courteous as you would have expected." "China Makes Peace with Patten," Associated Press, December 21, 1999.

36. Colum Lynch, "China Averts U.N. Human Rights Censure," *Washington Post*, April 19, 2000, A18.

37. Clay Chandler, "China, EU Sign Broad Trade Pact," *Washington Post*, May 20, 2000, A1.

38. Baehr, *The Role of Human Rights in Foreign Policy*, p. 124.

39. Patten, *East and West*, pp. xiv–xv.

40. "EU Toughens Myanmar Sanctions," Associated Press, April 10, 2000.

41. Der-Chin Horng, "The EU's New China Policy: The Dimension of Trade Relations," *Issues and Studies* 34, 7 (1998): 85–115; and Sutter, Robert G., *Chinese Policy Priorities and Their Implications for the United States* (Lanham, Md.: Rowman and Littlefield, 2000), p. 151.

42. As an example, when French Prime Minister Balladur visited Beijing in April 1994, he refused to intervene on behalf of Wei Jingsheng and Xu Wenli, two prominent Chinese dissidents who had been arrested again before his visit. Balladur argued that France's goal was to improve economic ties with Beijing. *Boston Globe*, April 9, 1994, p. 67.

43. Data are from <http://europa.eu.int>.

44. Hervé de Charette, "France as China's Multipolar Ally," *New Perspectives Quarterly* 14, 3 (1997): 28.

45. For example, see Peter R. Baehr, "Problems of Aid Conditionality: The Netherlands and Indonesia," *Third World Quarterly* 18, 2 (1997): 363–76.

46. Charette, "France as China's Multipolar Ally," pp. 26–27.

47. Lu Yaokun and Feng Zhonglin, "Deguo dui yazhou de zhanlue kaolu ji zhengce tiaozheng" [Germany's strategic considerations and policy adjustments toward China], *Xiandai guoji guanxi* 5 (1993): 15–20.

48. Christopher Burns, "France Won't Back UN on China," Associated Press, March 28, 1997.

49. Charles Trueheart, "France Polishes Its Diplomatic Image," *Washington Post*, October 28, 1999, A21.

50. As a Chinese international relations specialist noted, no one studies Sino-European human rights relations because they are not important. Discussion with the scholar, Beijing, May 27, 1999. He just returned from the annual meeting of the Chinese Association of European Studies. Among the more than 70 presenters, no one discussed the human rights issues at length.

51. See Dong, *Renquan zhongmei jiaoliang beiwanglu*; Jiang, *Shuishi yingjia zhongmei renquan jiaoliang jishi*; and Li, *Zhongmei guanxi zhong de renquan wenti*.

52. Wu Jiuyi, "Xiou duihua guanxi jinkuang yu qianjing" [Recent and

future developments in Western European relations with China], *Xiandai guoji guanxi* 7 (1993): 1–4; Song Xinning, "Zhongguo yu ouzhou mianxiang weilai" [China and Europe: facing the future), in Song and Zhang, eds., *Zouxiang ershiyi shiji de zhongguo yu ouzhou,* pp. 20–23; Wang Jinbiao and Feng Zhongping, "Oumeng tuixing geng jiji de duihua zhengce" [The European Union promotes a more active China policy], in Song and Zhang, eds., *Zouxiang ershiyi shiji de zhongguo yu ouzhou,* pp. 133–35; Wang Yi, "Zhongfa guanxi fazhan de dongli" [Momentum behind the development of Sino-French relations], *Guoji wenti yanjiu* 2 (1997): 31–36; and Feng Zhongping, "Jiuqi hou zhongying guanxi zouxiang" [Trend of Sino-UK relations after Hong Kong's return in 1997], *Xiandai guoji guanxi* 12 (1997): 19–23.

53. A senior diplomat with extensive posting experience in Western Europe recognized domestic pressure on Western European governments to deal with China's human rights but believed that European governments, unlike the U.S. government, are more in control of foreign policy and that economic interests drive their China policy. Interview, Beijing, May 1999. "Western European human rights pressure is not heavy," he commented.

54. Interview with a senior researcher and officer of the China Society for Human Rights Studies, Beijing, May 26, 1999. He based his observation on his trip to Northern Europe.

55. Dong, *Renquan zhongmei jiaoliang beiwanglu,* pp. 103–9; Jiang, *Shuishi yingjia zhongmei renquan jiaoliang jishi,* pp. 41–44; and Luo, *Dongfangren kan renquan,* pp. 17–18.

56. Disappointed human rights NGOs have considered China's economic statecraft as well as hard lobbying and political pressure as key factors for a weakening Western stance on human rights in China. For example, see Human Rights Watch, *Chinese Diplomacy, Western Hypocrisy and the UN Human Rights Commission* (New York: Human Rights Watch, March 1997).

57. Steven Mufson, "China Rewards France for Human Rights Backing with Aircraft Contract," *Washington Post,* May 16, 1997, A30.

58. *Washington Post,* May 17, 1999, A22.

59. Data are from <http://europa.eu.int>.

60. "China's Foreign Trade Up in 1999," *Beijing Review,* April 3, 2000.

61. Xinhua, May 10, 1999.

62. It also helped that Schröder indicated irritation over America's failure to provide a thorough investigation of the bombing of the Chinese embassy. William Drozdiak, "NATO Leaders Clash on Using Ground Troops," *Washington Post,* May 20, 1999, A1.

63. As one Chinese scholar maintains, while deeply convinced about human rights, leaders of major Western European nations have always been more flexible and pragmatic than Americans in actually dealing with human rights issues. Ren Feng, "Xiou lingdao dui oumeng waijiao zhanlue he ouzhong guanxi de kanfa" [Views of the main Western European leaders on the EU's foreign policy strategy and Euro-China relations], *Xiandai guoji guanxi* 4 (1998): 37.

64. *Human Rights Watch World Report 1999,* pp. 181–82.

65. *Washington Post*, February 25, 1998.

66. It should be noted that most European specialists in China are aware of the difficulties in European integration. This was reflected in most papers delivered at the 1997 annual conference of Chinese Association of European Studies. See Qiu Yuanlun and Shen Yannan, eds., *Ouzhou yu shijie* [Europe and the world] (Beijing: Zhonguo shehuikexue chubanshe, 1998).

67. Discussions with Chinese scholars and officials, May and June, 1999.

68. Yang Yiping, "Zhaoyan yu ershiyi shiji de ouzhong guanxi jiqi yingxiang" [Europe-China relations to the twenty-first century and its influence], in Song and Zhang, eds., *Zouxiang ershiyi shiji de zhongguo yu ouzhou*, pp. 106–20; Wu, "Xiou duihua guanxi jinkuang yu qianjing," pp. 1–4.

69. The new prime minister Tony Blair met the Chinese ambassador after the American ambassador. "Clearly, Britain is trying to turn Hong Kong from a stumbling block into a stepping stone into China." Frank Ching, "New Era for Britain and China," *Far Eastern Economic Review*, December 18, 1997, p. 37.

70. As an exception, in June 1996, the Chinese government canceled German Foreign Minister Klaus Kinkel's visit to Beijing, which had been scheduled for July, in retaliation for the German Parliament's adoption of a resolution condemning China's human rights record in Tibet. Earlier the Friedrich Naumann Foundation, which has close ties with Kinkel's Free Democratic Party, hosted a conference on Tibet in mid-June and invited the Dalai Lama to the conference. "Germany Pays for Loose Talk," *Economist*, June 29, 1996, p. 32.

71. Steven Mufson, "China Warns U.S. on Human Rights Resolution," *Washington Post*, April 11, 1997, A30.

72. Tian, *Zhongguo zai lianheguo*, pp. 220–21. Also, my interview with a European specialist of the Chinese Foreign Ministry who had been posted in Holland. Beijing, May 1999.

73. Interview, Beijing, May 1999.

74. Interview with a senior diplomat, Beijing, May 1999.

75. *Far Eastern Economic Review*, October 21, 1999, p. 8.

76. *Human Rights World Report 1999*, p. 181.

77. Feng Zhongping, "Dangqian oumeng duihua zhengce de sida tezheng" [Four characteristics in the EU's current China policy], *Xiandai guoji guanxi* 5 (1998): 13–14.

Chapter 5

1. Ishi Akira, "Taiwan ka pekin ka"[Taiwan or Beijing?], in Watanabe Akio, ed., *Sengo nihon no taigai seisaku* [Postwar Japanese foreign policy] (Tokyo: Yuhikaku, 1985), pp. 62–85; and Michael Schaller, *Altered States: The United States and Japan Since the Occupation* (New York: Oxford University Press, 1997).

2. Sun Pinghua, *Rizhong yohao suixianglu* [My reminiscences of Sino-Japanese friendship] (Beijing: Shijie zhishi chubanshe, 1987); Quansheng Zhao, *Japanese Policymaking: The Politics Behind Politics—Informal Mechanisms*

and the Making of China Policy (Hong Kong: Oxford University Press, 1996); Furukawa Mantaro, *Nitchu sengo kankeishi* [A history of postwar Sino-Japanese relations] (Tokyo: Hara shobo, 1988); Besshi Yukio, "Sengo nitchu keankei to hiseishiki sesshokusha" [Informal contact-makers in postwar Japanese diplomacy toward China], *Kokusai seiji* 75 (October, 1983): 99–113; Allen S. Whiting, *China Eyes Japan* (Berkeley: University of California Press, 1989); and Chae-Jin Lee, *China and Japan: New Economic Diplomacy* (Stanford, Calif.: Hoover Institution, Stanford University, 1984).

3. Shinkichi Eto, "Evolving Sino-Japanese Relations," *Journal of International Affairs* 37, 1 (Summer 1983): 49.

4. Sakamoto Yashikazu, "Nihon ni okeru kokuzai reisen to kokunai reisen" [The international Cold War and domestic Cold War in Japan], *Reisen seiji teki kosatsu* [The Cold War: political considerations] (Tokyo: Iwanami, 1963), pp. 331–75.

5. Tanaka Akihiko, "Nihon gaiko to kokunai seiji no renkan gaiatsu no seijigaku" [The connection between Japanese diplomacy and domestic politics: politics of external pressure], *Kokusai mondai* 348 (March 1989): 23–36.

6. Despite an improving bilateral relationship, several highly publicized "incidents" took place. See Tanaka Akihiko, *Nitchu kankei, 1945–1990* [Japan-China relations, 1945–1990] (Tokyo: Tokyo Daigaku shuppankai, 1991), pp. 120–64. Chinese books on contemporary Sino-Japanese relations normally contain substantial discussions of these disputes, focusing on why some elements in Japan continue to hurt the feelings of Chinese people and how the Japanese government has resolved the disputes partly to Beijing's satisfaction. For example, see Lin Daizhao, *Zhanhou zhongri guanxishi* [Postwar Sino-Japanese relations] (Beijing: Beijing daxue chubanshe, 1992); and Wu Xuewen, Lin Liande, and Xu Zhixian, *Zhongri guanxi* [Sino-Japanese relations] (Beijing: Shishi chubanshe, 1995).

7. For discussions of Japan's balancing act, see Tanaka, *Nitchu kankei*, pp. 172–87 and Takagi, "Human Rights in Japanese Foreign Policy."

8. See Inada Juichi, "Ajia josei no hendo to nihon no ODA" [The changes in Asia and Japan's ODA] *Kokusai mondai* 360 (March 1990): 58–59; and Quansheng Zhao, "Japan's Aid Diplomacy with China," in Bruce M. Koppel and Robert M. Orr, Jr., eds., *Japan's Foreign Aid: Power and Policy in a New Era* (Boulder, Colo.: Westview Press, 1993), pp. 163–87.

9. Yasunobu Sato, "New Directions in Japanese Foreign Policy: Promoting Human Rights and Democracy in Asia—ODA Perspective," in Edward Friedman, ed., *The Politics of Democratization: Generalizing East Asian Experiences* (Boulder, Colo.: Westview Press, 1994), pp. 103–5. In a recent case, the Tokyo High Court rejected an appeal from a Chinese dissident for political asylum, who lost his initial application in 1991 on technical grounds. Since the 1989 Tiananmen incident, the Japanese government has not accepted any Chinese dissidents as political refugees, although it did allow a few dozen Chinese dissidents to renew their stay in Japan on a half-year renewable basis. *Human Rights Watch World Report 1997*, p. 171.

10. Tanino Sakutaro, "Mutual Effort Will Be Needed to Further Bolster Sino-Japanese Relations," *Japan Times*, Oct 1, 1990, p. 8.

11. *Renmin ribao*, overseas ed., March 16, 1990, p. 6.

12. Maureen Dowd, "Bush Accepts Japanese Aid to China, with Limits," *New York Times*, July 8, 1990, A6. The summit issued a political declaration that acknowledged a lessening of Chinese repression and agreed to ease sanctions if improvement continued. This declaration resulted from heated negotiations among the summiteers. Japanese wanted to reward China while the French and others wanted to maintain a hard-line position. Roberto Suro, "Aid Accord Eludes Leaders at Summit," *New York Times*, July 11, 1990, A4. Also wishing not to isolate China, Bush quietly supported Kaifu's plan to resume aid to China. "Why Aid to China Is a High-Stakes Gamble for Japan," *Business Week*, July 30, 1990, p. 39.

13. "Why Aid to China Is a High-Stakes Gamble for Japan," p. 39.

14. Japanese Ministry of Foreign Affairs, *Financial Statistics of Japan*, 1993, pp. 72–75, and 1989, p. 95.

15. Takagi, "Human Rights in Japanese Foreign Policy," pp. 102–4; and Inada Juichi, "Democratization, Marketization, and Japan's Emerging Role as Foreign Aid Donor," U.S.-Japan Program Occasional Paper 93–03, Center for International Affairs, Harvard University. Moreover, some leading Japanese scholars also saw human rights diplomacy as interference in the internal affairs of developing countries by rich nations. See Okabe Tatsumi, "Tenanmon jiken to kongo no chugoku" [The Tiananmen incident and future China], *Kokusai mondai* 358 (January 1990): 2–16.

16. *Xinhua yuebao*, January 1990, p. 149.

17. "Deng on Handling International Relations," *Beijing Review*, October 2, 1989, p. 5.

18. *Renmin ribao*, overseas ed., July 7, 1990, p. 1.

19. *Renmin ribao*, overseas ed., July 13, 1990, p.1.

20. For examples, see *Renmin ribao*, overseas ed., December 12, 1989, p. 6; July 3, 1990, p. 1; July 7, 1990, pp. 1, 4.

21. Tai Ming Cheung and Louise do Rosario, "Kaifu's China Visit Lessens Peking's Isolation: Seal of Approval," *Far Eastern Economic Review*, August 22, 1991, p.10.

22. It is reported that Jiang Zemin expressed "understanding" of Japan's decision to cooperate in maintaining international sea-lanes during his talk with Nakasone in May 1991. Ono Iwao, "Jiang Acknowledges Japan's Motives in Gulf," *Daily Yomiuri*, May 4, 1991, p. 1.

23. Richard P. Cronin, *Japan, the U.S., and Prospects for the Asia-Pacific Century: Three Scenarios for the Future* (New York: St. Martin's Press, 1992), pp. 65–66.

24. Reflecting the general mood, a *Business Week* article warned in July 1990 "if Japanese businesses get a big jump on U.S. companies, who are being hampered in China by U.S. policies, they risk a backlash from U.S. executives." "Why Aid to China Is a High-Stakes Gamble for China."

25. Kaifu Masahiko, "Kaifu Apologizes for Past Aggression, Urges China to Help in New World Order," *Daily Yomiuri*, August 12, 1991, p.1. In the end, the two governments compromised in the mid-1990s with a two-phase strategy for the Fourth Yen Loan.

26. Cheung and do Rosario, "Kaifu's China Visit Lessens Peking's Isolation," p. 10.

27. David Arase, "Japan's Foreign Policy and Asian Democratization," in Edward Friedman, ed., *The Politics of Democratization: Generalizing East Asian Experiences* (Boulder, Colo.: Westview Press, 1994), pp. 81–101; and Robert M. Orr, Jr., "Political Agendas: A New World Order Through Foreign Aid?" in Barbara Stallings et al., *Common Vision, Different Paths: The United States and Japan in the Developing World* (Washington, D.C.: Overseas Development Council, 1993), pp. 83–97.

28. *Far Eastern Economic Review,* June 9, 1994, p. 48.

29. See David Arase, "Japanese Policy Toward Democracy and Human Rights in Asia," *Asian Survey* 33, 10 (October 1993): 935–52.

30. Human Rights Watch, *Human Rights Watch World Report 1995,* p. 163.

31. Much has been written about this debate. For example, see Amartya Sen, "Human Rights and Asian Values," *New Republic,* July 14, 1997, pp. 33–40; Peter R. Moody, Jr., "Asian Values," *Journal of International Affairs* 50, 1 (Summer 1996): 166–92; John D. Montgomery, ed., *Values in Education: Social Capital Formation in Asia and the Pacific* (Hollis, N.H.: Hollis Publishing Company, 1995); and Hsiung, *Human Rights in East Asia*; and Bauer and Bell, *The East Asian Challenge for Human Rights.*

32. William Branigin, "Asians Welcome China Decision," *Washington Post,* May 29, 1994, A49.

33. Susan J. Pharr and Ming Wan, "Japan's Leadership: Shaping a New Asia," in Hideo Sato and I. M. Destler, eds., *Leadership Sharing in the New International System: Japan and the U.S.*, Special Research Project on the New International System, University of Tsukuba, Japan, September 1996, pp. 133–70.

34. Yasuhiro Ueki, "Japan's UN Diplomacy: Sources of Passivism and Activism," in Gerald L. Curtis, ed., *Japan's Foreign Policy After the Cold War: Coping with Change* (Armonk, N.Y.: M.E. Sharpe, 1993), p. 351.

35. Liu Jiangyong, ed., *Kuashiji de riben zhengzhi jingji waijiao xinqushi* [Japan to the next century: new trends in politics, economics, and diplomacy] (Beijing: Shishi chubanshe, 1995), p. 427.

36. Some Japan specialists in China believed that this was the best period in the history of Sino-Japanese relations. Jiang Lifeng, *Zhongri guanxi sanlun* [Past, present, and future of Sino-Japanese relations] (Harbin: Heilongjiang jiaoyu chubanshe, 1996), p. 207.

37. IMF, *Direction of Trade Statistics Yearbook,* 1996, pp. 267–69; and 1997, pp. 157–59.

38. *Financial Statistics of Japan,* various years.

39. Ming Wan, "A Comparison of Sino-Japanese and Sino-American High-Level Official Contacts Since 1972," U.S.-Japan Program Occasional Paper, 94–15, Program on U.S.-Japan Relations, Center for International Affairs, Harvard University, 1994.

40. For different views on the emperor's visit, see four articles written by Tanino Sakutaro, Eto Shinkichi and Kobori Keiichiron, and Nakajima Mineo in *Japan Echo* 19, 4 (Winter 1992): 8–26. Opponents were also con-

cerned about financial liabilities of any imperial apology, China's territorial dispute with Japan, and potential manipulation of the emperor for political purposes.

41. A Japanese diplomat confirmed privately that human rights in China was not an important bilateral issue. His main concern was a rupture in Sino-U.S. relations. Beijing, March 24, 1994.

42. Based on my own observation and discussions with Chinese scholars and officials in Beijing, March 1994.

43. Interview with a senior officer of the UN Human Rights Division, Ministry of Foreign Affairs, Beijing, May 1996. Nanjing was the capital of the Republic of China. The Japanese army massacred Chinese civilians in the city in December 1937. "Comfort women" refers to the Asian women forced into prostitution by the Japanese army during the war.

44. Matt Miller, "Overdue Interest," *Far Eastern Economic Review*, January 8, 1998, pp. 62–64.

45. Sidney Jones, "Culture Clash," *China Rights Forum* (Summer 1993): 8–9 and 22; Gordon Fairclough, "Standing Firm: Asia Sticks to Its View of Human Rights," *Far Eastern Economic Review*, April 15, 1993, p. 22.

46. *Human Rights Watch World Report 1994*, p. 170.

47. Talks with Foreign Affairs Ministry Officials. Makuhari, Japan, September 1996.

48. *Human Rights Watch World Report 1994*, pp. 169–70.

49. Interview with a senior officer from Human Rights Watch/Asia on April 21, 1995, who had confirmed this from several sources in Japan and the U.S.

50. Interview with an official of the Japan Desk of the State Department, Washington, D.C., May 9, 1995.

51. "Japan Suggests Leeway for China on Rights," *Boston Globe*, March 22, 1994, p. 14.

52. Interview cited in note 50.

53. Note that Japan's prison situation and its treatment of minorities and foreigners have also received international criticism. See State Department, "Japan Report on Human Rights Practices for 1996," January 30, 1997 and Human Rights Watch/Asia, "Prison Conditions in Japan," March 1995.

54. Junji Nakagawa, "Legal Problems of Japan's ODA Guidelines: Aid and Democracy, Human Rights and Peace," *Japanese Annual of International Law* 36 (1993): 77.

55. Liu, "Renquan wenti yu riben de lichang jiqi duihua taidu."

56. Takashi Inoguchi, "Japan's Foreign Policy in East Asia," *Current History* 91, 569 (December 1992): 408.

57. Mike M. Mochizuki, "Japan and the Strategic Quadrangle," in Michael Mandelbaum, ed., *The Strategic Quadrangle: Russia, China, Japan, and the U.S. in East Asia* (New York: Council on Foreign Relations Press, 1995), pp. 134–35.

58. Arase, "Japan's Foreign Policy and Asian Democratization," pp. 96–97.

59. See Motoko Shuto, "Human Rights NGOs in Southeast Asia and

Japan's Approaches to Democratization," paper presented at the annual conference of the International Studies Association, Minneapolis, March 18, 1998, p. 7.

60. Michael H. Armacost, *Friends or Rivals? The Insider's Account of U.S.-Japan Relations* (New York: Columbia University Press, 1996), pp. 138–39.

61. Interview with an official at the Japan Desk, State Department, Washington, D.C., May 9, 1995.

62. This was repeatedly confirmed in interviews and discussions with Chinese and Japanese foreign ministry officials in Beijing in May 1996 and May 1999, in Makuhari, Japan in September 1996, and in Washington, D.C. throughout 2000. Most of the officials, some very senior, have been directly involved in bilateral discussions and negotiations.

63. Interestingly, Li did not discuss the history issue. Koichi Iitake, "Li Peng, Hashimoto Set Aside Differences in Talks," *Asahi shimbun online,* November 12, 1997.

64. Japan is now hedging against a rising China. See Michael J. Green, "Managing Chinese Power: The View from Japan," in Alastair Iain Johnston and Robert S. Ross, eds., *Engaging China: The Management of an Emerging Power* (London: Routledge, 1999), pp. 152–75.

65. For Japan's environmental ODA to China, see Susan J. Pharr and Ming Wan, "Yen for the Earth: Japan's Proactive China Environment Policy," in Michael B. McElroy, Chris P. Nielsen, and Peter Lydon, eds., *Energizing China: Reconciling Environmental Protection and Economic Growth* (Cambridge, Mass.: Harvard University Committee on the Environment, Harvard University Press, 1998), pp. 601–38.

66. Tokyo was particularly annoyed about Beijing's disregard of earlier Japanese warnings. Interviews with Japanese diplomats at the Japanese embassy, Washington, D.C., May 22, 1995 and in Cambridge, Mass., June 2, 1995. Japan resumed grant aid to China in March 1997 after China signed the Comprehensive Test Ban Treaty.

67. Jiang wanted to have an apology from Japanese similar to the one Korean President Kim had received earlier. But the Japanese side saw a major difference between China and South Korea. Kim was rewarded because he had adopted measures to improve relations with Japan such as opening the market for Japanese cultural products and it was believed that this apology would close the chapter. In contrast, the Japanese felt that China would continue to raise the history issue and did not want to yield at that time due to strong domestic opposition, especially in the Diet. Chinese experts admitted that Jiang had miscalculated Tokyo's possible reactions. Interviews with Chinese analysts in Beijing and Shanghai, May and June 1999, and with Japanese diplomats familiar with Jiang's visit to Japan in Washington, D.C. in May, July, and September 1999.

68. Jiang, *Zhongri guanxi sanlun,* pp. 207–10, 221–24.

69. This point is based on my interviews of and discussions with a number of Japanese Foreign Ministry officials, including five officials who deal directly with China. Their views on the issue have been consistent in 1994–99. In fact, one gets the strong impression that they really do not think about this option at all.

70. Interview with a senior Chinese official of the UN Human Rights Division, Ministry of Foreign Affairs, Beijing, May 1996.

71. Li, *Zhongmei guanxi zhong de renquan wenti*, pp. 127–51.

72. Steven Mufson, "Gingrich Tells China U.S. to Defend Taiwan," *Washington Post*, March 31, 1997, A17.

73. Elaine Kurtenbach, "China Suspends Denmark Exchanges," Associated Press April 15, 1997.

74. Japan Ministry of Foreign Affairs Press Conference, October 24, 1997.

75. Discussion with a Japanese diplomat specializing in China affairs. Washington, D.C., September 25, 1999.

76. Discussion with a China specialist in the Japanese Foreign Ministry. Washington, D.C., September 21, 1999.

77. *Human Rights Watch World Report 1996*, p. 165.

78. Talk with an NSC staff member, March 28, 1997; talk with an official at the Japan Desk of the State Department, January 22, 1999; and talk with a Japanese embassy official, May 14, 1999.

79. Takagi, "Human Rights in Japanese Foreign Policy," pp. 100–101.

80. Prime Minister's Office, "Summary of Public Opinion Survey on Diplomacy," March 1994, pp. 19–20.

81. For example, a Japanese diplomat who specialized in China noted that he used to believe that the Chinese Communist Party could achieve reform but Tiananmen taught him a big lesson, that is, communism is communism. Discussion with the official, February 8, 2000.

82. Discussion with a Japanese diplomat, Washington, D.C., July 1, 1999. But he recognized that Japanese media criticism of China is not conducive to a strong relationship.

83. Some leading Japanese experts on China also believe that current Chinese leaders, unlike their predecessors, are not familiar with how things work in Japan and how to push the right buttons.

Chapter 6

1. For a book on the international human rights regime, see Donnelly, *Universal Human Rights in Theory and Practice*.

2. Samuel S. Kim, "China and the United Nations," in Elizabeth Economy and Michel Oksenberg, eds., *China Joins the World: Progress and Prospects* (New York: Council on Foreign Relations, 1999), p. 45.

3. Kent, *China, the United Nations, and Human Rights*, pp. 40–42.

4. Lu, *The Dynamics of Foreign-Policy Decisionmaking in China*, pp. 56–57.

5. Discussion with the diplomat, Beijing, June 2, 1999. He also emphasized the impact of the Cultural Revolution.

6. Tian, *Zhongguo zai lianheguo*, pp. 34–35, p. 200. Note that this book was written by Chinese diplomats heavily involved in UN diplomacy.

7. Kim, "China and the United Nations," p. 46.

8. This is a point emphasized by virtually every Chinese book on China's relations with the UN. For example, see Wang Xingfang, ed., *Zhongguo yu*

lianheguo jinian lianheguo chengli wushi zhounian [China and the UN: in commemoration of the fiftieth anniversary of the UN] (Beijing: Shijie zhishi chubanshe, 1995), pp. 1–25. This book was reviewed by the UN Association of China.

9. Tian, *Zhongguo zai lianheguo*, pp. 204–5.

10. Wang, *Zhongguo yu lianheguo*, p. 348; and Li, *Zhongmei guanxi zhong de renquan wenti*, pp. 130–31.

11. For China's relations with Eastern Europe at this turning point, see Alyson J. K. Bailes, "China and Eastern Europe: A Judgement on the 'Socialist Community,'" *Pacific Review* 3, 3 (1990): 222–42.

12. Kent, *China, the United Nations, and Human Rights*, p. 61.

13. Reed Brody, Maureen Convery, and David Weissbrodt, "The 42nd Session of the Sub-Commission on Prevention of Discrimination and Protection of Minorities," *Human Rights Quarterly* 13, 2 (May 1991): 274.

14. Dong, *Renquan*, p. 65.

15. Tian, *Zhongguo zai lianheguo*, p. 217.

16. See Bin Yu, "China and its Asian Neighbors: Implications for Sino-U.S. Relations," in Yong Deng and Fei-Ling Wang, eds., *In the Eyes of the Dragon: China Views the World* (Lanham, Md.: Rowman and Littlefield, 1999): 183–210; and Jie Chen, "Human Rights: ASEAN's New Importance to China," *Pacific Review* 6, 3 (1993): 227–37.

17. Interview with a senior research fellow at the Institute of West Asian and African Studies of Chinese Academy of Social Sciences, Beijing, March 21, 1994. Also see Huang Shaoyu, "Mianxiang ershiyi shiji de zhongguo yu feizhou guanxi" [China's relations with Africa to the 21st century], *Xiandai guoji guanxi* 5 (1996): 26–30.

18. Kent, *China, the United Nations, and Human Rights*, p. 65; and Dong, *Renquan*, pp. 65–68.

19. Dong, *Renquan*, pp. 75–89.

20. Li, *Zhongmei guanxi zhong de renquan wenti*, pp. 134–36.

21. Tian, *Zhongguo zai lianheguo*, pp. 208–9.

22. Fan Guoxiang, "Thoughts on Human Rights Conference," *Beijing Review*, April 1, 1991, pp. 14–15.

23. The text of the speech published in *Beijing Review*, December 21, 1992, pp. 12–13.

24. Jin Yongjian's speech at the Asian Regional Preparatory Meeting for the World Conference on Human Rights in Bangkok, March 30, 1993. Excerpts in *Beijing Review*, April 19, 1993, pp. 10–11.

25. Kent, *China, the United Nations, and Human Rights*, pp. 165–68.

26. Fairclough, "Standing Firm."

27. Dong, *Renquan jiben wenxian yaolan*, pp. 206–8.

28. Luo, *Dongfangren kan renquan*, p. 83. The direct quote was translated by this author.

29. Kent, *China, the United Nations, and Human Rights*, pp. 173–81.

30. Tian, *Zhongguo zai lianheguo*, pp. 211–15.

31. See Solomon, *Chinese Negotiating Behavior*.

32. Dong, *Renquan jiben wenxian yaolan*, pp. 319–20.

33. Luo, *Dongfangren kan renquan*, pp. 13–20.

34. The commentary was translated into English. *Beijing Review*, March 16, 1992, p. 11.

35. Interview, Beijing, May 1996.

36. "Western Anti-China Draft Rejected," *Beijing Review*, March 21, 1994, p. 37.

37. Merle Goldman, "Behind the Scenes at the UN Human Rights Conference," *CFIA Dossier* (Harvard University), April 29, 1993, pp. 1–2.

38. Ibid., p. 2.

39. *Human Rights Watch World Report, 1996*, p. 147.

40. Human Rights Watch/Asia, "Chinese Diplomacy, Western Hypocrisy, and the U.N. Human Rights Commission," March 1997.

41. Tian, *Zhongmei guanxi zhong de reckon wenti*, p. 140; and Li, *Zhongmei guanxi zhong de renquan wenti*, pp. 139–40.

42. Interview, Beijing, May 1996.

43. The assertive Chinese behavior was highly publicized in the Chinese media and highlighted in Chinese writings. See Tian, *Zhongmei guanxi zhong de reckon wenti*, pp. 141–42; and Dong, *Renquan*, pp. 115–23.

44. Kent, *China, the United Nations, and Human Rights*, pp. 74–75.

45. Li, *Zhongmei guanxi zhong de renquan wenti*, p. 146.

46. "An Interview with China's Zhu Rongji," *Wall Street Journal*, April 6, 1999, A23.

47. Walden Bello, "China at 50: A Success Story," *Far Eastern Economic Review*, October 14, 1999, p. 60.

48. Hishammuddin Hussein, "Calm Approach to Rights," *Far Eastern Economic Review*, October 9, 1997, p. 39.

49. *Washington Post*, July 30, 1997, A1.

50. Thomas W. Lippman, "Albright Treads Carefully among African Leaders," *Washington Post*, December 15, 1997, A24.

51. Human Rights Watch/Asia, "Chinese Diplomacy, Western Hypocrisy, and the U.N. Human Rights Commission"; and Human Rights in China, "U.N. Commission on Human Rights Fails to Discuss China Resolution," April 23, 1996.

52. *Human Rights Watch World Report, 1999*, p. 181.

53. Guo Guanqiao, *Yige daguo jueqi de kunyou* [The difficulties and worries of a rising power] (Beijing: Shishi chubanshe, 1999), pp. 203–4.

54. Kent, *China, the United Nations, and Human Rights*, p. 247.

Bibliography

Arase, David. "Japan's Foreign Policy and Asian Democratization." In Edward Friedman, ed., *The Politics of Democratization: Generalizing East Asian Experiences*. Boulder, Colo.: Westview Press, 1994, pp. 81–101.

———. "Japanese Policy Toward Democracy and Human Rights in Asia." *Asian Survey* 33, 10 (October 1993): 935–52.

Armacost, Michael H. *Friends or Rivals? The Insider's Account of U.S.-Japan Relations*. New York: Columbia University Press, 1996.

Baehr, Peter R. "Problems of Aid Conditionality: The Netherlands and Indonesia." *Third World Quarterly* 18, 2 (1997): 363–76.

———. *The Role of Human Rights in Foreign Policy*. New York: St. Martin's Press, 1994.

Bailes, Alyson J. K. "China and Eastern Europe: A Judgement on the 'Socialist Community.'" *Pacific Review* 3, 3 (1990): 222–42.

Bauer, Joanne R. and Daniel A. Bell, eds. *The East Asian Challenge for Human Rights*. New York: Cambridge University Press, 1999.

Besshi Yukio. "Sengo nitchu keankei to hiseishiki sesshokusha" [Informal contact-makers in postwar Japanese diplomacy toward China]. *Kokusai seiji* 75 (October 1983): 99–113.

Brody, Reed, Maureen Convery, and David Weissbrodt. "The 42nd Session of the Sub-Commission on Prevention of Discrimination and Protection of Minorities." *Human Rights Quarterly* 13, 2 (May 1991): 260–90.

Bush, George and Brent Scowcroft. *A World Transformed*. New York: Vintage Books, 1998.

Chan, Alfred L. and Paul Nesbitt-Larking. "Critical Citizenship and Civil Society in Contemporary China." *Canadian Journal of Political Science* 28, 2 (June/July 1995): 293–309.

Charette, Hervé de. "France as China's Multipolar Ally." *New Perspectives Quarterly* 14, 3 (Summer 1997): 26–29.

Chen, Jie. "Human Rights: ASEAN's New Importance to China." *Pacific Review* 6, 3 (1993): 227–37.

Chen, Jie, Yang Zhong, and Jan William Hillard. "The Level and Sources of Popular Support for China's Current Political Regime." *Communist and Post-Communist Studies* 30, 1 (1997): 45–64.

China Social Investigation Institute. *Zhongguo guoqing baogao* [Report on China's conditions] (Shenyang: Liaoning renmin chubanshe, 1998).

Chiu, Hungdah. "Chinese Attitudes Toward International Law of Human Rights in the Post-Mao Era." In Victor C. Falkenheim, ed., *Chinese Politics from Mao to Deng.* New York: Paragon House, 1989, pp. 237–70.

Christensen, Thomas. "Chinese Realpolitik." *Foreign Affairs* 75, 5 (September/October 1996): 37–52.

Chu Shulong. "Zhongmei hezuo yu fenqi" [Cooperation and differences between China and the U.S.]. *Xiandai guoji guanxi* 6 (1998): 2–6.

Cohen, Roberta. "People's Republic of China: The Human Rights Exception." *Human Rights Quarterly* 9, 4 (November 1987): 447–549.

Cronin, Richard P. *Japan, the U.S., and Prospects for the Asia-Pacific Century: Three Scenarios for the Future.* New York: St. Martin's Press, 1992.

Dai Bingran. "Lengzhanhou shiqi zhongou guanxi zhanlue qichu chutan" [The strategic basis of Sino-Eurorean relations in the post-Cold War era]. In Song Xinning and Zhang Xiaojin, eds., *Zouxiang ershiyi shiji de zhongguo yu ouzhou* [China and Europe toward the twenty-first century]. Hong Kong: Xianggang shehui chubanshe, 1997, pp. 98–105.

Davis, Michael C., ed. *Human Rights and Chinese Values: Legal, Philosophical, and Political Perspectives.* Hong Kong: Oxford University Press, 1995.

De Bary, William Theodore. *Asian Values and Human Rights: A Confucian Communitarian Perspective.* Cambridge, Mass.: Harvard University Press, 2000.

De Bary, William Theodore and Tu Weiming, eds. *Confucianism and Human Rights.* New York: Columbia University Press, 1997.

Deng Xiaoping. *Deng Xiaoping wenxuan* [Deng's selected works], vol. 3. Beijing: Renmin chubanshe, 1993.

Deng, Yong and Fei-Ling Wang, eds. *In the Eyes of the Dragon: China Views the World.* Lanham, Md.: Rowman and Littlefield, 1999.

Donnelly, Jack. *International Human Rights.* 2nd ed. Boulder, Colo.: Westview Press, 1998.

———. "International Human Rights: A Regime Analysis." *International Organization* 40, 3 (Summer 1986): 599–642.

———. *Universal Human Rights in Theory and Practice.* Ithaca, N.Y.: Cornell University Press, 1989.

Dong Yunhu, ed. *Renquan jiben wenxian yaolan* [Collection of basic human rights documents]. Shenyang: Liaoning renmin chubanshe, 1994.

———, ed. *Renquan zhongmei jiaoliang beiwanglu* [Human rights: memorandum on Sino-U.S. contest]. Chengdu: Sichuan renmin chubanshe, 1998.

Drinan, Robert F. and Teresa T. Kuo. "The 1991 Battle for Human Rights in China." *Human Rights Quarterly* 14, 1 (February 1992): 21–42.

Edwards, R. Randle, Louis Henkin, and Andrew J. Nathan. *Human Rights in China.* New York: Columbia University Press, 1986.

Eto, Shinkichi. "Evolving Sino-Japanese Relations." *Journal of International Affairs* 37, 1 (Summer, 1983): 49–65.

Fang Jue. "A Program for Democratic Reform." *Journal of Democracy* 9, 4 (October 1998): 9–19.

Feng Zhongping. "Dangqian oumeng duihua zhengce de sida tezheng"

[Four characteristics in the EU's curent China policy]. *Xiandai guoji guanxi* 5 (1998): 12–14.

———. "Jiuqi hou zhongying guanxi zouxiang" [Trend of Sino-UK relations after Hong Kong's return in 1997]. *Xiandai guoji guanxi* 12 (1997): 19–23.

Fewsmith, Joseph. "China and the WTO: The Politics Behind the Agreement." National Bureau of Asian Research, *NBR Report*, 1999.

Finnemore, Martha and Kathryn Sikkink. "International Norm Dynamics and Political Change." *International Organization* 52, 4 (Autumn 1998): 887–917.

Foot, Rosemary. *The Practice of Power: U.S. Relations with China Since 1949.* Oxford: Clarendon Press, 1997.

Forsythe, David P. *The Internationalization of Human Rights.* Lexington, Mass.: Lexington Books, 1991.

Friedman, Edward, ed. *The Politics of Democratization: Generalizing East Asian Experiences.* Boulder, Colo.: Westview Press, 1994.

Friedman, Edward, Paul Pickowicz, and Mark Selden. *Chinese Village, Socialist State.* New Haven, Conn.: Yale University Press, 1991.

Furukawa Mantaro. *Nitchu sengo kankeishi* [A history of postwar Sino-Japanese relations]. Tokyo: Hara shobo, 1988.

Gao Hongjun. "Zhongguo gongmin quanli yishi de yanjin" [The awakening of consciousness of rights among Chinese citizens]. In Xia Yong, ed., *Zouxiang quanli de shidai zhongguo gongmin quanli fazhan yanjiu* [Toward an era of rights: research on development of civil rights in China]. Beijing: Zhongguo zhengfa daxue chubanshe, 1995, pp. 43–68.

Ginsberg, Roy H. *Foreign Policy Actions of the European Community: The Politics of Scale.* Boulder, Colo.: Lynne Rienner, 1989.

Goldman, Merle. "Human Rights in the People's Republic of China." *Daedalus* 112, 4 (Fall 1983): 111–38.

———. "Politically Engaged Intellectuals in the Deng-Jiang Era: A Changing Relationship with the Party-State." *China Quarterly* 145 (March 1996): 35–52.

Goldman, Merle, Perry Link, and Su Wei. "China's Intellectuals in the Deng Era." In Lowell Dittmer and Samuel S. Kim, eds., *China's Quest for National Identity.* Ithaca, N.Y.: Cornell University Press, 1993, pp. 125–53.

Goldstein, Avery. "Political Implications of a Slowdown." *Orbis* 43, 2 (Spring 1999): 203–22.

Green, Michael J. "Managing Chinese Power: The View from Japan." In Alastair Iain Johnston and Robert S. Ross, eds., *Engaging China: The Management of an Emerging Power.* London: Routledge, 1999, pp. 152–75.

Guo Guanqiao. *Yige daguo jueqi de kunyou* [The difficulties and worries of a rising power]. Beijing: Shishi chubanshe, 1999.

Harbour, Frances V. *Thinking About International Ethics: Moral Theory and Cases from American Foreign Policy.* Boulder, Colo.: Westview Press, 1998.

Harding, Harry. *A Fragile Relationship: The United States and China Since 1972.* Washington, D.C.: Brookings Institution Press, 1992.

———. "The Halting Advance of Pluralism." *Journal of Democracy* 9, 1 (January 1998): 11–17.

Horng, Der-Chin. "The EU's New China Policy: The Dimension of Trade Relations." *Issues and Studies* 34, 7 (July 1998): 85–115.

Hsiung, James C., ed. *Human Rights in East Asia: A Cultural Perspective.* New York: Paragon House, 1986.

Hu, Yuanxiang. *Legal and Policy Issues of the Trade and Economic Relations between China and the EEC: A Comparative Study.* Deventer, Netherlands: Kluwer Law and Taxation Publishers, 1991.

Huang Shaoyu. "Mianxiang ershiyi shiji de zhongguo yu feizhou guanxi" [China's relations with Africa to the 21st century]. *Xiandai guoji guanxi* 5 (1996): 26–30.

Human Rights Watch. *Human Rights Watch World Report.* New York: Human Rights Watch, various years.

Human Rights Watch/Asia. "Human Rights in the APEC Region: 1994." New York: Human Rights Watch, November 1994.

———. "Prison Conditions in Japan." New York: Human Rights Watch, March 1995.

———. "Chinese Diplomacy, Western Hypocrisy, and the UN Human Rights Commission." New York: Human Rights Watch, March 1997.

Inada Juichi. "Ajia josei no hendo to nihon no ODA" [The changes in Asia and Japan's ODA]. *Kokusai mondai* 360 (March 1990): 45–59.

———. "Democratization, Marketization, and Japan's Emerging Role as Foreign Aid Donor." U.S.-Japan Program Occasional Paper 93–03. Program on U.S.-Japan Relations, Center for International Affairs, Harvard University.

Inoguchi, Takashi. "Japan's Foreign Policy in East Asia." *Current History* 91, 569 (December 1992): 407–12.

Ishi Akira. "Taiwan ka pekin ka" [Taiwan or Beijing?]. In Watanabe Akio, ed., *Sengo nihon no taigai seisaku* [Postwar Japanese foreign policy]. Tokyo: Yuhikaku, 1985, pp. 62–85.

Japanese Ministry of Foreign Affairs. *Financial Statistics of Japan.* Various years.

Jiang Haiyang. *Shuishi yingjia zhongmei renquan jiaoliang jishi* [Who is the winner? report on Sino-U.S. human rights contest]. Beijing: Dangdai shijie chubanshe, 1998.

Jiang Lifeng. *Zhongri guanxi sanlun* [Past, present, and future of Sino-Japanese relations]. Harbin: Heilongjiang jiaoyu chubanshe, 1996.

Jones, Sidney. "Culture Clash." *China Rights Forum* (Summer 1993): 8–9, 22.

Kapur, Harish. *China and the European Economic Community: The New Connection.* Dordrecht: Martinus Nijhoff, 1986.

Keck, Margaret E. and Kathryn Sikkink. *Activists Beyond Borders: Advocacy Networks in International Politics.* Ithaca, N.Y.: Cornell University Press, 1998.

Kelliher, Daniel. "Keeping Democracy Safe from the Masses: Intellectuals and Elitism in the Chinese Protest Movement." *Comparative Politics* 25, 4 (July 1993): 379–96.

Kent, Ann. "Australia-China Relations, 1966–1996: A Critical Overview." *Australian Journal of Politics and History* 42, 3 (1996): 365–84.

————. *Between Freedom and Subsistence: China and Human Rights.* Hong Kong: Oxford University Press, 1993.

————. *China, the United Nations, and Human Rights: The Limits of Compliance.* Philadelphia: University of Pennsylvania Press, 1999.

Kim, Samuel S. "China and the United Nations." In Elizabeth Economy and Michel Oksenberg, eds., *China Joins the World: Progress and Prospects.* New York: Council on Foreign Relations Press, 1999, pp. 42–89.

————. "Chinese Foreign Policy in Theory and Practice." In Samuel S. Kim, ed., *China and the World: Chinese Foreign Policy Faces the New Millennium.* 4th ed. Boulder, Colo.: Westview Press, 1998, pp. 3–33.

Lampton, David M. "America's China policy in the Age of the Finance Minister: Clinton Ends Linkage." *China Quarterly* 139 (September 1994): 597–621.

Lee, Chae-Jin. *China and Japan: New Economic Diplomacy.* Stanford, Calif.: Hoover Institution, Stanford University, 1984.

Lei, Guang. "Elusive Democracy: Conceptual Change and the Chinese Democracy Movement, 1978–79 to 1989." *Modern China* 22, 4 (October 1996): 417–47.

Li Shenzhi. "Fengyu canghuang wushinian guoqingye duyu" [Weathering fifty years: solitary words in the night of the national day]. *Dangdai zhongguo yanjiu* 68 (March 2000): 74–83.

Li Yunlong. *Zhongmei guanxi zhong de renquan wenti* [Human rights issues in Sino-U.S. relations]. Beijing: Xinhua chubanshe, 1998.

Lieberthal, Kenneth. *Governing China: From Revolution Through Reform.* New York: W. W. Norton, 1995.

Lin Daizhao. *Zhanhou zhongri guanxishi* [Postwar Sino-Japanese relations]. Beijing: Beijing daxue chubanshe, 1992.

Ling Zhijun and Ma Licheng. *Huhan dangjin zhongguo de wuzhong sheng yin* [Shouts: five voices in present China]. Guangzhou: Guangzhou chubanshe, 1998.

Liu Jiangyong. "Renquan wenti yu riben de lichang jiqi duihua taidu" [Human rights issues, Japan's position and its attitude toward China]. *Riben wenti* 32 (August 1990): 1–15.

————, ed. *Kuashiji de riben zhengzhi jingji waijiao xinqushi* [Japan to the next century: new trends in politics, economics, and diplomacy]. Beijing: Shishi chubanshe, 1995.

Liu Jiangyong and Wang Hongjun. "Cong dongjing huiyi kan xifang qiguo de xietiao yu maodun" [Coordination and divisions of the Tokyo G7 summit]. *Xiandai guoji guanxi* 8 (August 1993): 13–19.

Liu Shulin et al. *Dangdai zhongguo renquan zhuangkuang baogao* [Report on the human rights situation in China]. Shenyang: Liaoning remnin chubanshe, 1994.

Lu, Ning. *The Dynamics of Foreign-Policy Decisionmaking in China.* Boulder, Colo.: Westview Press, 1997.

Lu Yaokun and Feng Zhonglin. "Deguo dui yazhou de zhanlue kaolu ji zhengce tiaozheng" [Germany's strategic considerations and policy adjustments toward China]. *Xiandai guoji guanxi* 5 (1993): 15–20.

Luo Yanhua. *Dongfangren kan renquan* [Orientals view human rights]. Beijing: Xinhua chubanshe, 1998.

Ma Licheng and Ling Zhijun. *Jiaofeng dangdai zhongguo sanci sixiang jiefang shilu* [Clash: records of the three thought liberations in modern China]. Beijing: Jinri zhongguo chubanshe, 1998.

Mahbubani, Kishore. "The West and the Rest." *National Interest* 28 (Summer 1992): 3–13.

Mao Yushi. "Liberalism, Equal Status, and Human Rights." *Journal of Democracy* 9, 4 (October 1998): 20–23.

Mochizuki, Mike M. "Japan and the Strategic Quadrangle." In Michael Mandelbaum, ed., *The Strategic Quadrangle: Russia, China, Japan and the U.S. in East Asia.* New York: Council on Foreign Relations Press, 1995, pp. 107–53.

Montgomery, John D., ed. *Values in Education: Social Capital Formation in Asia and the Pacific.* Hollis, N.H.: Hollis Publishing Company, 1995.

Moody, Peter R., Jr. "Asian Values." *Journal of International Affairs* 50, 1 (Summer 1996): 166–92.

Nakagawa, Junji. "Legal Problems of Japan's ODA Guidelines: Aid and Democracy, Human Rights and Peace." *Japanese Annual of International Law* 36 (1993): 76–89.

Nathan, Andrew J. "China and the International Human Rights Regime." In Elizabeth Economy and Michel Oksenberg, eds., *China Joins the World: Progress and Prospects.* New York: Council on Foreign Relations Press, 1999, pp. 136–60.

———. *China's Crisis: Dilemmas of Reform and Prospects for Democracy.* New York: Columbia University Press, 1991.

———. *China's Transition.* New York: Columbia University Press, 1997.

———. "Human Rights in Chinese Foreign Policy." *China Quarterly* 39 (September 1994): 622–43.

Nathan, Andrew J. and Tianjian Shi. "Cultural Requisites for Democracy in China: Findings from a Survey." In Tu Wei-ming, ed., *China in Transition.* Cambridge, Mass.: Harvard University Press, 1994, pp. 95–123.

Okabe Tatsumi. "Tenanmon jiken to kongo no chugoku" [The Tiananmen incident and future China]. *Kokusai mondai* 358 (January 1990): 2–16.

Orr, Robert M., Jr. "Political Agendas: A New World Order Through Foreign Aid?" In Barbara Stallings et al., *Common Vision, Different Paths: The United States and Japan in the Developing World.* Washington, D.C.: Overseas Development Council, 1993, pp. 83–97.

Patten, Christopher. *East and West: China, Power, and the Future of Asia.* New York: Times Books, 1999.

Pharr, Susan J. and Ming Wan. "Yen for the Earth: Japan's Pro-Active China Environment Policy." In Michael B. McElroy, Chris P. Nielsen, and Peter Lydon, eds., *Energizing China: Reconciling Environmental Protection and Economic Growth.* Cambridge, Mass.: Harvard University Committee on the Environment, Harvard University Press, 1998, pp. 601–38.

———. "Japan's Leadership: Shaping a New Asia." In Hideo Sato and I. M. Destler, eds., *Leadership Sharing in the New International System: Japan and the U.S.*, Special Research Project on the New International System, University of Tsukuba, Japan, September 1996, pp. 133–70.

Qiu Yuanlun and Shen Yannan, eds. *Ouzhou yu shijie* [Europe and the world]. Beijing: Zhongguo shehuikexue chubanshe, 1998.

Ren Feng. "Xiou lingdao dui oumeng waijiao zhanlue he ouzhong guanxi de kanfa" [Views of the main Western European leaders on the EU's foreign policy strategy and Euro-China relations]. *Xiandai guoji guanxi* 4 (1998): 34–37.

Ross, Robert S. "National Security, Human Rights, and Domestic Politics: The Bush Administration and China." In Kenneth A. Oye, Robert J. Lieber, and Donald Rothchild, eds., *Eagle in a New World: American Grand Strategy in the Post-Cold War Era.* New York: HarperCollins Publishers, 1992, pp. 281–313.

———, ed. *After the Cold War: Domestic Factors and U.S.-China Relations.* Armonk, NY: E. M. Sharpe, 1998.

Sakamoto Yashikazu. "Nihon ni okeru kokuzai reisen to kokunai reisen" [The international Cold War and domestic Cold War in Japan], *Reisen seiji teki kosatsu* [The Cold War: political considerations]. Tokyo: Iwanami, 1963, pp. 331–75.

Sato, Yasunobu. "New Directions in Japanese Foreign Policy: Promoting Human Rights and Democracy in Asia—ODA Perspective." In Edward Friedman, ed., *The Politics of Democratization: Generalizing East Asian Experiences.* Boulder, Colo.: Westview Press, 1994, pp. 102–21.

Schaller, Michael. *Altered States: The United States and Japan Since the Occupation.* New York: Oxford University Press, 1997.

Sen, Amartya. "Human Rights and Asian Values." *New Republic,* July 14, 1997, pp. 33–40.

Seymour, James D., ed. *The Fifth Modernization: China's Human Rights Movement, 1978–1979.* Sanfordville, N.Y.: Human Rights Publishing Group, 1980.

———. "Human Rights in Chinese Foreign Relations." In Samuel S. Kim, ed., *China and the World: Chinese Foreign Policy Faces the New Millennium.* 4th ed. Boulder, Colo.: Westview Press, 1998, pp. 217–38.

Shambaugh, David. *Beautiful Imperialist: China Perceives America, 1972–1990.* Princeton, N.J.: Princeton University Press, 1991.

———. "A Bibliographical Essay on New Sources for the Study of China's Foreign Relations and National Security." In Thomas W. Robinson and David Shambaugh, eds., *Chinese Foreign Policy: Theory and Practice.* Oxford: Clarendon Press, 1994, pp. 603–18.

———. "China and Europe." *Annals of the American Academy of Political and Social Science* 519 (January 1992): 101–14.

Shi, Tianjian. *Political Participation in Beijing.* Cambridge, Mass: Harvard University Press, 1997.

Shi Xiuyin. "Zhongguo shehui zhuanxing shiqi de quanli yu quanli" [Public power and rights during the transformational period in China]. In Xia Yong, ed., *Zouxiang quanli de shidai zhongguo gongmin quanli fazhan yanjiu* [Toward an era of rights: research on development of civil rights in China]. Beijing: Zhongguo zhengfa daxue chubanshe, 1995, pp. 69–129.

Shih, Chih-yu. "Contending Theories of 'Human Rights with Chinese Characteristics.' " *Issues and Studies* 29, 11 (November 1993): 42–64.

Shuto, Motoko. "Human Rights NGOs in Southeast Asia and Japan's Approaches to Democratization." Paper presented at International Studies Association Convention, Minneapolis, March 18, 1998.

Sikkink, Kathryn. "The Power of Principled Ideas: Human Rights Policies in the United States and Western Europe." In Judith Goldstein and Robert O. Keohane, eds., *Ideas and Foreign Policy: Beliefs, Institutions and Political Change.* Ithaca, N.Y.: Cornell University Press, 1993, pp. 139–70.

Solomon, Richard H. *Chinese Negotiating Behavior: Pursuing Interests Through "Old Friends."* Washington, D.C.: U.S. Institute of Peace Press, 1999.

Song Xinning. "Zhongguo yu ouzhou mianxiang weilai" [China and Europe: facing the future]. In Song Xinning and Zhang Xiaojin, eds., *Zouxiang ershiyi shiji de zhongguo yu ouzhou* [China and Europe toward the twenty-first century]. Hong Kong: Xianggang shehui chubanshe, 1997, pp. 5–32.

Sun Pinghua. *Rizhong yohao suixianglu* [My reminiscences of Sino-Japanese friendship]. Beijing: Shijie zhishi chubanshe, 1987.

Sutter, Robert G. *Chinese Policy Priorities and Their Implications for the United States.* Lanham, Md.: Rowman and Littlefield, 2000.

———. *U.S. Policy Toward China: An Introduction to the Role of Interest Groups.* Lanham, Md.: Rowman and Littlefield, 1998.

Takagi Seiichiro. "Posuto reisen kozo to chugoku gaiko no 'shinkaidan' " [The post-Cold War structure and the "the new stage" in Chinese foreign policy]. *Kokusai mondai* 394 (January 1993): 18–32.

———. "Human Rights in Japanese Foreign Policy: Japan's Policy Towards China After Tiananmen." In James T. H. Tang, ed., *Human Rights and International Relations in the Asia-Pacific Region.* London: Pinter, 1995, pp. 97–111.

Tanaka Akihiko. "Nihon gaiko to kokunai seiji no renkan gaiatsu no seijigaku" [The connection between Japanese diplomacy and domestic politics: politics of external pressure]. *Kokusai mondai* 348 (March 1989): 23–36.

———. *Nitchu kankei, 1945–1990* [Japan-China relations, 1945–1990]. Tokyo: Tokyo daigaku shuppankai, 1991.

Tang, James T. H., ed. *Human Rights and International Relations in the Asia-Pacific Region.* London: Pinter, 1995.

Teles, Steven M. "Public Opinion and Interest Groups in the Making of U.S.-China Policy." In Robert S. Ross, ed., *After the Cold War: Domestic Factors and U.S.-China Relations.* Armonk, N.Y.: M.E. Sharpe, 1998, pp. 40–69.

Tian Jin et al. *Zhongguo zai lianheguo* [China in the UN]. Beijing: Shijie zhishi chubanshe, 1999.

Ueki, Yasuhiro. "Japan's UN Diplomacy: Sources of Passivism and Activism." In Gerald L. Curtis, ed., *Japan's Foreign Policy After the Cold War: Coping with Change.* Armonk, N.Y.: M.E. Sharpe, 1993, pp. 347–70.

Van Ness, Peter. "Addressing the Human Rights Issue in Sino-American Relations." *Journal of International Affairs* 49, 2 (Winter 1996): 309–31.

Van Ness, Peter and Nikhil Aziz, eds. *Debating Human Rights: Critical Essays from the United States and Asia*. London: Routledge, 1999.

Vincent, R. J. *Human Rights and International Relations*. New York: Cambridge University Press, 1986.

Walder, Andrew G. and Gong Xiaoxia. "Workers in the Tiananmen Protest: The Politics of the Beijing Workers 'Autonomous Federation.' " *Australian Journal of China Affairs* 29 (January 1993): 1–29.

Waltz, Kenneth N. *Theory of International Politics*. Reading, Mass.: Addison-Wesley, 1979.

Wan, Ming. "A Comparison of Sino-Japanese and Sino-American High-Level Official Contacts Since 1972." U.S.-Japan Program Occasional Paper 94–15. Program on U.S.-Japan Relations, Center for International Affairs, Harvard University, 1994.

———. "Human Rights and Sino-U.S. Relations: Policies and Changing Realities." *Pacific Review* 10, 2 (1997): 237–55.

———. "Human Rights in China 1997: Domestic Politics and Foreign Policy." In Joseph Y. S. Cheng, ed., *China Review 1998*. Hong Kong: Chinese University Press, 1998, pp. 209–33.

———. "Policies, Resource Commitments, and Values: A Comparison of U.S. and Japanese Approaches to Human Rights in China." In John D. Montgomery, ed., *Human Rights: Positive Policies in Asia and the Pacific Rim*. Hollis, N.H.: Hollis Publishing Company, 1998, pp. 43–70.

Wang, Jianwei. *Limited Adversaries: Post-Cold War U.S.-China Mutual Images*. Hong Kong: Oxford University Press, 1999.

Wang Jinbiao and Feng Zhongping. "Oumeng tuixing geng jiji de duihua zhengce" [The European Union promotes a more active China policy]. In Song Xinning and Zhang Xiaojin, eds., *Zouxiang ershiyi shiji de zhongguo yu ouzhou* [China and Europe toward the twenty-first century]. Hong Kong: Xianggang shehuikexue chubanshe, 1997, pp. 130–36.

Wang Xigen. "Lun deng xiaoping de renquanguan" [On Deng Xiaoping's view of human rights]. *Xiandai guoji guanxi* 4 (1997): 29–33.

Wang Xingfang, ed. *Zhongguo yu lianheguo jinian lianheguo chengli wushi zhounian* [China and the UN: in commemoration of the fiftieth anniversary of the UN]. Beijing: Shijie zhishi chubanshe, 1995.

Wang Yi. "Zhongfa guanxi fazhan de dongli" [Momentum behind the development of Sino-French relations]. *Guoji wenti yanjiu* 2 (1997): 31–36.

Weatherley, Robert. *The Discourse of Human Rights in China: Historical and Ideological Perspectives*. New York: St. Martin's Press, 1999.

Whiting, Allen S. *China Eyes Japan*. Berkeley: University of California Press, 1989.

Wu Jiuyi. "Deguo xinyazhou zhengce chuxi" [Germany's new Asian policy]. *Xiandai guoji guanxi* 12 (December 1993): 29–31.

———. "Xiou duihua guanxi jinkuang yu qianjing" [Recent and future developments in Western European relations with China]. *Xiandai guoji guanxi* 7 (July 1993): 1–4.

Wu Xuewen, Lin Liande, and Xu Zhixian. *Zhongri guanxi* [Sino-Japanese relations]. Beijing: Shishi chubanshe, 1995.

Wu, Yuan-li et al. *Human Rights in the People's Republic of China.* Boulder, Colo.: Westview Press, 1988.

Xia Yong. *Renquan gainian qiyuan* [The origin of the concept of human rights]. Beijing: Zhongguo zhengfa daxue chubanshe, 1992.

——, ed. *Zouxiang quanli de shidai zhongguo gongmin quanli fazhan yanjiu* [Toward an era of rights: research on the development of civil rights in China]. Beijing: Zhongguo zhengfa daxue chubanshe, 1995.

Xiao, Zhi Yue. *Current EC Legal Developments: The EC and China.* London: Butterworths, 1993.

Yan Xuetong. *Zhongguo guojia liyi fenxi* [Analysis of China's national interests]. Tianjin: Tianjin renmin chubanshe, 1997.

Yang Manke. "Zuihuiguo wenti de lixiang jieju" [An ideal outcome of the MFN issue]. *China Spring* 9 (1991): 33–35.

Yang Yiping. "Zhaoyan yu ershiyi shiji de ouzhong guanxi jiqi yingxiang" [Europe-China relations to the twenty-first century and its influence]. In Song Xinning and Zhang Xiaojin, eds., *Zouxiang ershiyi shiji de zhongguo yu ouzhou* [China and Europe toward the twenty-first century]. Hong Kong: Xianggang shehuikexue chubanshe, 1997, pp. 106–20.

Yu, Bin. "China and Its Asian Neighbors: Implications for Sino-U.S. Relations." In Yong Deng and Fei-Ling Wang, eds., *In the Eyes of the Dragon: China Views the World.* Lanham, Md.: Rowman and Littlefield, 1999, pp. 183–210.

——. "The Study of Chinese Foreign Policy: Problems and Prospect." *World Politics* 46, 2 (January 1994): 235–61.

Zhao, Quansheng. "Japan's Aid Diplomacy with China." In Bruce M. Koppel and Robert M. Orr, Jr., eds., *Japan's Foreign Aid: Power and Policy in a New Era.* Boulder, Colo.: Westview Press, 1993, pp. 163–87.

——. *Interpreting Chinese Foreign Policy.* Hong Kong: Oxford University Press, 1996.

——. *Japanese Policymaking: The Politics Behind Politics—Informal Mechanisms and the Making of China Policy.* Hong Kong: Oxford University Press, 1996.

Zhao, Quansheng with Barry Press. "The U.S. Promotion of Human Rights and China's Response." *Issues and Studies* 34, 8 (August 1998): 30–62.

Zheng, Yongnian. "Development and Democracy: Are They Compatible in China?" *Political Science Quarterly* 109, 2 (Summer 1994): 235–59.

Zhong, Yang, Jie Chen, and John M. Scab II. "Political Views from Below: A Survey of Beijing Residents." *PS: Political Science and Politics* 30, 3 (September 1997): 474–82.

Zhou, Kate Xiao. *How the Farmers Changed China: Power of the People.* Boulder, Colo.: Westview Press, 1996.

Zhou, Wei. "The Study of Human Rights in the People's Republic of China." In James T. H. Tang, ed., *Human Rights and International Relations in the Asia-Pacific Region.* London: Pinter, 1995, pp. 83–96.

Index

Acknowledgments

This book began with postdoctoral work comparing U.S. and Japanese approaches to human rights in China at the Human Rights Policy Program of the Pacific Basin Research Center based at the Kennedy School of Government of Harvard University in 1995–96. I thank Professor John D. Montgomery, the director of the center, for support and advice and other fellows for constructive comments.

The work conducted in this intellectually stimulating environment at the center led to continuous research interest in human rights issues. An important part of the research for the book resulted from a paper on Chinese views on human rights and democracy written for the "China Views the World" project (1997–98), which examined Chinese views on a variety of foreign policy issues and helped focus my own research on China's human rights foreign policy. I am grateful to project leaders Deng Yong and Fei-Ling Wang and other project members for valuable feedback.

I made numerous presentations on parts of my research for the book over a five-year period: Kennedy School of Harvard in December 1995 and June 1996, the International Symposium on U.S.-China Relations organized by Chinese academic associations in the U.S. in October 1996, George Mason University in November 1996 and March 1997, the annual conference of the Association for Chinese Political Studies in November 1997, a workshop at Georgia Institute of Technology in February 1998, the International Studies Association conferences in March 1998 and March 2000, and Soka University of America in December 1998. I thank Davis Bobrow, Jie Chen, Christine B. N. Chin, Thomas Christensen, Francis Harbour, Richard Higgott, Peter Li, Xiaobing Li, John Montgomery, Ryo

Oshiba, John Paden, Motoko Shuto, Ezra Vogel, Fei-Ling Wang, and others for useful suggestions.

I conducted field research in China, Japan, and the United States, interviewing officials of the Chinese Foreign Ministry, Japanese Foreign Ministry, U.S. State Department and other government officials; scholars from think tanks and universities; and human rights activists. Interviewees are not identified by name, but I thank them for providing useful information and helping me understand China's human rights exchange with the West.

I would like to thank Professor Scott Keefer and other colleagues in the Department of Public and International Affairs, George Mason University for their support. In particular, the Department granted me a course reduction in 1999–2000 that allowed me more time to work on my book.

It is difficult to name all those who have made the book possible. But I am particularly thankful to Professors Robert O. Keohane and and Susan J. Pharr, who guided me in my earlier academic research and continue to be my models for intellectual excellence. Patricia Smith of the University of Pennsylvania Press encouraged my project early on and provided me with prompt and most valuable editorial guidance. I am grateful for the useful suggestions made by the two reviewers of the book manuscript. My thanks also go to Alison A. Anderson, Laurel Frydenborg, and others at the press for excellent assistance. Last but not least, I dedicate this book to my wife Anne, who offered me sharp intellectual critique and steady emotional support for the book project and has inspired me in life as well as in work.

Three chapters are based on previously published work, substantially revised and enlarged. I am grateful for permission of the following publishers. "Chinese Opinion on Human Rights," *Orbis* 42, 3 (Summer 1998): 361–74; permission by Foreign Policy Research Institute. "Human Rights and Sino-U.S. Relations: Policies and Changing Realities," *Pacific Review* 10, 2 (1997): 237–55; permission by Taylor & Francis Ltd. "Policies, Resource Commitments, and Values: A Comparison of U.S. and Japanese Approaches to Human Rights in China," in John D. Montgomery, ed., *Human Rights: Positive Policies in Asia and the Pacific Rim* (Hollis, N.H.: Hollis Publishing Company, 1998), pp. 43–70; permission by John Montgomery. "Human Rights and U.S.-Japan Relations in Asia: Divergent Allies," *East Asia: An International Quarterly* 16, 3/4 (Autumn/ Winter 1998): 137–68; permission by Transaction Publisher.